Routledge Revivals

The Sisters d' Aranyi

First published in 1969, *The Sisters d' Aranyi* traces the careers, personalities and musical development of Jelly d' Aranyi and Adila Fachiri, outstanding violinists in Britain and Hungarian great nieces of Josef Joachim, with insight and a wealth of anecdote and description. The book contains fresh lights on figures such as Joachim himself, Elgar, Ravel and Vaughan Williams, Casals, Suggia, and Myra Hess, Aldous Huxley, Einstein and Schweitzer, Balfour, Asquith and Neville Chamberlain. There are illuminating comments on music from Bach to the present day, and also a chapter on the mysterious affair of the Imprisoned Schumann Violin Concerto, and how it was found and liberated. These two consummate musicians were, however, part of a movement towards greater sincerity in music- a tendency not yet sufficiently recorded by musicologists. To set them in their time, this biography contains a most readable history of music in Britain with some original observations on the nature of music itself in performance. This book is an essential read for students of music, music history, literature, performance studies, for violin players and also for general music lovers.

The Sisters d' Aranyi

by Joseph Macleod

First published in 1969
By George Allen and Unwin Ltd.

This edition first published in 2021 by Routledge
2 Park Square, Milton Park, Abingdon, Oxon, OX14 4RN
and by Routledge
605 Third Avenue, New York, NY 10017

Routledge is an imprint of the Taylor & Francis Group, an informa business

© George Allen & Unwin Ltd. 1969

All rights reserved. No part of this book may be reprinted or reproduced or utilised in any form or by any electronic, mechanical, or other means, now known or hereafter invented, including photocopying and recording, or in any information storage or retrieval system, without permission in writing from the publishers.

Publisher's Note
The publisher has gone to great lengths to ensure the quality of this reprint but points out that some imperfections in the original copies may be apparent.

Disclaimer
The publisher has made every effort to trace copyright holders and welcomes correspondence from those they have been unable to contact.

A Library of Congress record exists under LCCN: 79480569

ISBN 13: 978-1-032-13326-3 (hbk)
ISBN 13: 978-1-003-22868-4 (ebk)
ISBN 13: 978-1-032-13327-0 (pbk)

DOI: 10.4324/9781003228684

The Sisters d'Aranyi

JOSEPH MACLEOD

London
GEORGE ALLEN AND UNWIN LTD
RUSKIN HOUSE · MUSEUM STREET

FIRST PUBLISHED IN 1969

This book is copyright under the Berne Convention. Apart from any fair dealing for the purposes of private study, research, criticism or review, as permitted under the Copyright Act, 1956 no portion may be reproduced by any process without written permission. Enquiries should be addressed to the publishers.

© George Allen and Unwin Ltd., 1969

To
Alice M. F. Dukes of Rugby
in gratitude
and to
Adrienne and Adila Jane Camilloni
in hope

PRINTED IN GREAT BRITAIN
in 11/12 *point Plantin Type*
BY WILLMER BROTHERS LIMITED
BIRKENHEAD

Foreword

BY

THE RT. HON. SIR EDWARD BOYLE, BART., M.P.

I feel pleased and honoured that I should have been invited to contribute a short introduction to Joseph Macleod's most sympathetic and perceptive study of *The Sisters d'Aranyi*, which I have read with the greatest interest.

My father shared chambers in the Temple with Alexander Fachiri, and this was the foundation of a close friendship between our respective families. Both my parents were music lovers. My father had an unusual gift for playing by ear, and my mother was a good amateur 'cellist who had been trained by Georg Wille in Dresden immediately before the 1914 war; one of the proudest and happiest moments in her life occurred when Adila Fachiri invited her to play at the same desk as Alexander, in the small string orchestra which accompanied her and Jelly d'Aranyi at the Haslemere Festival. Incidentally Alexander's own abilities as a performer, and even more his musicianship, should not be underrated. My mother much admired him as a chamber-music player, and always said she had never heard anyone do greater justice to the Second Cello part in Schubert's great String Quintet (especially the *adagio*).

But the close intimacy between our families was based principally, not just on admiration for Jelly and Adila as performers, but on a deep affection for them as persons—an affection which extended to Alexander and also to Adila's daughter, Adrienne (now Signora Fachiri-Camilloni), who remains today as she has always been, a particularly valued friend and close contemporary both of my sister and myself. I shall always remember Adila—exuberant, uninhibited, not always discreet—as one of the warmest personalities and loyalest friends I have ever known. Jelly's personality, as Mr Macleod's pages bring out so well, was something rather more rare. I shall not attempt to emulate his description, but readers of this book will be able to sense the atmosphere, which Jelly always radiated, of goodness, ethereal charm, and also wit; I particularly like Mr Macleod's story of her remark to Einstein, after playing quintet with him: "Your time was relative only once or twice."

One was always struck, not only by the mutual devotion of the two sisters, but also by how much they were able to give to one another. Jelly could always count on Adila for technical help and advice; Adila would have been the first to admit how much she owed to Jelly's qualities of character. Each was absolutely devoid of any spirit of jealousy, or even emulation where the other was concerned. I can recall listening to a broadcast of a performance in Holland by Jelly of the Mendelssohn Violin Concerto and Adila's concern that we would not be tuned in properly before the slow movement "which Jelly plays so divinely"; she added "It is my own least good Concerto". Mr Macleod has rightly devoted some space to their performance of the Bach *Concerto for Two*

Foreword

Violins, with which they became so intimately associated. I agree with all that he writes, though I think it is the slow movement that lives on in my own memory the most vividly.

Mr Macleod brings out the size of their repertory, especially Jelly's—in this one respect they were very different from their great-uncle Joachim. Some of their items would strike a contemporary audience as old-fashioned though I believe there are a number of present-day critics who would be glad occasionally to hear Spohr's Duos which Tovey so much admired. But we are also reminded of Jelly's enterprise in learning and introducing a number of contemporary works—like Ravel's *Tzigane*, and the two Sonatas for Piano and Violin by Bartok which still sound among the most difficult works of this great composer. Incidentally, remembering Jelly's performance of the Second Sonata, and having recently heard the recording of it by Bartók and Szigeti, I would endorse Mr Calvocorvessi's judgment, quoted by Mr Macleod, that Jelly's was the more tense. There is an amusing description of Jelly's relations with Elgar—she could never 'take' his Violin Concerto (neither, despite her admiration for the youthful Menuhin's performance, could my mother).

One Concerto in which Jelly specially excelled, not mentioned by Mr Macleod, was the Saint-Saens in B Minor—not even Ysayë can have played the opening theme more effectively. I once asked Jelly why Tovey, in his musical writings, seemed to evince such a disproportionate hostility to Saint-Saens' music; she said she thought it was a reaction against the praise of those in Tovey's circle who took Saint-Saens too seriously, especially Speyer. Mr Macleod deals factually and tactfully with the curious story of the 'rediscovery' of the Schumann Violin Concerto. Actually, it was in my home that Adila first came downstairs and announced "Schumann has come to us". It did not prove a fortunate visitation—though, as a music lover, I cannot regret the disinterment of this Concerto if only for the sake of the opening bars of the slow movement.

There is a tinge of sadness surrounding the final chapters of this book, and Mr Macleod writes sympathetically about the "strange fading-out" of Jelly as a front-rank artist from about the time of the start of the 1939 war. As Mr Macleod's earlier chapters show, uncertain health may have had something to do with this. Undoubtedly Alexander's prolonged illness and death early in 1939 caused a great strain for the whole family, and perhaps for Jelly most of all. And my mother always held the view—she once plucked up courage to say this to Adila, who did not contradict her —that Jelly was never quite the same player after she abandoned her Bergonzi instrument for the 'Strad' to which her friends contributed; somehow the new instrument never seemed entirely to suit her, and she would privately admit she was nervous of it. It has to be remembered, also, that Jelly did not have a single violin lesson after she was fourteen years old; her relative lack of formal training, by present-day standards, probably made it harder for her to fight back technically. And there were, in addition, personal factors, like the tragic rupture with Myra Hess, with whom Jelly had previously formed such a successful partnership.

Foreword

But if Jelly was in her hey-day as a performer during the period between the wars, the same is not true of Adila who gave some of her most memorable recitals after 1945, especially the 1951 recital, fully described by Mr Macleod, at which she played the entire sequence of Brahms—Joachim Hungarian Dances. Those members of my family who were present, always remembered this recital as a quite astonishing achievement, and one of the major musical experiences of their lives. There are certain particular movements from sonatas that I shall always associate with Adila—the slow movement of Beethoven's Sixth Sonata Op. 30 No. 1, which she sometimes played as an encore, and the *alla breve* finale of Brahms's A Major Sonata Op. 100; this movement can easily be allowed to sound 'sticky', but in Adila's performance, and on Joachim's magnificent instrument, it never did. In her later years, Adila seemed to take ever more pleasure in discussing music, and I remember her comparing Joachim's performance of the Beethoven Violin Concerto with the general run of performances today: "He took the finale more slowly, but the opening movement a little faster." My wartime billetor, Mr J. St. O. Dykes, a pupil of Raff in the 1880s, and for fifty years a distinguished member of the staff of the Royal College, used to say exactly the same.

When, first, Adila and then Jelly died at Bellosguardo, I can think of no old friends of the family whose passing saddened me more. Adila may not always have been wise—she could even on occasions be exasperating—but these were great artists and good people, who inspired not only admiration but devotion. Happily the history of the family is not yet complete. Adrienne has never gained the fame as a violinist that her talents would justify, but no one who has ever heard her play the Dvořák Violin Concerto, or the Beethoven 'Spring' Sonata, can doubt that, given single-minded application, she could have been one of the notable players of her generation. And as for her delightful small daughter Jane ('little Adila')—well, from what I have seen of her (she is my god-daughter) I should judge her to be capable of anything.

EDWARD BOYLE

ACKNOWLEDGMENTS

Lack of space prevents more than a mention of thanks to those who have made possible the compiling of this book: especially to the bright, accurate warmth of Mrs Gell (Anna Robertson) and the tireless care of Evelyn Jowett; the shrewd advice of Sir Ralph Hawtrey, friendliness of Lady Fisher of Lambeth, generosity of Adrienne Camilloni—all very near to the Sisters d'Aranyi.

No less to Sir Edward Boyle for his Introduction; and to the kindness of the following: Sir Adrian Boult; the Librarian and Recording Department of the B.B.C.; Mrs Jean Cleland; Dr Howard Ferguson; Brigadier Hardy-Roberts; Mrs Marya Hornes; Frank Howes: the Editor of *Music and Letters*; Professor Sidney Newman; the Editor of *The Spectator*; Count Teleki; and Kenneth Wright. With a special word to Lady Malise Graham, whose vivid glimpses of Jelly as a girl arrived too late, alas, to be included.

For permission to quote from letters I would also like to thank Lady Asquith of Yarnbury, Mrs John Booth, Mrs Pamela Diamond, Mrs Laura and Sir Julian Huxley, Mrs Law, H. G. Mallory, Lord Monteagle, Max Rendall, Sir John and Michael Rothenstein, Lord Russell, Mrs Ursula Vaughan Williams, Mrs Volterra and Lady (Stevart) Wilson. I have done my best to get in touch with others.

However, in each case, mere mention carries deeper meaning.

Contents

PART I   THE THREE SISTERS

     1   *Childhood in Budapest*   page 13
     2   *Music Prospect*   26
     3   *Violins and Fiddles*   37
     4   *To the Death of Joachim*   46
     5   *Viâ Elsewhere to England*   55
     6   *Music in Britain and Abroad*   66
     7   *An Advantage of High Society*   78
     8   *Enemy Aliens*   91
     9   *Wartime Music*   101

PART II   JELLY D'ARANYI

     10   *Drawing Flames*   115
     11   *Béla Bartók*   131
     12   *Ravel: Vaughan Williams: Szymanowsky*   143
     13   *Variations on Various Themes*   153
     14   *Myra Hess and America*   171
     15   *The Truth About the Schumann Concerto*   186
     16   *The Pilgrimage of Compassion*   204

PART III   ADILA FACHIRI

     17   *Divisions on a Ground*   217
     18   *The House in Netherton Grove*   242
     19   *Last Years*   254

EPILOGUE AT BELLOSGUARDO   267
INDEX OF MUSIC AND MUSICIANS   287
ADDITIONAL NOTES AND REFERENCES   295
INDEX   315

Illustrations

1 *Duo in canon written for Adila by Béla Bartók 1902*   *page* 29

2 *Adila in Budapest*
3 *Adila in London*
4 *Jelly as a child*
5 *The Music Room at Netherton Grove*
6 *The effect of the Sisters' playing: friends listening at Netherton Grove*
7 *Musicians off duty*
8 ⎫
9 ⎬ *Three Studies of Jelly playing*
10 ⎭
11 *Last years at Bellosguardo*

between pages 152-3

PART I

The Three Sisters

I

Childhood in Budapest

The three sisters were born in Budapest: Adila in 1886, Hortense Emilia in 1887, and Jelly in 1893. Reference books and obituaries which give other dates are incorrect.

Whether it matters that people are born in a place depends on how they came to be born there. English girls born in Pekin are not Chinese: but if like the daughters of Timothy Richards (Li Ti) they are immediately brought up as befits the daughters of an honorary mandarin of an appropriate button, wearing the colours of Chinese seniority and thinking in Mandarin as readily as in English, then they cannot be called, except in a legal sense, entirely British. They are, deeply and almost equally, the products of two localities.

Locality is not nationality, nor is it mere place. It is place as that place has come to be at that point of time. It derives from history, geography and tradition, modified by science and rebellions of generations, but is still mentally and spiritually there.

To get to know these three sisters, therefore, we must get to know something of their locality. If they were Hungarians, why did they all turn British? what like was the Hungary of their day? and what like the Britain? We do not change much. Most of us merely swell. To know anyone adequately we must know something of his or her youth, or we may get confused by mere today.

However, excavating other people's childhoods means also disturbing one's own. To write about Michelangelo is to greet

The Sisters d'Aranyi

one's own father, or to avoid him. In the present case two of the sisters took a prominent part in my own young manhood in music; and the new attitude to interpretation, of which they were heirs and symptoms, is today required of the best musicians all over the world. So my job, in interpreting their generation to yours, is also to interpret my own to my own. But after all, anyone expecting a biographer not to be involved in his subject is asking either for the impossible or for a dead book.

Budapest, when the sisters were born, had not been a city long. Until 1872 it was two cities, more different than those of London and Westminster. Buda stood on a height above the Danube: seat of government, with ministries and museums and a seldom occupied royal palace. Pest lay flatter on the left bank, the commercial centre, but with Parliament House, various schools and institutes, and most important for us the Academy of Music founded by Liszt in 1875. Most Hungarian nobles had their town houses in Vienna, 130 miles away. But despite this, Buda might have been called aristocratic, Pest educational and artistic. The three sisters were born as much artistic as aristocratic.*

Hungary today is a tiny country, not so big as England without Wales. But it had once been a huge European empire, after which it was ruled for over a century by the Turks, and after that by Austria.

When the Emperor Franz Josef had himself crowned King of Hungary in what historians call 'the Compromise', only nine years before Adila was born, this sop of a 'Double Monarchy' was as little to the taste of good Hungarians as the hideous late-Hapsburg edifices stuck about the capital of Hungary by his bureaucrats and collaborators. School children like Adila had their Hungarian cock-snook for it. 'The Emperor!' they acclaimed, fingers to forehead in a smart salute. Then the fingers crept down to the end of the nose in a derisive twiddle: 'The King of Hungary!'

Grown-ups had as deadly a jeer. The Hungarian pack of playing

---

*Jelly objects. 'Nobles but not aristocrats'. The family had a title but no vast estates or court positions. I maintain however that Osbert Sitwell is an aristocrat, while we all know nobles who do not belong to the aristocracy.

Childhood in Budapest

cards starts with the seven, and has no Queen but two Knaves in each suit. It was the thing to recite the names of these to the tune of the Austro-Hungarian anthem, rising with a shout to the Ace above the King. Only, the Hungarian word for Ace means also Swine.

A repressed people keeps its locality innerly. You find it in literature, music or painting according to local developments. Hungary's was in music: popular gipsy music, and also cultured European music, which in the eighteenth and part of the nineteenth century was predominantly Viennese.

The sisters' family, like many Budapest families, was musical. It also had roots in localities quite other than Hungarian.

One of their great-great-grandfathers was the eighteenth-century numismatologist and archaeologist Georg Zoëga, who was born in Denmark of Italian origin (Zuegga). He re-Italianized himself by settling in Rome, where he acted as Danish ambassador. The neo-classic sculptor Thorvaldsen was his *protégé*, and made a bas-relief of him, which may be seen in the Museum at Copenhagen, together with a drawing of him and his friend the geographer Humboldt.

Already there is a thin family link with music; for Georg Zoëga's first cousin was the Danish *chargé d'affaires* Von Nissen, Mozart's biographer, who befriended Mozart's widow and married her in 1809.

On their father's side the most vivid figure was Grandfather Lajos. According to Hungarian usage the correct form of his name was Hunyadvàri ('noble' title) Arànyi (family name) Lajos. Austrian manners, which prevailed, hardly used the title, but prefixed 'von' to the family name to indicate good family. There was no derivation from the hero Hunyadi, and no connection with the poet Arany (dissyllabic because lacking the final 'i') who wrote in parallel with Pushkin and Byron.

Grandfather Lajos was an ardent nationalist, who became head of Pest University. A very odd man. Having an encyclopaedic knowledge of peculiar things, when one of his sons died at the age of five, hydrocephalic and so of more interest to his father as case than child, this devoted scientist embalmed the body with his own hands and presented it to his University. Years later, Adila and Hortense on a school tour of the Museum squealed with delighted dismay at seeing their monstrous little uncle in a glass case sitting on a chair surrounded by children's toys.

Also Grandfather Lajos was antisemitic. The Hungarian upper classes had always been and continued so: which gave Admiral Horthy an extra grip for his dictatorship in the nineteen twenties and thirties. But Grandfather Lajos had a less violent backlash from the Diaspora than Hitler's. 'You can't exterminate them,' he used to say, 'better to dilute their blood, till it finally disappears, by intermarriage.' Not altogether theory or grim joke. He married Johanna, sister of Josef Joachim the Jewish Hungarian violinist. She had two sons by a former marriage. Grandfather Lajos converted these to Christianity and made priests of both: another alternative to extermination.

The three sisters adored their priestly uncles, and when one died (by tragic conjunction on a sinister number) on Jelly's thirteenth birthday, they were much moved to hear that he had left them his entire priestly fortune. This amounted to 1,000 *gulden*, about fifty pounds in those days, which their father invested for them in twelve fine persian rugs, some of which are still in the family. Both 'uncles' became headmasters of schools founded by the Scolopi, or Piaristi, an international Catholic Order instituted in 1621 to provide boarding schools free for the poor, the most famous being the Nazarene College in Rome. We meet them later.

Grandfather Lajos named his three sons after Hungarian patriots. The eldest, Arpàd, was thus to be kept in mind of the first Prince of the Magyars who, in the ninth century, founded a dynasty of four hundred years. The second, Zoltan the hydrocephalic, was named after one of the leaders in the same period; and the third, Taksony*, father of the three sisters, after another.

Young Taksony wanted to be a lawyer, but he took a job because he wished to marry. He became Chief of Police in Budapest.

*Dissyllabic. The nearest phonetic spelling would be Tocson.

Childhood in Budapest

The girl of his choice was Adrienne Nievarovich de Ligenza, who was no less than the fourteenth child of a Pole of good family from the Cracow district. Her father, the sisters' grandfather on their mother's side, was said to have sat as a child on the knee of Napoleon. Certainly when Cracow was re-annexed by Austria in 1846 he managed to escape, dressed as a footman or valet, to France. Here he married Sophie Zoëga, the numismatologist's grand-daughter, whose mother was French. But many Polish nobles and gentlefolk went to Hungary, and after a while he joined his friends there.

The reason for Taksony's change of profession was one of the economic crises in the nineteenth century, when family fortunes collapsed. Taksony's Jewish mother wrote for a loan to a relative in England. This was her other brother Henry Joachim, a business man, who had married a descendant of Sir George Smart: another thin link with music, because Smart was the conductor and organist who had begun his musical career in 1791 by substituting for a missing drummer when Haydn was rehearsing in London, and who raised high the standard of British orchestras by his life-long devotion to provincial festivals from 1823 onward. A timely loan might have sufficed. But Henry was not like Josef. Indeed it was said that his only merit was his love for his brother, and his brother's only failing his love for him. A sum was given, but not enough. Strict economies were in force for many years.

The decline of the Aranyi family income is seen in the addresses of the sisters' births. Adila was born in Andrassy Street, a mile and a half long and fifty yards wide, centre of Budapest's Belgravia, tented across in summer by the odour of robinia blossom in the gardens. Hortense on the other hand, (whom Adila, and thereafter almost everyone called Titi*, as I will though I never knew her) was born in Sziv Utca, a short street off the Andrassy, pleasant enough but not so fashionable; while Jelly

---

*All the members of this family had pet names for each other, the origins of which as with most pet names are so personal as to have been forgotten. 'Toto' their mother had more than fourteen names for Jelly alone. On occasion such a name could become an *alter ego* who could alternate with the real name and even sign the same letter jointly.

on May 30th ('a date' she says 'which I shared, like my initials if little else, with Jeanne d'Arc, who was therefore my heroine') in the humbler Wesselényi Utca in the same district. This had no garden.

Madame von Aranyi was more at home in French, and for both Adila and Titi this was their mother tongue: but the family spoke Magyar. They did not feel Hungarian because of that. In relation to the Austrians they behaved as the Hungarians they were. But just as the Abbé Liszt, of whom it is said that though Hungarian-born he had not a word of that tongue when his own capital city presented him with a Sword of Honour, and burst into tears, was educated as an Austrian, but lived equally at home in Weimar, Rome and Budapest, so the three sisters, in contrary motion, were later to feel wholly at home in a land of their adoption, where they lived technically, and for a time might have lived perilously, as enemy aliens.

Hungarian society during the long reign of Franz Josef was even more ceremonious and stiff than British society during the shorter one of Queen Victoria. 'Our maids' says Jelly, sitting among June roses in a villa on a hill above Florence before the *maggiordomo* serves dinner in white cotton gloves, 'had to kiss our father's hand.' But then in another villa on another hill above Florence another British subject is trying to dissuade a young Sicilian maid from kissing her son's hand in the mornings. That old order has not yet vanished from all the world.

In nineteenth-century Budapest chaperons shadowed each step, look and gesture of young ladies at balls, in trams, in drawing rooms with young men. In their father the sisters had a martinet of the proprieties. Should a daughter cross her knee in company, he would catch her eye and frown. The frown was enough: for though, if anyone were ill, he could be indescribably dear and gentle ('a saint' Jelly says), his family went in awe of him. He could be severe. He could lose his temper. He once lost his temper so emphatically at breakfast that he broke his watch, and spent the rest of the meal trying to mend it.

He was a forthright man. 'My youngest daughter', he several

Childhood in Budapest

times introduced Jelly to a newcome visitor, 'the ugliest and the best.' If there were any humour intended, it came from disregard. For Jelly knew that she tried to be good: therefore by child logic it followed that she succeeded in being ugly. An opinion which remained with her all her life, but was never shared by anyone I ever met. At this time she had a childish-passionate, almost slavonic, beauty with eyes sultry in full cheekbones.

Taksony was an emotional man, too; or at least he showed his emotions more than his graceful wife did. When moved by a pathetic line or situation in a play, he would bring up opera-glasses to conceal tears: and when he recited the *Erl-König* in Goethe's tongue, he did so with so much feeling that little Jelly wept, understanding the story but as yet no word of German.

The other two sisters were decidedly 'beauties', Adila as a child so much so that people stopped in the street to look at her. From her father, Adila took her forthrightness, as we will see. She too could lose her temper, if she felt that somebody had let her down, or let themselves down, or worse and more frequently had let down something precious. Her inner fear of being afraid made her character firm and strong under her high spirits and love of fun. But she was impulsive, and talked impulsively and much, and put others before herself all her life, a habit of thought which greatly influenced her playing. This she got from her mother.

The mother was small, gay and witty. The portrait in the music-room in the villa above Florence shows a lovely, sensitive face, with limpid brown eyes: a tender face, but of a type one would have called Italian more than French or Polish. She would have agreed with the Greek folk poem, that the fourth-best thing in the world is to be young when friends are young; only with her the friends were her children and this was the first-best.

She dedicated herself to her children. In the lean years she renounced luxuries and even fineries for herself, so that they could go well-dressed. Once she even refused a diamond ring which her husband had brought home for her when the financial cattle were fattening. This mystified and hurt him, though he

The Sisters d'Aranyi

knew self-denial to be part of her character. But if she renounced things and kept herself in the family background, she did not renounce people or deny her own self. She was too lively and vital. At parties, attractive though her daughters might be, there was always a delighted group round the chair she sat in. Wit and vivacity, people coming in, goings-out to people, remained an enchantment to her three daughters, whether in poverty or affluence, all their lives.

Titi renounced things too, but for a very different reason. She could never believe in herself: and so this self became her inner fear. It affected her music. It made her the most complex of the three, with scenes, temperaments, nervous anxieties. But she too when at her ease was amusing and vivacious. As they grew up, she was considered the prettiest.

Jelly had few inner fears: of horses, perhaps. Lack of traffic rules in that Budapest made the crossing of a street a peril to a small girl, at whom horses seemed to rush viciously from all sides at once. But at night horses became friends. Perhaps at night Jelly feared loneliness more than anything (perhaps in daytime too, later in her life). Then the sound of a clip-clop cab coming nearer and nearer along the street below was reassurance that there were other people in her world and awake: and as the cab passed, she felt safe and happier. On many nights she did not sleep well, and would reach out to touch her mother in the next bed. Later, when big enough to share a room with her eldest sister, she would anchor a hand to Adila's pigtail, and hold on out into oblivion.

There was an intimacy between Jelly and Adila from the moment Jelly was born. Adila happened to be the first person to kiss her, wrapped in swaddling clothes and laid in another room before her mother saw her, a third daughter and not the son Taksony had hoped for. Adila had to stand on tiptoe to reach her. We do not yet know much about the effects of the first impact of its world on a new-born infant: but it is possible that this primal welcome by other than a mother was some cause of the unusual sympathy between the two sisters.

Childhood in Budapest

We are already anticipating the last chapter of this book, when Adila was dead: but as for dreading loneliness, it is modest people who do this; and a modest person Jelly remains. 'I don't like this business of resting on one's laurels: they are so prickly.' Only modest people feel themselves crowned with holly.

The laurel tree was now growing, if the leaves were not yet won, cut and worn. But for the rest, the sisters lived like other children of good family in Budapest, in a way of life comfortable, congenial, and reasonably calm. They had the usual ailments, but an out of the ordinary affliction struck Adila when suffering cold or shock. She went completely rigid, unable to move limb or joint: a kind of passing paralysis which she got from her father; for when his wife was expecting her first child and the time had come, Taksony found himself seized up like an overheated piston, and quite a time elapsed before he could run off to fetch the doctor.

When Adila was four, she had a serious attack of diphtheria, as a result of which her voice stayed unusually deep in pitch. She was sent to her aunt's country house to convalesce. Titi went with her mother to see her for the first time in a long while; and the family was interested to know how these devoted sisters would greet each other. All Titi said was *'Tu as des beaux souliers rouges.'*

The Aranyis had no carriage. Their transport was the electric tram, as it was for all the professional classes; a kind of club on wheels, where you met your friends on various errands. They used most the yellow tram, like many good Glaswegians of the same period: and, as in Glasgow, an underground railway, of a sort, was in construction.

One place where electric trams were not allowed was St Margaret's Isle in the middle of the Danube, summer playground of Budapest for rambling, bathing, eating pastries. Here, overhead wires would have spoiled the line of the ancient horse-chestnut trees and vulgarized the collection of roses, one of the finest in the world. So only horse-drawn trams still plied here, constant as ox-carts, for many years after other cities had gone tram-electric throughout.

But the Aranyi family did not like this beauty spot very much: 'too many mosquitoes' says Jelly. To escape the suffocation of a city summer they would rather take day trips down the Danube in river boats. In the bleak cold of winter they skated in the *bois*, a woody part near the Zoo.

The Zoo named Jelly. There was a tiny African nation called Dahomey, on the Gulf of Guinea, which has recently become an independent republic. In those days Dahomey was a kingdom, famous for the monarch's bodyguard of valiant female warriors. But in 1892, when European nations were vying with each other in a building of empires, the French invaded it and two years later deposed the king. Some kind of propaganda mission of protest was touring Europe and arrived at the Budapest Zoo with a show. The nursemaids of Adila and Titi and of other small children made friends with this company, one of their favourites being a Dahomeian girl called Jeli, said to be a princess of that small royal house.* Taksony's third child was about to be born, and he was already calling it, as fathers often do, by an affectionate nickname. When the child was born, he kept the name officially; and being anglophilic spelt it in what he believed to be the british way, with two *l*s and a *y*; though he knew neither sound nor meaning of the word in english. Expected fun was made of this when the sisters first played in London: but British music-lovers learned to pronounce *J* as Y, thinking it all exotically Hungarian and traditional.

Coming to London in Edwardian days, Jelly was to hear the last street-cries of lavender-women and knife-grinders, just as she recalls the rag-and-bone men of Budapest streets chanting '*Handlee! Handlee!*' in Yiddish accents. But she does not recall any of the tellers of fairy-stories, who, I had heard, recited in public parks. If any existed, these children had no need of them: for Adila was a great retailer of fairy stories, and like all good

---

*So at least Jelly was told. But a former king of Dahomey had a name very like Jeli, and her father may have misunderstood.

Childhood in Budapest

story-tellers also made them up. Years later, if Jelly were ill, even when they were in the full current of their fame, Adila often sat at her bedside and told her a new one.

There being no boy in the house, playthings were mostly dolls; scores of dolls large and small. Adila liked dressing and hatting them, especially small ones. She must have made at least a hundred hats out of scraps of cloth and cocks' feathers, feathered hats being then in vogue. Before long she had both parents involved in the supply of materials. Taksony had to order dozens of samples of silks and velvets from Switzerland, and then found himself morally obliged to make real orders, of dress lengths for his wife. To the end of her days Adila, faithful to little dolls, carried one or more in her handbag.

Once Adila had a doll as big as a modern 'walkie-talkie'. When Jelly was two, there was a grand public celebration of a national anniversary, and the children were taken out in their best frocks to see the decorations. Jelly's phenomenal memory retains to this day the illuminated fountain, and also the pink satin dress she wore, with a green velvet collar. It had come off Adila's doll.

Adila and Titi went on playing with their younger sister long after the age when today they would consider themselves much more grown up. They played the usual international children's games like hide-and-seek, and a Hungarian one called how-like-you-this? Once a young student, smitten with Adila, was teased to confusion by the question 'How like you Adila?' This was Béla Bartók, four years her senior, shy, precise, and with no sense of humour.

Again we anticipate a later chapter: when the famous and impressionable Bartók met the famous and radiant Jelly. But Jelly could take little interest in a person with no sense of humour, her own having developed very early. When she was a small child, the family was coughing and sneezing from all sides of the sitting-room. Jelly could not read for the noise. She opened an umbrella and sat in its shelter and went on reading.

The Aranyi family often went into the country, where an invitation to afternoon coffee usually finished as a full supper be-

The Sisters d'Aranyi

fore they left, for which a chicken or duck would be killed: Hungarian hospitality being like Spanish, or like what Spanish hospitality used to be. Country customs were known to them. On Easter Monday young men used to raid the homes of their chosen girls and duck them (no less) in ponds or wells. In the cities water was replaced by a deluge of scent. The girl had to respond with a gift of a carnation; and debonair lads paraded the evening streets sporting several.

They sometimes went for a holiday in the foothills of the Western Carpathians, some miles to the north of Budapest, in a region now Czechoslovakian for its language. One night after they had arrived and gone to bed, Adila being about seventeen, Titi and Jelly about fifteen and ten, their father came into the bedroom anxious and grave. The house, he said, (which was a kind of superfarmhouse standing by itself) was surrounded by brigands. Not a paternal leg-pull. It might well have been true. Even within a few score miles of the capital, brigands there were; and a middle-class family from the city isolated with no help, and of course no telephone, would have been easy prey. Nor was Taksony the kind of police chief to have a bodyguard nor even a private sleuth.

However, this turned out not siege but serenade: a serenade by gipsies hired by some local people to perform, who suddenly burst into music and song all round the house. If you did not at once put a candle of acknowledgement in a window they started up a wicked little gipsy satire that ran 'O Sajo, my dog, how fast asleep you are!'

On this holiday Adila, who had a liking for snails as pets, put salt on some she had collected. She never knew why. To her torment, and theirs, they shrivelled and died.

Financial straits apart (and finances steadily improved) it was a sheltered life. Liked or not, the Austro-Hungarian Empire seemed as permanent as the British Empire seemed in Britain, and was not inconvenient for some Hungarians. Social unrest was not yet organized. Politics were politics, and families for the most part families. The Aranyi family grew closer and closer to each other,

Childhood in Budapest

feeling the same way about most things that mattered, so that there was little need of discussion. Schooling could not, as it can and sometimes does, disrupt the younger generation against the older.

Adila and Titi went to school when they were eight, but Jelly was taught for four years at home by her mother. Mother-education at home was no bad preparation for school, as those who have had it will know. Reading, writing, arithmetic, history and geography became part of family life. There was no gap between 'learning=school' and 'playing=home'. There was no need to co-ordinate or puzzle out discrepancies between what the teacher said and what your parent or nursemaid said. In a sense little Jelly had better than the best of four worlds, for she went to school only for examinations.

It was no use. Book-learning was not for her. Or not yet. To each examination she went equipped with one of her father's big handkerchiefs to weep into, making nor head nor tail of any kind of education. So it was decided to send her to a private day-school not far from home.

Ten days only she went there. Most of the time she spent crying in the lavatory. On the eleventh day, enduring despair no farther, she trotted by herself the ten-minute pavement home, and never went back. Her parents said she had better become a musician like her sisters; and that was the end of her formal education. However, like the celebrated Etonian who wrote of himself in *Who's Who* 'mainly self-educated in the holidays', she acquired a by no means inconsiderable culture, and like her sisters refused all her life to read and to talk only musical 'shop'.

For long enough this narrative has been neighing and shaking its mane at the mention of music, and the time has come to give it its head. A direction no doubt as welcome to reader as to rider.

2

Music Prospect

Nobody remembered when, why or how Adila first held a violin; she seemed to have been born with a bow in her hand. So here are no sprats to catch psychologists, except those few who find genius born, not made by conations or inhibitions or anything else. It may have been that the visits of Josef Joachim to his relatives encouraged her musical impulse: but music was a normal part of education and life in that household. Everyone, with greater or less talent, played the piano. Even Taksony liked to strum: also on the *cimbalom,* that ancient Persian dulcimer which most performers play jangily and only Hungarians well. Sometimes he irritated his wife by the noises he made, for she was better on the keyboard than he.

All the sisters learned the piano; and that was why Béla Bartók came regularly to the house, as a senior music student with an upturned nose and prim grey face, to give lessons to Titi. The Bösendorfer grand stood in the drawing-room, and through the glass pane of the door that led in from the dining-room Adila, with Jelly standing on a chair, made faces and gestures of derision during lessons, so that when he looked up, as he had to do, he was confused and did not know where to put himself. He was a delicate lad, and for a couple of years Adila often saw him take nothing at meals but a glass of milk.[1]

By the age of twenty-two Béla Bartók was much in love with Adila, and sent her postcards. Some were from other towns where he happened to go, Berlin or Pozsony; the majority were posted in Budapest. Some were amusing: caricatures of public figures in a series called *La Lune Journaliste*. At Christmas he made her a devil's broom out of three twigs pasted on red paper and worked with red ribbon on to a card. On most, the printed words *carte postale* have been scored out in ink, and the words *levelezò-lep* substituted: for Bartók was already a nationalist. On the rest the Hungarian cancels the French with an over-printing as by a rubber stamp.

Sometimes his love-cards were musical. In 1902 he sent a short *duo* for violins, the score exquisitely clear in his neat manuscript on an ordinary postcard. In this form of canon by retrogression, or rather *per recte et retro*, the second violin's part is literally in reverse: it is the first's, turned upside down. Reverse the card, and the same notes make the other voice.

In the same year, after hearing Adila at a concert, he sent in homage a longer piece, for solo violin, on three postcards linked together. This Adila studied, making figures and signs for fingering and bowing: but whether she did so then, or half a century later when she played it for the first time in public, I do not know. Certainly he took more than an adorer's interest in her progress. 'Are you practising hard?' he wrote fiercely, 'I will beat you with a broomstick if you are not.'

Some of these cards were addressed in the usual way: but on some, when he felt like it, he wrote the city first, then Adila's name, then the street and house number; 'because' says Jelly, with a more or less detached affection, 'Béla always wanted to be different.'

The lively Adila was fond of him, but not in love with him; and nothing came of this. But Bartók never forgot her, though he fell in love with at least two other violinists in his life. One, according to a letter in *The Observer*[2] was Stefi Geyer, a Hungarian pupil of Hubay at the Academy, who was two years younger than Adila, and to whom he dedicated his first, and posthumously published, *Violin Concerto*. The third, later, was Jelly.

Though all three sisters were normal, sincere and passionate

The Sisters d'Aranyi

girls, continually falling in and out of love with young men, they were of the time and place and background in which they were brought up. Indeed all three were innocent and young for their age at all ages. The time had not yet come when an artist had to feel restricted, had to have her reputation sullied as not being fully alive, if she did not change bed-partners every week or two—or oftener. In this narrative there are no ramstam sex affairs. This is bound to be a gentle book. For it is about people of a generation and ambiency in which such things were in fact rare, and kept as private as prayer, or regarded in public with fully as much wonderment as disapproval: and if any reader dislikes such un-existentialist facts, he had better return it to the library; for I cannot fabricate life to his taste.

So innocent was Adila, that when in the garden of a country summer hotel she was grabbed and kissed on the mouth by some impetuous young man, who afterward protested he had mistaken her for somebody else (he as naïf as she naïve, perhaps), she was convinced like other girls of her generation and some of a generation more recent too, that he had made her pregnant. For days she kept her agony to herself, but finally had to confess to someone. She chose her Aunt Tatiana, the Pole, who being so advanced as to use rouge, might be counted on for worldly wisdom if not comfort. Aunt Tatiana listened and questioned her. Finally she said gravely that she doubted if Adila were pregnant this time, but she must never let such a thing occur again.

Béla Bartók came almost every day for five years to the Aranyi house as teacher and as friend, partly because of Adila, partly because of the Joachim connection, and partly as Halsey Stevens says[3] because 'they all absolutely refused to speak German, and with his budding nationalism Bartók felt a kinship for them.' Already he was fascinated by Balkan folk music, and within a couple of years was to start investigating and preserving authentic melodies, for which he would set off, bearded, in high boots, with spectacles and a walking stick, and a raincoat over his arm. By 1918 he would have brought home over six thousand.

In his book *Neue Musik*, H. H. Stuckenschmidt shows how

Music Prospect

1. Duo in canon written for Adila by Béla Bartók, 1902.

The Sisters d'Aranyi

Bartók was discovering that this pure folk music was in advance of the 'cultured' tradition of Europe, and quite unrelated to the bastard 'gipsy' music of Liszt and others. For one example, the alternation of *tempi* (2/8; 3/8; 2/8); for another, a tendency to hover on the frontiers of tonality: these opened out a new set of terms for musical thinking. Not arid experimentation, nor from lack of ideas inside the old set; but as a matter of musical logic in a locality where the new set was already functioning. This was to make him, like all true innovators and explorers in the arts, traditionalist as deeply as he was rebel: so that his *Second String Quartet,* the sounds of which seemed neurotic, not to say pathological, to its first hearers, became wholly intelligible if they heard recordings of certain Rumanian folk music.

Bartók was already becoming known as a young composer, and his patriotic and rather Straussian symphonic poem called *The Kossuth Symphony** would be presented at Budapest in January 1904. It caused some scandal in official quarters by caricaturing a German national hymn.

But there may have been another reason for his liking the Aranyi home. Great Britain interested him, and Britain was much discussed there. This was the time of the Boer War, or just after. Anglophile though he was, Taksony von Aranyi like many other thinking people in Europe could not pardon the unprovoked British aggression. The British Empire in its state of financial-industrial *lebensraum* was regarded by thousands with the same loathing as was Mussolini later over Abyssinia. To be pro-Boer was to be pro-decency, and ladies all over the Continent were wearing 'Boer' hats to show solidarity. Nevertheless one voice was raised in Sziv Utca on the British side. This was Adila's. Staunch to a country she could not remember ever not having believed in and dreamed over, she argued against her father time after time till both grew acrimonious.

Adila was in love with England. If its politics were wrong, she still loved it, as often happens between woman and man. She

*Kossuth was one of the Hungarian leaders who challenged the Austrian Empire.

could not formulate her reasons. She merely wanted, longed, needed, to go to Britain. And when she did, it was largely due to her great-uncle Joachim, who must now come into close-up.

Josef Joachim was not just another brilliant violinist in the long line from Baltzar* or Corelli through Viotti and Paganini to Kreisler and your preferred virtuoso of today. Brilliant he was, but always before brilliance and above it he put sincerity and musical meaning, thereby helping to make public, if not indeed to make possible, the new instrumental music of the later nineteenth century. The results last on all good violinists living.

'I too think', Schumann wrote in his last letter to Joachim⁴ then only twenty-three years old, 'that the caterpillar Virtuosity will gradually die and give place to the fair butterfly Composition. But don't let it be too much of a black butterfly: let brighter tones have their turn.' Joachim was so burningly serious in his youth that old-style critics said he took himself too seriously.

Joachim was born on June 28, 1831 near Pozsony (=Pressburg=Bratislava) now in Czechoslovakia, about sixty miles from Vienna and once the capital of the Hungarian kingdom. When he was seven, he played a duet in public with his teacher Serwaczynski, leader of the Pest Orchestra. When he was ten, he went to study in Vienna. Two years later he made his début as a boy prodigy at Leipzig with none other than Mendelssohn himself accompanying him. Mendelssohn introduced him to London the following March at Drury Lane Theatre, and Joachim played at other London concerts in May. This was the Hungarian boy' whom Bunn engaged to play between the acts of *The Bohemian Girl,* for which Bunn had written the libretto. The boy played *Grand Variations on a Theme from Rossini's Otello,* devised by the violinist Ernst.

In his published correspondence there is reproduced a caricature of the boy prodigy by the English artist Crossley. He wears

*The German Thomas Baltzar (1630–63), commonly known as 'The Swede' because born in Lübeck, was one of the earliest if not the first of what we would call violin virtuosi. Evelyn heard him playing on March 4, 1656, and Anthony à Wood describes part of his technique in 1659. See Ernst H. Meyer, *English Chamber Music,* 1946, pp. 209, 211.

The Sisters d'Aranyi

a boy's suit, carries his head bowed slightly towards the ground near his right foot: already, as always, a characteristic position. Whether or not he already had a spark of the flame that was to burn throughout his life, peeling off like varnish the incrustations of technical trickery and revealing the original grain of meaning in music, we do not now know. Probably he had. But London was not ready for such a thing. London was not even ready for the meaning of music. A critic described one work he played as 'a thankless work, rather trivial, and more curious than beautiful.' This was the Beethoven *Violin Concerto*, nearly forty years after it was written. Joachim went on playing it until it was accepted.*

But Joachim liked England nevertheless; and in his maturity it was largely through him that Brahms had a hearing and a following in London[5]: for Joachim loved Brahms, and when in 1897 he was playing in St James's Hall (where the Piccadilly Hotel now is) and heard that his friend had died in Vienna, he and his public mourned the news in the slow movement of the *D minor Sonata*.

From 1847 to 1862 he went to Britain frequently, and thereafter every year. For some time he was leader of the Grand Duke of Weimar's Orchestra, and then Konzertmeister to the King of Hanover. In 1868 he became head of the Berlin Royal High School of Music which King William of Prussia founded and Joachim helped to organize and plan[6], and lived in Berlin for the rest of his life.

The condition of music was little better in the rest of Europe than in London. Paganini, whose demoniac fingers led him to stopped harmonics and other expansions of range and tone, now required of all public executants, had died in 1840 while Joachim was still a student. But the Paganini world continued. A virtuoso was expected to play tricks: anything that would set off his dexterity. Even the admirable violinist Spohr, then elderly,

---

*Donald Tovey, writing to Robert Bridges in 1904. He very likely heard the description from Joachim himself, if indeed he had not been shown the cutting. See Mary Grierson, *Donald Francis Tovey*, London, 1952, p. 110.

Music Prospect

played Beethoven *Quartets* solo 'with pianoforte accompaniment.'

With some exceptions like the Leipzig Gewandhaus Orchestra, which had given music in the old market hall since the end of the Seven Years' War, and the Berlin Friends of Music Orchestra (Mendelssohn and Joachim), and the Vienna Philharmonic founded in 1860, concerts were chaotic. This was because many orchestras were either small private household bands for princes and grand-dukes, which could manage little after Haydn and Mozart, or opera-house units more at home in the tum-ty harmonies of Spontini and Meyerbeer. In these latter viola-desks were often manned by retired or failing or failed players of violins or even of wind instruments.

Conductors were no better. Spohr claimed to be the first to take a baton in hand to direct an orchestra: till then and after him, directing was done by the leading violin literally hammering the beat, when necessary, on his music desk, and sometimes in a frenetic attempt to synchronize a rabble, breaking his bow. Too little interest was taken in correct *tempo*, because too little interest was taken in the feel of the music as written, which dictates *tempo*. Mendelssohn himself was an offender in this.

Going to a concert was like going to an opera or melodrama: a social occasion not only in court circles but also in the bourgeois world. Spohr complained that in London he had to spend £10 on providing free refreshments in the interval because the audience expected it, and that even if they were music-lovers and took no advantage, the caterers did.[7]

Chopin's works were treated as displays of sprinkled notes like pretty fireworks, not felt-over in the simple and sensitive way he himself had played them. But Chopin was dead, like Schubert and Weber, and the Romantic Movement was soon to end its great days with the end of Mendelssohn. Schumann, who had hailed both Chopin and Brahms when they were unknown, was now near his unhappy death. European music, like European drama, was resting on hackneyed and hashed classics or was frisking about on *bravura*.

The Sisters d'Aranyi

A change was needed, and a change was in the air. Many were conscious, but four led: Wagner in conducting and composing, Liszt in conducting, composing and at the piano, Brahms as pianist and composer, and Joachim principally with the violin. Joachim's example, said Donald Tovey, 'sufficed to expel for ever the old association of the musical performer with the mountebank.'[8]

Their call for a greater seriousness in the approach to music did not imply any disregard for technique nor puritan restrictions on composition. Quite the contrary. Wagner marched on, expanding chromatic harmony to a point from which today's music could send out and found its own colonies; and for all his elimination of claptrap arias by popular tenors and primadonnas, he demanded of voices and instruments alike a new technical ability for the intervals, as yet unused, which the meaning of his music demanded.

Even in performing the older music the attitude of the performer had to alter. 'Liszt when interpreting the classics' says Saint-Saens, 'did not substitute his own personality for the author's, as do many performers, he seemed rather to get at the heart of the music and find out its real meaning.'

If Wagner dared all for the future, Brahms remained more timidly in the past, and they hated each other: but both faced the same way in their earnestness for music. Liszt invented the symphonic poem, leading up to Elgar and down to lesser men. Joachim invented little. He austerely, dedicatedly, devoted one of the finest violin techniques of all time to the actuality of the music, and found thereby deeper and richer meanings throughout his life. But all four refused to be put off by what had become exhausted and therefore false conventions. The sounds in our concert halls today are due to them.

Musicologists have not yet invented a term for this new attitude, which had a parallel in other arts. Pre-raphaelites and impressionists in differing ways were melting off the rules that had crystallized round and were suffocating the principles of good painting. Tennyson published *The Princess*, in which oriental or

Music Prospect

romantic epics were for ever thrown out of fashion, and a long poem of great beauty was made about the emancipation of women. Tolstoy was preparing to write *War and Peace*, Flaubert, *Madame Bovary*. The new attitude sought truthfulness.

This was what Schumann meant in his letter to Joachim, and was what Joachim and Brahms found in each other when they first met in 1853, Joachim being twenty-two and Brahms twenty.

When Joachim founded his string quartet in Berlin in 1869*, Europe heard for the first time real ensemble playing as we know it. For uniformity of tone, a quality undemanded and thitherto unheard-of, all the members had Stradivarius instruments of the same, and the best, period. It was no accident that they should be invited to the Meiningen Music Festivals. At that time the Duke of Saxe-Meiningen and his actress wife were weaving the first acting ensemble on the European stage: or at least the first for several centuries, for we do not know enough about this side of early theatres. But the theatre in general, being always more conservative than other arts, had to wait longer for fruition. It was not for another generation that the parallel of seriousness appeared with men like Stanislavsky and Chehov, like Granville Barker and (if it is granted that the Great Buffoon was able to be such only because he took the theatre more seriously than any man of his time) Shaw.

Joachim was tall, broad-shouldered, grave and courtly, with a deep voice which could be gruff but never pompous. His personality was imposing, authoritative by nature, without 'side' and without cant: 'a king' says Jelly. Indeed royalty in his presence did on at least one occasion seem by comparison rather ordinary people.

He respected all who respected music. This included also the memory of Paganini for his better works such as the *Capricci*. When he taught in Berlin, he was no class-room teacher. Assuming that his pupils knew how to play the violin, or they would not be there, he taught them how to play music.

In his turn he was respected, internationally admired, honoured

*Or 1870. Grove says the former, *Encyclopaedia Britannica* the latter.

The Sisters d'Aranyi

and rewarded. He was a Senator of the Berlin Royal Academy of Arts, and Honorary Doctor of Music at Oxford, Cambridge, Glasgow and Göttingen. He was given the Prussian order *'Pour la Mérite'*. He was fêted all over Europe. In Britain he had powerful admirers like Lord Plymouth and Lord Spencer and the musical Mr Behrens of Manchester. In Germany he was loved, bowed to and waved to by the public in the street, and saluted by the Imperial Guard when he passed in his carriage.

Such, in very brief, was the historic Onkel Jo who often came to Budapest to see his sister's son and the son's family and to give concerts. A genial and congenial figure in the house, and one who made music respectable even to Hungarian aristocrats.

The gap between artists and the bourgeoisie was wide enough: but the aristocracy was so snobbish, right up to its extinction in the last revolution, that none could be anything but Army, Church or Politics. 'When Viscount Hambledon visited Hungary in the 1930's, Jelly says, 'a Hungarian nobleman asked his beautiful wife (who was a Pembroke Herbert) what her husband did. She replied "He's in business"* and the nobleman would have nothing more to do with them.'

In the nineteenth century it was worse. But the Aranyis were not snobs. Only the Aunt Tatiana from Poland, when her nieces took to the profession of music, called them *'les filles perdues'*. Both parents were pleased. Even the priestly uncles approved. So when Onkel Jo offered to train Adila in Berlin, he had little difficulty in getting his offer accepted. Thus at the age of twenty she became a pupil of the greatest violinist of the age, and possibly of any age so far.

At the same time Adila had been brought up in Budapest, and had that locality in her soul and ears, however non-Hungarian or dream-British she may have felt. So before we take her to Berlin we must occupy a few pages with what she heard in her native city.

*W. H. Smith & Son.

3

Violins and Fiddles

The sisters were told that when their father was a boy of about ten, about 1870, Joachim and Brahms came to Budapest to perform, and all three went out to a dinner-party at the 'Hungaria', a fashionable dining-place with the best gipsy orchestra in the city. Joachim and Brahms listened, Brahms with a beer-mug on the table in front of him. After a while they left the party at the long table and went to a smaller one near the music, to listen better. Silent they sat, hands to foreheads, concentrated on listening. 'That was the night' Jelly says 'when the Brahms-Joachim *Hungarian Dances* were begotten.'

I believe her. The story is not contradicted by Florence May[1] when she states that Brahms was first interested in Hungarian dances by the violinist Remenyi and performed a four-hand version on the piano of some of them in 1858. At the 'Hungaria' it was the fiddle side that absorbed the two musicians.

Budapest was a city of fiddles. Every restaurant and café of any quality had its gipsy band—of real gipsies. And just as there were two kinds of gipsy: on the one hand the savage, vindictive, free-wandering romany who in Hungary at least was happy to take a life in revenge for an insult with the police powerless; and on the other the musical gipsy who could be vagrant but could also have a constant musical job and live in the gipsy quarter Jozsefsvàros: so there were two types of gipsy music, the florid and the simple. But both were played in the gipsy style of fid-

The Sisters d'Aranyi

dling which is all but inimitable. It is quite different from the romantic lushness called 'gipsy' in light music ensembles; and no concert violinist can impart its quality without quite changing his outlook, any more than a pipe-major used only to marches could impart the quality of the *piobhaireachd*.

Yasha Krein, whose small light-music group used to delight Britain on the radio, once when I was present after a run-through, slid quietly into a real gipsy tune. As a man I had heard nothing like it; only in Spain as a boy. It was as if strings spoke words, as if both he and I were improvising from joint thoughts, he playing, with bright eyes holding mine, and I in some way helping. He played another. He had learned them from a gipsy in Russia. When I asked why he didn't invest this musical capital of his and educate us in it, instead of doing as plenty of others did, he replied that the public wouldn't like it. Maybe he meant he wouldn't like the public. For a good gipsy player, however cunning or showy, is not a mere entertainer. Intimate with his audience, he needs their intimacy.

The gipsy quality is hard to define. It is no mere matter of slurring and scooping notes till they sound like an electric guitar. It does not lie only in the almost quarter-tone *portamento*. Part of it, I think, lies in the unusual accuracy of *rubato*. One feels that the fiddler is tenoning his tune into a mortice of cimbalom harmonies, even, or especially, when playing without accompaniment: that he times the *tenuto* exactly, as if waiting for dulcimer strings to stop shivering. But this exactitude seems to have a law. His waiting, and that of his audience, tally. The timing is not merely for grace. In a way it has something in common with that of a good public speaker.

Of course 'cultured' music also has something of this. There is a difference between the last private run-through and the public performance, which is not mere keying up of the nervous system. But whereas some performers can take from an audience a sense of occasion that at times approaches the mystical, several eminent pianists have told me that they are quite unaware of people while playing, and some actually prefer an empty broad-

Violins and Fiddles

casting studio. Certainly a Joachim needs no public to get him nearer to the sonata he is studying. A gipsy fiddler playing to himself without an audience, would have, I fancy, to invent one.

Which does not mean that gipsy music is such only when heard by gipsies. For centuries the musicians preferred by Queen Elizabeth of Hungary and members of the Hungarian Parliament were gipsies. Bihari, reputed composer of the *Rakoczy March*, was one. Panna Czinka, possibly its real composer, was gipsy mistress to Prince Rakoczy.[2] In those days nobles and gipsies could address each other with the second person singular, a familiarity not permitted by the former to the middle classes. One noble, who prided himself as an amateur violinist, once took up the fiddle of his band-leader and acquitted himself so well to the liking of the band, that he found himself kissed and embraced and treated with 'thou' as an equal: 'But Excellency! thou'rt no gentleman, thou'rt romany.'[3]

There could also be camaraderie between gipsy fiddlers and gringo ones. In 1921, when Jelly, then famous, was back in Budapest on a visit, the most famous of all gipsy fiddlers Banda Marci became leader of his band again for one night in her honour, though he felt too old to lead and was playing second fiddle to his son-in-law Magyar Imré. He was a gipsy of the old style. As a little boy (so he told Jelly) he had stolen a cushion for the money to buy a fiddle. 'After that', he said, 'I never stole anything. Except with my ears.'

But gipsy fiddlers were already by then being tempted financially and socially into 'cultured' music. There were still a thousand of them to accompany Banda Marci to his grave in the nineteen-thirties, but ten years previously he had been proud that all his sons were going like gringo students to music schools to learn the violin 'properly'. Gipsies in Hungary, like gipsies in Russia for other reasons, were becoming 'artists'. The original fusion of performer and public was on the way out.

Neither Adila nor Jelly made a deliberate study of gipsy playing nor was ever an exponent of gipsy music. But neither could escape the larger influences of these. The influences were in the air of Hungary. A great artist usually appears as a concentration or distillation of the wild flowers of locality. There are exceptions like Sibelius and Grieg. But just as Poland produces pianists, so the proportion of violinists to other Hungarian soloists is remarkable in so small a nation. It is worth speculating whether there might have been no Joachim in nineteenth-century musical history if he had not been Hungarian. Certainly in his quest of sincerity he scaled the same mountain as the gipsies, though from another side and very differently equipped.

That a sensitive Hungarian could not live pleasurably without hearing fiddles round him may have contributed to making violinists of Adila and Jelly. Jelly pays her tribute to the gipsies. 'From listening to them I learned freedom, warmth and naturalness in playing.'

She may have learnt more. In 1931 an article in *Music and Letters*[4] by A. G. Browne on Béla Bartók tries to define the differences between 'Tzigane' and 'Magyar' music, meaning the style that became Brahms and Liszt and the style that became Béla Bartók. They are rhythmic and modal, and the latter style infinitely more subtle. 'This music', the author writes, 'depends for its effect upon the skill and imagination of the artist-executant, and it is significant that Bartók has written his two violin sonatas for Jelli d'Aranyi and Josef Szigeti respectively.* They know exactly how to bring to life the intricate decorations, how to regulate the frequent and subtle graduations of tempo, and, above all, how to suggest a flowing movement which is yet fascinatingly syncopated.'

The 'skill and imagination' demanded for the above and the 'freedom, warmth and naturalness' felt by Jelly have something in common. Both groups of qualities postulate a music which depends for full effect on the way it is performed and an artist who allows nothing else to come between the music and its proper performance.

Adila too was cradled in this tree. She was already an artist

*This is an error. Both sonatas were written for Jelly. Szigeti, like Adila and Jelly, was born in Budapest and studied under Hubay at the Academy there.

Violins and Fiddles

of more than high promise before she became Joachim's pupil. He set the seal. He opened new roads. He pruned wisely the vigorous shoots of her springtime. But he did not train her from the beginning, nor ever for very long.

With his approval Adila was sent to the Budapest Academy of Music, which had an international reputation. There she studied under Jenó Hubay, the Hungarian whom Joachim had taught in the seventies. 'Hubay's success as a violinist' however 'lay less in his solo playing than in his quartet leadership, at least that was Brahms's opinion.'[5] In Budapest he founded his quartet with David Popper, who taught the 'cello at the Academy. Under Popper Adila studied chamber music. He always liked to take part when she took part.

Once a young violinist has a sufficient technique, chamber music is not only one of the most magical of joys, but also the best of trainings. You cannot contribute mere skill to an ensemble. By the age of thirteen Adila had acquired a technique that approached prodigy level, but already she stood for more. This was partly due to the Joachim 'feel' of the Academy. It was also innate.

There are accounts of her as early as August 1900, when she took part in a concert at Crickvenica, an Adriatic town near Fiume, now Yugoslav. 'The public listened with astonishment' wrote the representative of the *Budapesti Hirlap*[6] 'to Arànyi Adila, the thirteen-year-old violinist, who played with great artistic precision and impeccable technique Bériot's *Scènes de Ballet*. Arànyi Adila has a definite personality; and one day, in fact very soon, will create a sensation by her beautiful playing.'

In November she played a concerto by the same French violinist Bériot at Vac, a town north of Budapest, where the Danube cuts through the foothills of the Carpathians some twenty miles from the present Czech frontier. A critic with a romantic style wrote: 'We realized how the great masters of violin-playing first began, enchanting their listeners at the outset of their careers, and the way in which they won their laurels of public enthusiasm and recognition. Hail to thee, young maiden; hail! We do not doubt but that the success and triumph of the virtuoso will be thy lot.'

The Sisters d'Aranyi

Two years later at the age of fifteen she had mastered Tartini's *Devil's Trill* Sonata, a maddening piece to most students, a kind of eighteenth-century anticipation of Paganini. This was at Kecskemét, south-east of Budapest, where the uplands run down into the Tibisco plains. Priest-uncle Guszti was headmaster there, and Jelly (for the family went too) remembers being worried because an island nearby was called Hell Isle. 'An already very remarkable technique', observed one critic: and another, unexpectedly knowledgeable for a provincial newspaper critic of that time, gives welcome details. Besides noting that her trills were 'brilliant', that the audience called for her again and again, and that among her encores was *Légende* by the nineteenth-century Polish violinist Wieniawski, he says she played with great feeling and 'variety of tone'.

Jelly pauses in her translation of the old press cutting, and says, 'Variety of tone! It's wonderful that she already possessed that. It was what Joachim and all of us stood for, and is ignored by many prominent violinists, who just establish a *vibrato* and stick to it.'

The critic seems to agree. 'A special feature of her playing is her bowing, so important and alas! neglected by many of today's players.'

A more rapturous account of this concert is worth reproducing both for its description of Adila's appearance and behaviour on a concert platform, and for a little light relief to the reader during this solemn assessment of Adila's gifts.

'The Society of Music Lovers' Concert last night exceeded all expectations. The whole evening gave great satisfaction, but everyone's heart quivered with delight when the little guest artist Arànyi Adila's violin spoke. Charming, lovable and brilliant is her appearance. A sweet little girl with a very, very old* violin, smiling, and her sparkling eyes prophesying a great artist's career. Gradually her expression changes. Her bright eyes look down,

---

*The 'very, very old violin' was in fact an eighteenth-century one: by Gobetti, a Venetian maker.

Violins and Fiddles

and little Adila leans her lovely small head on her violin with as much warmth and love as if she wanted to kiss that dry piece of wood. And so she played; and while the strings spoke under her hands, it seemed as if everyone had vanished away, and only those two were left, little Adila and her violin, on some enchanted height: Adila, and her best playmate, the old violin.'

Praising both her 'sorrow and playfulness' this sentimental person adds that at the end 'the little artist seemed pleased and grateful at having such a reception, and gave several encores, among them two by Hubay and Schumann's *Träumerei*.

But this picture, over-painted or not, will prove worth carrying in our minds when we come to Adila's maturity on the platform.

By the next year, at Körmöcbanya, to Adila's 'masterly' playing was added Titi's 'lovely and enchanting' accompaniment. 'And it is not surprising that the public was not satisfied with the Paganini *Moses* Variations, Hubay's *Hungarian Rhapsody* and Bazzini's *Ronde des Lutins*' (another display piece for such young virtuosi as can manage it), 'but clapped and shouted for more'.

However, just as in those days no British musical aspirant had arrived unless Berlin attested it, so any Hungarian of ambition had to be measured by Vienna. At Vienna Adila appeared on January 17, 1906. The *Wiener Fremdenblatt* gave a considered, and favourable, verdict.[7]

'The night before last we made the acquaintance at the Ehrbarsaal of a young violinist who has a great future. Adila von Aranyi* is a great-niece of Joachim, and it seems that a spark of her great-uncle's divine fire has fallen on her. So far as we may judge from her first appearance, her characteristic is her tone—warm, and full of deep feeling, with every now and then the flame of a glowing temperament breaking through. In the last movement of the Beethoven *Concerto* the young violinist was at war with her temperament. She took it by storm. . . . Here was a new and interesting, truly fresh, reading of the concerto, and very convincing, despite its departure from tradition.'

*Note the Austrian Imperial form.

The Sisters d'Aranyi

In which we see Adila growing fast from wonder child to serious musician, capable of getting nearer to Beethoven than the conventions of her time.

This reviewer elaborates on her tone in the Bach *"Air on the G String"*, and in Godard's *Adagio,* with special praise for her *ritardando* at the end, 'which can only be played by one who has a store of musicianship in her.' Hubay's *Zéphyre* and Schumann's *Träumerei* brought out the enthusiastic side of her playing, he says; and one of the Sarasate *Spanish Dances* the virtuoso side.

But Vienna had to administer a political rebuke; 'The only pity was the red, white and green on the laurel wreath presented to her' during wild scenes of rapture at the end. For these were the Hungarian national colours, and the Hungarians on the organizing committee did well to adopt them. In Hungary ladies avoided wearing the Austrian black and yellow, though many, including Madame von Aranyi, loved them in combination.

It was in this year of 1906 that Adila, then twenty, sat for the Artist's Diploma, a distinction which the Academy awarded seldom because few reached the high standard it required. A candidate had to know by heart a large number of concerti, and to prepare in ten days one that would be chosen as unfamiliar to him or her. Béla Bartók took Adila to a music shop and bought her all the violin concerti on sale.[8] But the one for her proved none of these. It was the Dvořák *Concerto* which had been written for Joachim.

She had to perform also the *Devil's Trill*, over which Béla Bartók sent her a postcard covered with babies' faces. 'Count these little maggots' he wrote. 'An even number, and you play well. An odd, and you don't.' But there are more than five hundred of them, some so tiny that an exact count is impossible. It would seem that the number was even.

She won the award easily. It is calligraphically a handsome document, in a beautiful square Hungarian lettering of red and blue. The red of the ink is echoed by, or at least by luck does not clash with, that of a perforated government stamp, which the law required to be fixed on it. Some artistic person at the Aca-

Violins and Fiddles

demy so placed this, that it becomes part of the general layout.

In the same year she gave her first recital in Budapest, at the Bösendorfersaal, equivalent to our Wigmore Hall. Joachim and all the pundits were present; and so nervous was Adila, that her performance, which should have lasted an hour and fifty minutes ended under the hour. Heresy to all that Joachim lived for in the matter of *tempo*.

But her gifts were immediately recognized. An impresario named Gross had a contract for her in his pocket, which he drew out for signing: but Joachim intervened and tore it up. He said afterward that Adila had better come and stay with him for a bit, to learn discipline and the calming of herself into proper *tempi*.

Already, then, Adila could have left the Academy for a career as a capable, indeed an exceptional, performer. But technical skill, with or without new interpretations of Beethoven, was not enough. Joachim saw greater possibilities. In becoming his pupil she joined an international cluster of stars, Danish, Polish, Argentinian, Italian, American, German: names known in Europe in later years. But few of them, I think, took with them such a violin as Adila's. The teachers at the Academy had no fears that she would fall short of the standards of the Berlin High School of Music. Not only did they give her the rare diploma; they got together a subscription and presented her with a Balestrieri violin of 1736.

For some while in Berlin Adila lived in a *pension* near Joachim's house; but for most of her time there she was his resident pupil. And his only private one. Ever.

4

To the Death of Joachim

Meanwhile Jelly also had become a violinist. If ever a player was gifted as well as talented (may the distinction hold?) it was she. At a recital she gave in a Portland Place private house during the summer of 1938 I noticed her fingers and for the first time touched them. Their sinews, when flexed, were like those of a young seagull I once caught on a Scottish island. They had always been like that: nor was I the first to notice them. The fingers made the violinist, and not the other way about.

One day in Budapest Adila, who had graduated from Grunfeld's class into Hubay's, was taken by her late professor to Zimmer's violin shop to buy a new bow. Jelly went with them. It was Jelly's eighth birthday, and she was holding a bag of sweets. She was to go to the Academy herself in the autumn to study the piano. But when Grunfeld saw her hands, he was struck with them. 'This child' he announced 'must learn the violin, not the piano'; for he found her hands fashioned by nature to that end. Jelly was eager, and the family willing: so for the rest of the summer holidays Adila showed her how to begin playing, and she practised like a devoted demon for six weeks.

At the end of that time she had to pass an entrance examination, an ordeal rather severe, since all the eminent musicians who were professors at the Academy heard all the candidates. Including Popper and Hubay himself. To give her confidence, Jelly's mother asked if Adila might be with her; but this was refused

To the Death of Joachim

as against the rules: 'especially to the great-nieces of Joachim' they said. So Jelly went by herself. The test piece was called *Syncopated Study,* and she had to play it at sight; but syncopation did not worry her: she had already mastered that on the piano. This must be a very rare case: a child of eight, who is not only accepted, but given an entrance scholarship, by a celebrated musical academy when she has had a violin in her hands only six weeks. But a scholarship she was given: so that her musical education never cost her family a farthing. Grunfeld was her first teacher. He called her his 'little gipsy' because she played *Ta-Ra-Ra-Boom!-de-Ay* with such abandon.

That made all three sisters students at the Academy; for Titi was already studying the piano there under Arpàd Szendy, who had been a pupil of Liszt. She never gave recitals; but at Academy concerts played such works as the Chopin *Fantaisie in F minor,* and on another occasion, Jelly recalls *The Ruins of Athens* in an arrangement for two pianos. She became as beautiful a pianist as person, but was nervous and self-conscious on the platform. Unable to trust her memory, she preferred chamber music and accompanying, and avoided solo work when she could.

Little Jelly learned as quickly as she had begun. In her second year she broke a leg while skating. The only result was a double remove next term. The year following, the Joachim Quartet was in Budapest on its way to an engagement in Vienna. A breakfast party was given in the Aunt's house, at which Adila played the first movement of the Beethoven *Concerto,* probably with Titi in place of orchestra. Taksony asked Jelly also to play, seeing that she was already working on the first movement of one of the Spohr Concerti*, and Onkel Jo had not yet heard her playing.

'At that time,' says Jelly today, sitting, with her hair cut necklength, under the portrait de Laszlo painted of her in the 'twenties, when she wore dark coils over her ears, 'I wore a fringe. Onkel Jo parted the fringe and kissed me on the forehead, saying I looked

---

*Being about ten years old, and having studied the violin for less than two years.

nicer without it. He spoke in German. His comment on the way I played, was "Never too much *vibrato!* That's circus music".'
And he went on to show her how in bowing the wrist must be flexible, with the middle finger pressing, not bent stiffly back to shove the bow.

Joachim's own bowing was one of the secrets of his phenomenal variety of tone. An account of it was given by Adila in a letter to *Music and Letters* in 1950, to dispose of a misrepresentation by Harold Bauer.[1] Bauer had described Joachim's bowing arm as 'tightly glued to his side when playing.' Adila replied:

'Naturally the upper arm must, when one is playing on the E string, be kept near the body, but Joachim raised it with a harmony of movement truly wonderful as he shifted to a lower string. His instructions to me were that the arm should be in such a position that a ruler placed across the arm would stay there horizontally. I owe it to my great-uncle to refute Mr Bauer's imputation. Joachim's bowing was not unlike Gioconda de Vito's. It was exquisite.'

On this his last visit to Budapest Joachim said he would like to take Jelly to Berlin and train her himself. 'Talent like hers', were his words 'occurs once in a century'. So Jelly tells me. She adds: 'A century starts every day'.

But the parents could not consent: Jelly was too young. So she stayed with Grunfeld and Hubay, and it was Adila who went, and only she. But Joachim when touring told everyone about his brilliant great-nieces, especially in England; thereby leaving them a legacy of very great value, which he was never to know they inherited.

In Berlin Adila soon made her mark, and enjoyed herself. She met Grieg there the year before he died, and Humperdinck in his early 'fifties, a most impressive man: but the most important friend she made among her great-uncle's friends was undoubtedly Donald Tovey, then in his early thirties, as tall, dominating, authoritative and knowledgeable as Joachim himself.

To the Death of Joachim

This young Englishman was scholar, composer, pianist and conductor, of equal merit. Also one of the best educators in his musical generation. Joachim said of him that he knew more about music than any man living. According to Casals, Joachim also said that he could easily talk about music with Schumann and Brahms, but not with Tovey, 'he knows too much'.[2]

When Adila entered the room to meet this paragon for the first time, her great-uncle said, 'I want you to meet the greatest musician since Brahms'. Tovey was kindly, however, and respectful when Adila joined the two in the Bach *Double Concerto in D minor*. He was tolerant and self-restrained and interested in other people's points of view; and he and Adila became great friends. But Adila regarded him for the rest of his life with awe. It was her own word.

When Tovey was only thirteen he had played a sonata of his own with Joachim: and later in his life Casals, whose declared opinions must be respected, made the startling comment: 'The Brahms *Concerto* played by Schnabel was remarkable, but Tovey's rendering was superior to his.'[4] In 1905 he was already a figure well-known in London, Berlin and Vienna chamber concerts, at a time when chamber music had to be fought for; but this, like the effect of his Bach on the musical public and the help he gave to the sisters, will be shown later.

Adila attended all her uncle's recitals, and sat on the platform with a spare violin. She herself made some appearances with display works like the *Devil's Trill*, or Saint-Saens' *Rondo Capriccioso*, and more serious ones like the unaccompanied Bach *Adagio and Fugue in G minor*. Joachim particularly liked the way she handled Sarasate's *Zapateada* from the *Spanish Suite:* so much so, that once when they were staying in a house-party outside Berlin he made her play it seven times over. They were good friends as well as good musicians.

Their friendship did not stop Joachim from treating her as severely as any other pupil if she did not reach the very high standard of accuracy he had laid down for himself and others. They were practising the Bach *Concerto for Two Violins and Orchestra*

The Sisters d'Aranyi

in D minor*. At the opening of the first movement the following interruption took place:

Joachim: What is this? How are you playing this?
Adila: Legato.
Joachim: And how is it marked?
Adila: Staccato.
Joachim (grave): Why do you play it *legato*?
Adila: Because I can't play it *staccato*.
Joachim (very quiet): In that case (*removing the music and substituting another work*) we will not practise the *Double Concerto*.

By no means all our major violinists do play these passages *staccato*, either because they do not think it important, or because they would lose speed if they did. As Jelly says, they lose fire instead. But Adila always did so after this, and Jelly with her later: which work was perhaps the finest in their joint repertoire, as many who heard it in the Queen's Hall or elsewhere may agree. The very copies Adila used with Joachim went with them through life and exist today, a little worn, but clean and intact, as not all well-studied sheet-music is preserved.

An event which Adila remembered the rest of her life was a recital in Berlin by the Bohemian violinist Jan Kubelik. At the age of twenty-five, as he then was, he had already an outstanding technique which he had acquired under Sevcik at Prague. It was capable of 'magical effects', and he avoided that 'nauseating *vibrato*' which Onkel Jo had called circus music to Jelly. 'Well do I remember', Adila wrote in 1950 'my great-uncle Joachim talking to me about it. We sat in the first row, and Kubelik when he saw Joachim was obviously panic-stricken. He began with Bruch's *G minor Concerto,* and on the long-sustained G in the first bar his bow was shaking.' Joachim however was enthusiastic

---

*Since this work is bound to be often mentioned in this book, I will generally call it 'the Bach *Double Concerto*', leaving its partner in C major to be differentiated by its full title.

about Kubelik's 'clear, flute-like tone'. Later in life, according to Adila, Kubelik became mechanical, 'a matter of losing his nerve —and with it his control.'[5]

At Christmas that year Joachim had no fewer than a hundred presents, including a model carriage-and-pair which stood on the table to represent the real equipage sent him by the two brothers Mendelssohn, rich bankers, nephews of the composer. One of these, Robert, was a good amateur 'cellist. At the Bonn Festival, when Joachim and Adila were staying with him, Adila and his two daughters frivolously asked him if he were never nervous at night and locked his bedroom door. Hearing he was not and did not, the three girls that night floured their faces and crept into his bedroom in long white nightdresses each holding a lit candle. Robert Mendelssohn woke up screaming with terror at three Angels of Death round his bed.

This conduct Joachim thought unbecoming to a young lady of twenty. He adapted the punishment by leading Adila into the breakfast-room next morning by the ear.

In all her life Adila never quite caught up with her own age. She was fond of jokes and fond of falling in love. When she was sixteen and at the Academy, her sisters found in a drawer a piece of pink vellum edged with gilt, on which she had written a list headed 'People I Have Been In Love With'. There were already about twenty names. Her sisters added others, including the two janitors at the Academy, who, all agreed, were 'horrid'.

So now in Berlin, though growing in dignity and intellect as a musician, she kept the emotional course of an adolescent. She conceived an indomitable and unrequited passion for Karl Klingler, a young pupil of Joachim. Hopeless passion being a kind of death, she paid tribute to it, one night of Wertherian despair, by making her will. Having written home at the same time, she put the will in the wrong envelope, and discovered her mistake only in time to telegraph the family not to open what arrived.

But the proper letter arrived too late. Her parents assumed she was having an affair with some undesirable, and took the next train to Berlin. When they got there in the morning, Adila was out at a studio having her portrait painted by the German artist Nelson.

The first time anyone sits for a portrait is a flattering experience. It gives one a new and re-assuring interest in one's self. Adila, properly chaperoned of course, was furious to find her parents possessed of her secret. The storm blew over from both directions; but meanwhile little Jelly in Budapest was in such a nervous apprehension over her sister's fate (whether death or worse than) that she came out in a rash. A thing that often afflicted her throughout her life when she was run down.

Adila now appeared properly before the Berlin public. She gave a joint recital with a Hungarian woman pianist Valéri Ipolyi, who did not long pursue her career because of a family tragedy. Each played solo, and combined as a duo only in the Beethoven *'Spring' Sonata*.

She gave other smaller concerts elsewhere, conscious of her growing ability but not conceited about it. A postcard written to Jelly from Dresden railway station, saying: 'I played better than ever', was not a demand for admiration from herself or from anyone else. It was an honest, wondering pride that progress was being made and maintained: as all will understand who have appeared often on stage or platform in any public ploy.

But now the time was coming when Joachim could give her his official introduction to the musical world. They chose a programme. The orchestra would be the Berlin Philharmonic, which Joachim would direct. The date was fixed for a day in October 1907. It was almost as if Edmund Kean had launched his son Charles by producing him in *Richard III*. Without real personality and worth in the young performer such a début would have been mere nepotism, a delusion and disaster, perhaps a derision. But all who had heard her knew that Adila had a talent approaching her great-uncle's and a similar if less mature use of it. The same could not be said of all his pupils.

It was not to be. Joachim fell ill in May 1907. The doctors said he had cancer of the lung. This Adila refused to believe, saying he did not have the symptoms she had seen in a real case. The doc-

To the Death of Joachim

tors laughed at her. But in the end it was they who were wrong. This was a disease much rarer than cancer; one of the few recorded cases (the ninth of which they knew, they said) in which a human being contracts *actinomycosis,* called in cattle foot-and mouth disease. Joachim on country walks, of which he was fond, had a habit of chewing grass, and this, for want of any better, was given as the means of infection. In those days no official action was taken against an infected herd, and there was no cure.*

Adila did not want to leave Berlin, but her mother insisted that she join the rest of the family for their usual summer holiday in Austria. She had been there only a week, when she heard that Joachim was not expected to live. She made the long night journey alone, wearing the wedding ring her mother lent her against molestation. She was sure it was the end. And so it was.

Almost the last thing Joachim said was to ask if Jelly really understood and followed what he had said to her in Budapest about bowing, that single time he had heard her. For though quite apart from loving and guiding Adila he thought his elder great-niece had a big future, he could never forget the impression he had received from the ten-year-old Jelly.

On August 15, 1907 Adila sat by Joachim's body, devastated. She could not leave the bedside. The outer world mourned the death of the 'King of Violinists' at the age of seventy-six; but Adila's world was broken in pieces. Even so, she knew that now she had both a chance and a duty to hand on what she had learned from Joachim, and the better she trained and developed herself the more she could hand on: for she had learned as much in this one year as most students learn in an academic lifetime.

There was another who could not leave Joachim's deathbed. Donald Tovey was in Berlin at the time. He had come round at once. He sat there 'almost demented'. The world had lost a great musician, but he his best friend.

It is seldom that two men exceptional in the same art admire

---

*Apparently Lord Beaverbrook in 1918 suffered from the same trouble, but he was cured. See Kenneth Young, *Churchill and Beaverbrook*, London, 1966, p. 50.

and love each other as these two did. But Joachim inspired such friendship. Tovey found in him what Schumann might have, what Brahms did—only more.

Yet in his grief Tovey was also aware of a trust laid on him, a deeper thing than merely carrying out the wishes of a dead friend: to see that despite the unexpected death of their great-uncle Adila and in time Jelly should have as wide an opening to musical life as if he were still alive. And this, as we shall see in later chapters, he was able to help them to get.

5

Viâ Elsewhere to England

For a while Adila stayed on in Berlin. In November at the Singsacademie she gave without Joachim the big orchestral concert he had planned. It contained the Mozart *Concerto in A major* (K. *219*), the Beethoven *Concerto* and Joachim's exacting *Hungarian Variations*. The Berlin Philharmonic Orchestra was conducted by Ernst Kunwald, the Austrian who was its director that year and for five years after.

To the discerning ears of Berlin a style of her own sounded, a new musical personality. The press on November 23, commented with fairness and in favour. The *Vossichzeitung* said that her 'lovely talent' had been developed in the best of schools, and that she had given the Mozart an attractive performance. In the Beethoven she showed 'a real understanding of the greatness of her task', and there was no doubt about her very great talent.

It was a well-chosen programme. In the Mozart she could play with witty graces, in the Beethoven more heavily and deep, while the highly coloured *Variations* gave scope to her ebullient deftness.

On the same day the *B. Z. Mittag*, a more important paper and not given to superlatives, went further. 'This artist promises to be in the front rank of violinists. From her great master and great-uncle she has inherited her beautiful bowing, clear tone, perfect intonation and a fine technique. The Beethoven suited her best, and the success of this young artist was great and well-deserved.'

The Sisters d'Aranyi

Adila felt confirmed and encouraged by having passed with honour the test of this fastidious city, but it held no more for her. By this concert she had done all she could do without Joachim, and she returned home.

Her great-uncle had wished her to have his favourite and most precious companion, an Antonio Stradivarius of 1715. His family gave it to her, and it remained her greatest treasure. All the same, characteristically, she nearly lost it in the first months. On her way back to Hungary she stopped with some distant cousins in Vienna, who met her at the station to take her home. The evening talk was mostly of Joachim and this wonderful legacy. However, what should happen but that in the early hours of the morning there was knocking at the front door, and outside stood the droschke driver who had brought them from the station. He said Adila should be very grateful to him. He had found the instrument in his cab, guarded it all night, and only now had had time free to bring it round.

In Berlin, Adila had come across a little booklet which gave names and addresses of principal music societies in Europe. In those days princely and ducal patronages were fading out, and impresarios concerned themselves most with big money-makers. The best openings for new soloists were local philharmonic societies and music clubs, widespread in many countries, not only in big cities but also in quite small places. Adila wrote personally fixing engagements, as she continued to do for years, neither knowing of nor needing any concert agents. Her first tour abroad was to Holland, in February, 1908.

Here her accompanist was a Georges Enderlé, and her repertoire included sonatas by Fauré and Brahms, the *Rondo Capriccioso*, the *Zapateada* (in her playing of which her uncle must have stood near her) and a *Romance* by Joachim. They opened at Utrecht on the 10th, played at the Hague next day, in the small Concertgebouw at Amsterdam on the 19th, returned to Utrecht on the 22nd, and ended at Hilversum on the 26th. The Dutch critics were full of praise, saying she had virtuosity in her blood,

Viâ Elsewhere to England

but deep feeling and intellectual control as well, and was not merely the niece of the 'King of Violinists'.[1]

These three qualities of technique, sensibility and musical intelligence are those that make a good executant, and 'greatness' comes when they function in equal measure. But the equal measure is not common. Adila might have been satisfied. All could have been set for a fine voyage through life as a soloist, to rival Suggia, Myra Hess and others as a leading woman instrumentalist. Pleased of course she was, but not satisfied. She had at her hand a triad of players, all feeling the same way about musicianship.

Titi's hands and head were fully able to bring a whole orchestra out of a grand piano as 'accompaniment' to a concerto, provided she had the score in front of her. Such renderings of concerti were still the rule at recitals, partly because less costly, partly because the emphasis was still very much on the soloist in circles unconvinced by Joachim. With such fellow-understanding beside her Adila was better off than with a provincial orchestra under an incompetent or dogmatic conductor. And so was Jelly. Jelly was rising to as near prodigy level as her sister had done eight years before. So toward the end of the year Adila arranged for all three to visit the confines of Austria, places which have since had their names and nationalities altered several times by post-war politicians with mapping pens. Both parents went with them on this family adventure.

They opened at Trieste, then by law wholly Austrian, on November 12, 1908. Adila, besides the *Rondo Capriccioso* which was becoming her star piece, played the *adagio* from Max Bruch's *Concerto in D minor* (Bruch was a colleague of Joachim at the Berlin High School) and some of the Brahms-Joachim *Hungarian Dances*.

Jelly, playing on Adila's presentation Balestrieri, performed the Chaikovsky *Concerto in D*, Saint-Saens' *Habanera*, the *Adagio Patetico* of Godard, and some of the Sarasate *Spanish Dances*. She and Adila joined for Spohr's unaccompanied *Duo for Two Violins in G minor*, the reverent slow movement of which took

The Sisters d'Aranyi

its place later with the Bach *Double Concerto* among their greater moments.

A good mixed programme. Something meaty, something established, something to hold a special hush in the audience, and something suitably 'Hungarian' and personal. The local paper *Il Piccolo* (published as its name indicates in Italian) caught at once the difference in temperament between Joachim's pupil and Hubay's. 'Adila is the more finished of the sisters, the more refined. Jelly is a young lady who rushed unrestrained over vast plains. Both have an excellent technique—absolute masters of all the technical resources of their instruments.'

The difference lasted long: but one of the ways in which Adila could hand on from Joachim was to guide her sister as he would have guided her, had he been given the chance to take her to Berlin. Adila never domineered over Jelly: but she always, with the same self-withdrawal as their mother had, put her first, and for that reason passed on all she knew. Jelly when she matured had learned almost as much, if not fully as much as Adila, with a lustier passion for it to control.

From Trieste they went to Klagenfurt, which is still Austrian; to Marburg in Slovenia, which had been colonized by Germans since the tenth century, later became part of Yugoslavia, was annexed by Germany in the last war, and is now in Yugoslavia again.

A second concert at Trieste was followed by one in Gorizia, where the tour ended. Gorizia in Venezia Giulia then part of the Empire, was occupied by Italy in the First World War, taken by Yugoslavia after the Second, and is now a frontier town split in two. Part of the audience at least in those days was Italian, and the *Corriere Friulano* of November 28, 1908 confirms the opinion of Trieste. 'Adila is the great lady, calm, in control of the events she is interpreting, she guides the bow, commands it. Jelly no, Jelly lives, is excited, grieves, delights in, trembles. She does not confine herself to playing her instrument, she neither guides nor commands it, she lives with her violin.'

There is a physical description, too, which will be recognized

Viâ Elsewhere to England

by those who saw them in later days: Adila with her eyes closed most of the time, opening them only in moments of 'ecstasy'; Jelly with hers looking upward. For some reason one was made all the more aware of their sisterhood.

But both modest people, this newspaper reports; pleased and a little surprised by the warmth of applause, and not feeling they were in any way superior to other people.

This was as true in private as in public, and remained so. Conceit would not have been tolerated in the Aranyi household. Their father showed his pleasure in them perhaps more than their mother did, but neither praised them to their faces: nor could any of them ever bear the kind of admirer who comes into the artists' room and gushes. It was perhaps during this tour that one such gusher raved to Madame von Aranyi about Jelly. She answered *'Elle est une bonne petite.'*

Jelly first played in Vienna in October, 1908, sharing a concert with Adila and a singer. Adila allowed her to play her solo pieces on the Joachim Strad; but Jelly remembers, curiously for her fine memory, very little of what she played except the first movement only of the Beethoven *Concerto*, and that she and Adila played the Bach *Double Concerto* for Onkel Jo's sake.

Such little tours abroad were all very well. They helped to make a name. They began to bring in a little pocket money. But for Adila they were only try-outs for England. And to England they had to go.

It was not hard to get a few engagements by letter, thanks to Joachim. He had been very much loved in England, partly because he did not wade through roses like a primadonna. For years he had been the chief attraction of the London musical season, at the Crystal Palace, at the Philharmonic Society, at the Saturday and Monday 'Pops'. In 1906 his Quartet had given the complete cycle of Brahms' chamber music in the Queen's Hall. He had played the Beethoven *Concerto* in the same hall at the celebration of his seventy-fifth birthday, when Sir Hubert Parry read an address, and the Prime Minister Arthur Balfour presented Joachim with the portrait Sargent had painted of him. There is

The Sisters d'Aranyi

no doubt that he had looked forward to bringing Adila to London with him after her Berlin début. All his many friends in England were keen to hear her. So three concerts were arranged, to start at the end of February 1909.

The first was at Haslemere. Arriving at Charing Cross Station at six in the morning, the three sisters and their mother hired a room at the station hotel to wait for their connection. Adila was excited to be at last in England, but Jelly got the impression of a strange, serious-minded country, where educated workmen stopped on their way to the morning job, to read free copies of daily newspapers fastened into reading-desks round the main hall of the terminus.

There is a snapshot of Jelly during this first visit, rather blurred and ill-lit. She stands at a window with a violin, her hair falling on her shoulders, the very picture of an Edwardian child prodigy.

Haslemere was a small residential village, but there was no shame in making their English début there. British music was by no means limited to, or even dependent on, London. All over our islands from Dublin and Edinburgh to the Isle of Wight, from Bath to Bury St Edmunds, from Kendal to Hull, there had been music festivals, regular or sporadic, since the beginning of the nineteenth century. In recent years some of the most important new works had been first heard not in London but at Hereford or Leeds or Liverpool. From Hallé's day to Dan Godfrey's, first-class musicians were founding permanent orchestras in other places than Manchester or Bournemouth. Local choral societies invited the best conductors and singers for oratorio. Where there was no permanent body of music-makers, there often was a permanent body of music-lovers, who organized clubs and societies to finance visits by celebrated artists. Even the little Scottish burgh of Elgin in our own day could command prized international names, and not only when these happened to have a spare day from London.

In 1909 Haslemere was such a place. The Dolmetsch family had not yet settled there, to make its musical name synonymous with the building and playing of harpsichords, recorders, lutes

Viâ Elsewhere to England

and viols. But each season a series of concerts was arranged in the School Hall by Frances Dakyns and Annie Bristow. These two ladies had often heard Joachim talking of his great-nieces. They were devoted to music, especially the former, who later became unpaid agent for the Busch String Quartet.

The Aranyi ladies stayed in the Dakyns house and were enchanted by Frances's father, a small radiant figure with a long beard, whom before long they were calling 'Dakyns Bàcsi' (Uncle Dakyns). Donald Tovey was there to present and protect his new protégées, and before long an unusual noise outside the house announced the arrival in one of the early motorcars of another pianist, Frederick Septimus Kelly.

Of Kelly as a musician and in other ways we must speak later. He was a well-to-do Australian, who had been to Eton and Balliol, where he succeeded Tovey as Nettleship Scholar, and then studied music under Knorr and Eugesser at Frankfurt. But he was also a famous rowing Blue, who won the Diamond Sculls three times and the year before he came to Haslemere had rowed in the Leander Eight at the Olympic Regatta.

Frances Dakyns had arranged for him to play the *Kreutzer Sonata* with Adila, and most of the time was spent in rehearsals; but the rest was laughter and friendly high spirits. He spoke German and often pulled the sisters' legs when they tried to speak English—a language they had not studied and never did. In the evening, presumably to put young Jelly at her ease, they played hunt the slipper. A pleasantly informal and unpretentious way for three foreign musicians to pass an evening before making their début in Britain.

At first Jelly called him Mr Kelly. But she turned soon, like everyone else, to 'Sep' or 'Cleg'. She fell deeply in love with this handsome young man, his piercing blue eyes, his keen face; but saw no signs that her passion was returned.

The *Kreutzer Sonata* made an impression: so did the Spohr *Duo* and the Bach *Double Concerto*. The *Hungarian Dances* swept the audience off their feet, and Jelly's feeling in a Joachim *Romance* moved them. This was not the separate piece Adila had

The Sisters d'Aranyi

played in Berlin, but a movement from the *Hungarian Concerto*, which is still thought to be among Joachim's most durable compositions. The sisters had an acclamation, all the more welcome because it was English. England was the green and pleasant land they had expected, even in February: English people were kindly, natural, musical, and warm despite language difficulties; and there was Donald Tovey, attentive, solid and helpful, to take them onward from Haslemere.

Tovey took them to Newcastle, where Joachim's old friend Sir Andrew Noble, of Vickers-Armstrong, engaged them to play at a chamber music concert. Jelly, all her life stimulated by beautiful or historic places, never forgot her first sight of Durham from the train, ridge beyond ridge of streets like ground-rows on a stage with the Cathedral riding high in the mists. Little did she think of the time and the occasion when she would give one of her most moving performances as a mature artist in this cathedral. She never forgot the double-decker trams in Newcastle, either.

Then Tovey took them to Northlands School, at Englefield Green in Surrey, where he was living. Northlands was a strictly select school for strictly select girls of the privileged classes, directed by Sophie Weisse; and lucky the pupils were to have Tovey's brain to instruct them in music. But Miss Weisse provided the best of everything, and even the Joachim Quartet had played there. When Tovey was a boy at Worplesdon, Miss Weisse had been a kind of mother to him, and sometimes behaved as if she were a jealous mother. She had known Joachim well, and like Tovey always referred to him as Onkel Jo.

The stay at Northlands was anything but formal or dull. The sisters gave concerts in public, and played with Tovey in the evening privately to the girls. Tovey could be a great tease. He tried to teach Jelly English in far from pedantic ways. Jelly wished to learn the differences between British and Continental table manners, for instance, and Tovey gave outrageous advice. 'When they appear at your left elbow offering fish, you have to sniff it and say, "No thank you, I prefer my fish fresh"; and when you are given wine, taste a little and say "Corked!"'

Viâ Elsewhere to England

It was at Northlands that they began a lifelong and mutually admiring friendship with Casals, who at that time lived mostly in Paris.

The news of three Hungarian girls who were outstanding musicians soon got round, and they were able to stay in Britain for four months. Compatriots in the Austro-Hungarian Chamber of Commerce invited them to play at its annual dinner in the Imperial Restaurant, Regent Street, on March 21st. They played in Balliol Hall, Oxford, where that delightful Brahmsian Ernest Walker remembered having accompanied Joachim thirteen years before when Dr Walker was a mainly self-taught musician of twenty-six.[8] They appeared in Cambridge, and at several private houses in London and elsewhere. Society at that time was fond of entertaining its guests with private recitals, the interest of which varied very much according to the musical knowledge of the hostess or the set she moved in. The most eminent for the sisters was at Woking, where the Prime Minister's brother Gerald Balfour and his wife (who had been a Lytton) lived, lovers of music and friends of Tovey.

On June 10th, Adila and Jelly performed at a *Soirée Musicale* (another type of Edwardian social event) organized by the Francis-Joseph Institute in the Princes Galleries, Piccadilly. These and other successes were welcome and exciting, but of limited professional value, being nearly all obtained through friends or Joachim's friends or friends of friends. Sooner or later they must make a proper London début: and this took place at the Bechstein Hall, Wigmore Street*, with Tovey taking part.

Adila and Jelly played the Bach *Double Concerto in C minor,* of which the surviving version is for keyboard instruments, though Bach arranged it also for violin and oboe. The restoration of the original made by Carl Berner seems to have been known little in London, and more than one critic hoped it would find its way into the repertoire. Apart from their old favourites the sisters played Vieuxtemps' *Ballade et Polonaise* (Adila) and the Joachim *Romance* (Jelly). Adila and Tovey gave the Brahms *Sonata in D*

*Now known as the Wigmore Hall.

minor, and Tovey by himself played the little Beethoven *Sonata in F sharp* (op. 78) with due reverence for the absorbing harmonies.

London critics were unanimous in praise. 'Miss Jelly appears the most gifted, having in mind the fact that she is considerably younger than her sister', wrote the *Westminster Gazette,* of which leading cultural organ one might have expected a better literary style. 'Each has acquired a technique' (*Daily Telegraph*) 'in which there seems to be neither fault nor flaw'; while the *Morning Post* (as yet unmerged) gave a special commendation to Titi. So their first visit to England was a decided musical success, and news of this was eagerly printed by newspapers in Berlin and Budapest.

Certainly they had been lucky. In those days foreign, and indeed native, musicians had a hard struggle if they were not taken up by Society. There were no grand-dukes in England; but many a good foreign soloist could give a concert or two and go away no better known than when they arrived. The Aranyis were able to stay, not only because they were able musicians, but also because they were very distantly connected with the Russells. In this also their great-uncle had helped them.

Joachim's brother Henry had a daughter Gertrude, who married Rollo Russell, son of Bertrand Russell's uncle Lord John. This explains what might seem a flippantly bohemian scene described by Lady Ottoline Murrell at Bedford Square in 1914: with Bertrand Russell 'a stiff little figure jumping up and down like a child with an expression of surprised delight on his face at finding himself doing so ordinary a thing as dancing'—which the Aranyis had dragged him in to do.[4]

Lady Ottoline also describes Jelly in June 1909, at Crabbet Park near Crawley, where Neville Lytton, an aristocratic painter who had shared an exhibition some years before with Roger Fry, painted her portrait. He painted Jelly in 1919, also, and he recalled the happiness there had been at Crabbet Park which had then gone for good. 'The youngest of the three' wrote Lady Ottoline 'was about fifteen years old, with black hair falling straight

Viâ Elsewhere to England

down her dark cream face, making her look like a figure in a Puvis de Chavanne fresco. She played the violin with precocious knowledge, hardly realizing difficulties she had met and conquered. While I stood for Neville to paint me, she played duets with Tovey, who accompanied her on the clavichord.'[5]

Jelly denies the black hair, saying it was always dark brown: but in my own recollection it certainly could look black in concert lighting, black and glossy with a smoky fire in it.

Jelly also denies the clavichord; and so do I. You cannot hear a clavichord if anyone speaks in the room, let alone plays a violin or sings. But she seems to recall that the Lyttons had a harpsichord, which he and his wife Judith liked playing to their friends after dinner; and maybe Tovey accompanied her on that, though her very reliable memory does not tell her he did.

The sisters' social luck in no way detracts from their merits in concert or career. They still needed much hard work and quiet patience before they could find the solid favour of the musical world, to which there is no royal road, and no short-cut either through mere well-born friends. Snobs they despised: but felt at home in English society because they were at home in Hungarian. In time indeed they felt more at home and less foreign than in Budapest. And English society, soon the highest, welcomed them because they were well-bred, witty, musical and radiant: good company as that society liked its company to be. Further, to quote Tovey in his diary: they were 'in love with everyone and everyone with them.'

The friends they made on this first visit not only eased professional arrival and stayed faithful in later visits. Some were to be of great value when the First World War broke out in 1914.

6

Music in Britain and Abroad

The sisters d'Aranyi arrived as a kind of reinforcement to the rescue-workers and rebuilders of music in Britain.

Rescue was being done in three operations: improving performances of orchestras and soloists, making known the work of important contemporary or recent foreign composers, and giving British ones a better chance.

By the turn of the century the heavy-rescue squads found their tasks lightening, especially after the foundation in 1895 of a permanent, professional orchestra for Promenade Concerts in the Queen's Hall, which had been opened two years before. Henry J. Wood tuned his players to continental pitch and his listeners to good music. His results were extraordinary.

The Monday and Saturday 'Pops' in St James's Hall had been going for many years. They were strangely named 'Popular' when they were in fact almost the only chance the general musical public had of hearing the best European performers. Their standard rose steadily under the influence of Joachim, supported by the 'cellist Piatti who had much in common with him and had settled in England.

When these ended in 1898, the series was continued by a Joachim Quartet Society.[1] Joachim did not like the title because it drew too much attention to one ensemble; and in 1906 this was replaced by the Classical Concerts Society, in which younger men came to the front, such as Tovey and Kelly.

Music in Britain and Abroad

Casals said[2] 'This society only engaged artists of the highest rank. They had Jelly d'Aranyi (a relation of Joachim), Donald Tovey, Leonard Borwick (the best English pianist of that period), Fanny Davies etc. (Borwick and Fanny Davies had both been pupils of Clara Schumann).' He should have included also himself.

Fanny Davies, already loved at the Pops, campaigned not only for Brahms, Liszt and Schumann, but also for new orders of harmony and colour in Debussy and Skryabin. So did Frederick Dawson. Easier masters like Dvořák had long been known in London. John Dunn first played the Chaikovsky *Violin Concerto* there in 1900. Wagner was known, through Stanford. Over Brahms, London split, and remained split for many years. Tovey persevered with concerts of his own in Chelsea Town Hall, the Grafton Galleries and the Bechstein Hall.

The foundation of the Musical League in 1909 with Elgar (at last getting known)[3] as first President gave new British composers the chance they needed. This was organized by men who were more conductors than composers themselves. They backed younger musicians as diverse as Frank Bridge (chamber music), Arnold Bax, Vaughan Williams (*On Wenlock Edge, Thomas Tallis*), Percy Grainger the robust Australian, Ethel Smyth (operas) and the exotic studies of Cyril Scott. An important era in British music was beginning with these and Delius and Gustav Holst: more important than any since the Elizabethan, or the seventeenth century.*

Henry Wood was valiant. It is estimated that in the twenty-four years up to 1919 he introduced some 200 new British works to the British public.[4] He sometimes lost patience. When Skryabin's *Prometheus* had a hostile reception in 1913, he promptly re-raised his baton and played it all through again: after which it was acclaimed.[5]

Minor curiosity reached out even to the ultra-moderns.

---

*Bax said that the older generation (Parry, Stanford, Mackenzie) were all so respectable that they 'regarded gorgeous beauty of orchestral sound as something not quite nice'—adding that he was near-quoting Parry's own words.

The Sisters d'Aranyi

Schönberg's *Five Orchestral Pieces* were heard in London in 1912; Stravinsky's *Pulcinella* and *Le Sacre du Printemps* in 1911 and 1913. These were the first bulldozers against tonality. British interest in what was going on abroad had widened fast since 1892, when the Scot William Wallace wrote the first British symphonic poem *The Passing of Beatrice*.[6]

Space does not allow a full diagram of this fascinating momentum in British music, which was conscious and deliberate. I will deal with Tovey's sector only.

Tovey was the best musical scholar of his time, with a memory that startled people like Joachim and Adolf Busch. In 1913 as a pianist he was within memorizing distance of no fewer than sixty-five concerti, and once when asked how long it would take him to play his entire repertoire, estimated six to seven weeks. His analytical notes so crammed his concert programmes as pianist or conductor, however, that the London Press called him an Oxford pedant with no musicianship whatever. Maybe because he was responsible for the main articles on music in the *Encyclopaedia Britannica* (11th edition) and for an edition of the *Forty-eight Preludes and Fugues* which has never been surpassed.

Nor was his playing more to the liking of critics. He lacked, they said, 'pianism'—that is, showiness. His biographer Mary Grierson, herself no mean musician, described him as never intervening between composer and listener, and so illuminating the music that it reached one with unforgettable vividness, especially in Bach.[7] This is worth superimposing on what we have read of Liszt in the eyes of Saint-Saens, and on what has been said in previous pages about Joachim. Tovey did not mind being damned, as he was, in the company of Brahms and of Brahms's interpreter Joachim by older men. His own compositions were indeed all too Brahmsian.

It is in this sense that the sisters were reinforcements. They had set foot on the path that Tovey was clearing, and the walking seemed good. They arrived as an encouragement to him, and they departed encouraged.

The whole family went for its usual summer holiday in Aus-

Music in Britain and Abroad

tria, two months for mother and children, one for father: then back home. Hungary was eager to hear them, and they gave concerts in Budapest and elsewhere. At Arad (now in Rumania) the Hungarian Prime Minister Stefan Tisza himself attended: a popular statesman for his lifelong struggle toward a liberal democracy, and a measure of the Aranyis' fame. From here they had to catch an early morning train to Budapest and did not go to bed after the concert. Jelly was still young enough to be thrilled by sitting up all night, and remembers that they spent most of the time in a restaurant, dancing. The viola-player in the gipsy band was either exhausted or ill. Jelly watched his face getting paler and paler, till he was continuing to fiddle his simple figure in his sleep.

In November they again went abroad, to north-east Italy, launching the tour with a return visit to Klagenfurt. Adila had added to her repertoire Tartini's *Concerto in D minor,* Jelly had mastered that of Saint-Saens *in B minor,* and together they ended with Handel's *Sonata for two Violins in G minor,* which was to open many a joint concert of theirs in years to come.[8]

Titi also was growing in skill and sensibility; and at Trento, chief town of the woody and mountainous Trentino, one finds a tribute to her in the press: a rare thing in those days; for although music schools and conservatoires awarded diplomas for accompanists, these important artists who can reinforce or ruin a soloist went as a rule unnoticed. Many deserved to. Gerald Moores were scarce.

At Ferrara they played in the Teatro Comunale, which because Italy had re-established the twenty-four hour clock advertised the concert for 21.30. Jelly got special notice. 'Jelly is fifteen years old and has more than promise. She has value' (*valore,* which can also mean significance). 'It blazes in the eyes of this child like an undying fire.'

Verona specially enjoyed Jelly's playing of Bazzini's 'vertiginous' *Ronde des Lutins.*

On December 1st, they were at Padova in the hall of the Circolo Filarmonico. They played Sinding's *Serenade for two Violins.*

The Sisters d'Aranyi

They were to meet Sinding later, and found him as unimpressive as his music. This audience was startled by Adila in the *'Moses' Variations on a Single String*, which Paganini is said, mythically or not, to have broken three strings before beginning. Jelly played a *Spinning Song*, which the Hungarian pianist Dienzl had composed for Stefi Geyer, with whom he often appeared.

In going to Padova they should have changed trains, but forgot to do so and were carried on to Venice. They did not appear at Venice on this tour, but returned to visit it after Padova. This visit was not a success. Though the two bedrooms shared by the four women were large, they were in a dark, old-fashioned, second-category hotel. Adila, thirsty in the night, got up for a drink of water, which she took from a carafe on the wash-stand. This tasted of some chemical which she described as 'chloroform' and made her very ill. Before they left, they found that a man had died in that room shortly before they occupied it, and some kind of disinfectant had been left there. Apart from the impressionable girls' shudders at the nearness of a death, they were worried by Adila who was indeed ill.

The tour ended at Genoa, where they played twice: in the hall of the Circolo Artistico on the 12th, where the programme included a violin arrangement of Chopin's *A major Nocturne* played by Adila: and a week later in the Sala Sivori, a hall named after the Genoese violinist who had been Paganini's only pupil. In the full programme of this final concert one notices Godard's *Duettino for two Violins and Pianoforte*, a Zanytsky *Polonaise* and a *Valse Caprice* by Wieniawsky. With the exception of the Bach *C minor Concerto*, and the Chaikovsky and Tartini *concerti*, the works here tend to be lighter and showier than in the season before. This, whether deliberate or not, was probably sensible, because as young Jelly advanced in technique and felt her wings supple, she was apt to fly wildly.

From Italy they crossed into France and spent Christmas at Aigues-Mortes, where in the church Adila played Bach's so-called *Air on the G String*, and both sisters a pretty piece for two violins from a suite by Godard. This was called *Minuit*, and ended

Music in Britain and Abroad

with a single note repeated twelve times on the piano. They were very fond of it.

The small town of Aigues-Mortes in the swamps at the mouths of the Rhône is not an ideal place to stay in winter, despite the thirteenth-century ramparts that are reputed to rival Carcassonne's. But the family had a reason for being there. One of their mother's brothers, Adam, was *juge de paix* there, and she had not seen him since she was seven years old. He was to meet them on the train; and they heard a thin voice calling 'Annette! Annette!' (his old name for her) along the corridor before he came to the compartment. He was a very poor-sighted man with thick lenses to his spectacles; but an excellent amateur violinist. He also painted quite well.

Having no children of his own and hearing that his sister had three, he always wanted to adopt Jelly; but however fond Madame von Aranyi was of her brother at a great distance of time, she was not fond enough to let him have her daughter.

To make the visit possible and help with finance, Adila had arranged recitals at Nîmes, Montpellier and Avignon, all within fairly easy reach. Montpellier was a scene of anxiety. Adila found that she had lost a lily-of-the-valley brooch in clustered diamonds and pearls which Princess Liechtenstein had given her (Prince Liechtenstein was at the Austro-Hungarian Embassy in London and they were friends). Her mother was more concerned in searching for this than in attending the concert. But as it happened, the concert hall was just across the road from their hotel, and while digging into bags, baggage and drawers she could clearly hear the music—and the applause. The brooch had been left behind somewhere and was forwarded safely—only to be stolen some years later.

They played in Paris. They were invited on January 16th, 1910, to a private concert in the *salon* of a rich patroness, Mme Edouard Pearson, in the avenue Marceau. Adila had no means of organizing Paris concerts from Hungary, and the audience, if select, was limited. Press notices were found in *La Chronique Féminine* and *Le Journal Musical*. From these we learn that the

The Sisters d'Aranyi

sisters pleased their listeners with works in hand, plus Paganini's *La Campanella*.* A social occasion.

Parisian society took them to its bosom as English society had done, if for a shorter period. They met gay and interesting people and some famous ones. Aunt Tatiana in Budapest had often told them of the 'great French dramatist' René Fauchois, whose *Fille de Pilate* had made him head of the new school coming into vogue.** At a party given by another hostess, Mme Dorian Ménard, who should appear but this fascinating figure, and what could the young ladies do but fall figuratively at his feet? And what should he do but take all four ladies out to dinner and consternate them by suddenly, publicly and formally asking Madame von Aranyi for the hand of her youngest daughter in marriage? Her refusal was firm but kind but light-hearted. 'But we are inseparable' she cried 'You would have to take all four of us.'

This was Jelly's first proposal, if rather a strange one at the age of sixteen. It did not mean much, but it pleased her. Nor was Fauchois forbidden to see her. In fact a day or two later during a walk, he and Jelly drew ahead of the others, and he kept addressing her as *toi*. When Jelly protested at this breach of the proprieties, he said 'One always uses *toi* to one's God and one's loves.'

He wrote tender, wistful little missives to her in England or Hungary, starting, *Chère et lointaine petite amie* or, *Chère demoiselle et amie et grande artiste*.'⁹ Many of them refer to an exhibition in the Galerie Georges Petit where portraits of Adila and Jelly were on view, which he wanted to buy but bid too late. When they would be returning from London through Paris, he planned to get together a lot of poets and artists for them to play to after dinner. And then he fades out.

At the same party another scintillating figure proposed to tell fortunes by the reading of hands. He impressively warned Titi against voyages by water, saying it was written in her hand that

---

*La Campanella is often thought of as being by Liszt, who wrote and played a more famous piano version.

**The Late Christopher Bean was founded on one of his plays.

she would be drowned. She never was: but her high-strung credulity was unable to forget the prophecy and she was overcome with terror during rough Channel crossings and even in bad Atlantic weather in the *Berengaria*.*

France however was only a country on the way back to England, and they gave their second concert at Haslemere in the middle of February. F. S. Kelly was again there and took part with them. At this time Kelly had only published a *Cycle of Lyrics* and some minor pieces, but was becoming known as a pianist. He had been something of a prodigy, being able to play Mozart sonatas by heart at the age of five. According to an anonymous but patently knowledgeable contributor to the local paper (probably the *Surrey Advertiser*) his rendering of Bach 'it would be hard to excel, hard even to equal: he possesses in a marked degree a power of sober variety of tone, excellently well suited to the more complex works of this great master.' The variation of tone enabled him to bring out the personality of separate voices, so that even the most involved passages sounded clear and inevitable. He and Tovey obviously faced the same way, but their friendship was uneasy. When Tovey was in love, Jelly says he could be 'very tiresome'; and Kelly objected to the attentions Tovey paid to Kelly's sister Maisie.

When he and Jelly played one of the Mozart *Sonatas in E♭* (I think K 26) she was found to have developed a 'magnetic charm', and her *Hungarian Dances* brought the house down; but she refused to encore them, as the Mozart was to follow. All the same, the undying fire was overspilling from the grate and singeing her bird-like fingers. In the free passion and gusto she showed during this season, some lack of precision was detected. Adila warned her about it.

Titi's growth is noticed too, her 'delightfully sympathetic contribution'. But though Adila and Kelly did justice to the Brahms *Sonata in G*, Adila's playing of the Beethoven *G major Romance* was felt not to be so good as that of the *Kreutzer* the year before.

*Jelly is pretty certain that this was Jean Cocteau. According to *Who's Who* (1964) Cocteau would have been about twenty-one years old. So it is possible.

The Sisters d'Aranyi

Do we perhaps discern a slight wearing-off of the rapture of newness, like the second night of a good stage production? The sisters had to do better than this if they were not to lose headway made as novelties.

At the same time I must not give the impression that Jelly was in danger of becoming a romantic player. Her mind was opening fast, outside as well as inside music. 'Dakyns Bàcsi' noticing her interest in Ancient Greece gave her a translation of Plato's *Lysis*, the dialogue on friendship, an excellent introduction for a sixteen-year-old: and if maybe the music of the thoughts influenced her more than the dialectic, and the sentiment of emotional friendship more than the higher vision, nevertheless Plato remains a companion to Jelly ever since. When the war came, and Kelly left for the trenches, he carried with him a volume of Plato which Jelly had given him. He had little time to read it. It came back to her, years later, 'a little soiled'.

A fortnight after Haslemere the sisters played at a Popular Concert of the Cambridge University Musical Society. Adila who, the *Granta* recorded, played a *Berceuse* of Grieg as an encore, was given her due as a violinist of rare gifts; Titi is called, with insight, 'a clever accompanist, and more remarkable still a beautifully unselfish one'; but Jelly is again accused of sometimes losing precision.

This made London a more chancy test than it had been the year before. On March 15th a concert was organized for the sisters at No 10, Grosvenor Square by Mr and Mrs Robert Finney McEwan. No 10 did not belong to the McEwans, they had rented it from the Cazalet family. They were a rich Scottish couple (Mrs McEwan was a Dundas), who were patrons of music, he being an amateur pianist; and it was he who started the Nelson Hall Concerts for the Edinburgh working class.

New items here were the Bach *Sonata in C for two Violins*, Jelly playing the *andante* from Mozart's *Haffner Serenade* and Paganini's thirteenth *Capriccio*, and Adila in Corelli's *Variations* on '*La Follia*', a Portuguese dance originally of such barbaric violence that the dancers went frantic like dervishes. But Corelli

Music in Britain and Abroad

took the tune as a rather solemn one. No lack of precision is attributed to Jelly. On the contrary *The Times* said her playing of some of the *Hungarian Dances* 'recalled vividly the spontaneous buoyancy of their first interpreter.' It was only three years since Joachim had died, and thousands of London concert-goers remembered him well.

Clearly Adila's vigilance was working. Clearly also they did to some extent on this visit consolidate their position. They became known to the general public. Even *Punch* heard of them.

Punch was at that time a middle-upper-class paper, taken by country houses, doctors, dentists, clubs and all who believed in the British Empire and stability. 'Good enough for *Punch*' was the highest praise for a friend's joke, provided it was neither dirty nor witty. *Punch* specialized in humour, carefully explained and illustrated with black and white drawings worthy of the Royal Academy. The editor, who apparently thought Jelly was a singer, found her first name screamingly funny. A paragraph on June 16th announced that in consequence of the new fashion Mr Plunket Greene would henceforth be calling himself 'Junket', Madame Melba 'Pêche', and Madame Kirkby Lunn 'Sally Lunn' like the tea-cake, *de rigveur* and almost universal at Edwardian At Homes. However, this was fame, or at least acceptance into the English way of life. Now nobody could say they had not heard of Jelly Aranyi, except the lowest form of Edwardian life: 'a crossing-sweeper.'

The whole family again spent a holiday in Austria, this time at Leoben, a Styrian town near Graz, which they liked best. At least Adila and Titi did, because they always had a multitude of agreeable young men about them and were always falling in and out of love. But Jelly felt out of place and dull. They had rooms in the centre and used to play with the windows open in the evenings. If for any reason they did not play, they heard sad voices outside saying: 'What! no concert tonight?'

Next season, after performing in Budapest they made another tour of Italy, extending from the same cities as last time to Palermo, Bergamo, Parma, La Spezia and Pola. Rome could not be fitted in. Throughout this tour they were followed by an eccentric Italian who seemed fascinated by Titi. He never behaved other than well, but was ever entering the artists' room after concerts, and before long they thought him cracked and a bore. He seems to have been faithful, though: for, some seventeen years later, when Jelly was playing in Belgium, in he came unannounced saying he was now Italian consul.

The second Italian tour was more exciting than the first. At Pola (now Pula) later to belong to Italy, and later still to Yugoslavia, but then an important Austrian naval base on the Adriatic, they played to the Austrian Navy, and were rewarded by a grand party in the battleship *Bamberg*. At La Spezia they played to the Italian Navy, and were treated to a trip in a naval motor-launch, windy but exhilarating in February.

At that time Liguria was full of orange and lemon groves; and an orange tree stood on the terrace of their hotel at La Spezia. Under this the Aranyis were chatting with some brightly uniformed naval officers, when without any warning an orange detached itself and landed on Titi's lap. Jelly does not know why this completely unimportant incident should have remained so vivid in her memory. Maybe it was just joy of youth in happenings and in belonging. The fall of an orange can mean more than the gift of a brooch. Anyhow I record it.

In Bergamo they were waiting to be called on to the platform for the Bruch *Concerto in D minor*. When Jelly was not playing, she generally turned over for Titi. They were in the waiting room at the Palazzo Vecchio, but no call came. Then they remembered they had been examined about exact timings before the concert began. Outside in the Piazza stood the fifteenth-century Torre Comunale, which had a clock and chimes. There had always to be a pause, to prevent social time from crashing into musical.

It is interesting that musical taste should demand this at Bergamo in 1911. At Oxford in the twenties similar pauses were made at Balliol and elsewhere (though not everywhere) for Big Tom of Christchurch to boom for his 101 scholars at 21.15. Once when told to wait, Jelly said: 'Let's see if we can beat Tom', and began playing. On that occasion Tom was hardly noticed.

And now they were really treated like celebrities. At Parma they had been thinking that their Verona engagement was in the evening and were in no hurry to leave, when the telephone rang, bidding them take the next train, as it was an afternoon concert. They flung their things into a huge trunk, and were met at Verona station by the son-in-law of the Music Society President, an army officer in full uniform. He organized porters and cabs like orderlies and lorries to rush them to the Teatro Filarmonico, which was far from the station through streets often blocked by bullock-carts. There was no bullock-cart, but the cab carrying the trunk broke down. The undismayed young officer mobilized some passing soldiers to hoist it on to another, which they did with a will when they heard who the ladies were. Thanks to this forceful person the party did get to the theatre in time, but in the dressing room found all their concert dresses crushed and creased. Adila suggested 'ironing' them on the radiators; and so, breathless but in fairly good moral state, they came out on the stage.

In a criticism of this concert we have a rare account of Titi's actual playing. It was 'light, velvety and on occasion sparkling.'

This has been on the whole a musically uneventful chapter. But such things can happen when serious artists begin to get their own measure. Then what matters most is their art itself, to probe and enlarge and intensify, while their unknown public goes on forming unseen. But it is good to have anchors, too. And it was good for the sisters when they cast their anchor in 1911 again at Haslemere, where they were becoming annual features, desired by the subscribers.

7

An Advantage of High Society

Outside their concerts and hard practice the three sisters had plenty of time for social pleasures, the elegant, luxurious and sometimes enervating attractions of Edwardian society, which have been portrayed with charm by Lady Violet Bonham Carter and with wicked wit by George Dangerfield.* They were *de mode,* invited everywhere, sometimes to play, sometimes to be played with. Particularly so at the Coronation of George V in 1911, when London Society, always gay, went mad. Party followed party. On one day the sisters gave three recitals in private houses, one in the afternoon and two in the evening.

The Coronation procession itself they saw, after an early breakfast in Swan Walk, Chelsea, where they were staying, from the window of an office in the Admiralty belonging to their naval friend William Fisher, whose Coronation duties were so heavy that his health suffered.** This was not the ugly, violent Admiral Fisher ('Never explain! Never apologize!') who with Winston Churchill foresaw and forewarned about the first world war. This Captain Fisher did in fact become an Admiral of the Fleet, but he had also musical connections. One of his sisters was Adeline, first wife of Vaughan Williams, who was then becoming recognized as an important composer: while his sister-

---

Winston Churchill As I Knew Him, London, 1965; and *The Strange Death of Liberal England*, 1935, and 1961.
**Ursula Vaughan Williams: *R. V. W.*, London, 1964, p. 214.

An Advantage of High Society

in-law, wife of Desmond McCarthy, brought literary figures into the picture.

The Aranyis felt they really belonged to London when they leaned out of the window to wave to a personal friend passing on horseback: Prince von Liechtenstein. 'The new King looked very old to me' Jelly says, 'but at that age everybody did.'

Jelly recalls the effervescent smartness of that period, and the impression made on her by enormous house parties at Alderley Park in Cheshire. House parties were not at that time mere weekend affairs. Few hosts and no hostesses had offices on Monday mornings. At Alderley Park the sisters spent a fortnight amid profusions of gowns, jewellery, good wines, rich food. They met people as different as the charming A. A. Milne and the amusing, often detested First Lord of the Admiralty, Winston Churchill. Jelly took little account of Churchill; she remembers more clearly his little red-headed daughter Sarah. And his secretary too, Edward Marsh, 'with his squeaky voice'. But best of all their beautiful hostess Lady Sheffield, who was an aunt of Gertrude Bell. All this because of the old friendship between Lord Sheffield and Onkel Jo.

It was really a shooting-and-fishing party, and the men were out all day. The conversation, in English, French or German, was of the subtle, allusive kind sometimes given a capital letter and ranked among accomplishments. It had an extra-functional grace like diving.

When the men returned and had had too convivial an evening, they sometimes got out of hand. One guest, for a bet, or a boast, jumped off the musicians' gallery. He did no damage to himself but ruined the floor.

'If we were blue-stockings' Jelly says, 'I was a very pale-blue, silk one.' What Wyndham Lewis was later to sneer wittily at as the 'Upper Bohemia' did not yet exist, though the Morells and young Stephens were starting the new way of life. Some younger aristocrats had to fight for their revolution; and how much they suffered, and were called, and so became, eccentrics, has been shown by Lady Ottoline. But many of the governing class were as much

The Sisters d'Aranyi

interested in the arts as in politics or blood sports, and in their homes artists found a welcome, especially if both hosts and guests were 'well bred'.

Society danced in a void. Below that void lay an increasingly bitter awareness of reality. The arts could avoid this reality. They could also be a way to it. Another way was slumming.

Many smart young London women spent an afternoon a week entertaining or instructing or consoling or 'improving' what they called 'poor people' in the East End. The sisters Aranyi took their share in this operation, giving concerts in what were literally ragged quarters, and feeling unhappy about their own good clothes.

Further than this few went. The politicians themselves danced in a void, a professional Horn Dance long bare of meaning, internal and external affairs alike being controlled by the Irish, who danced in their own void and loathed each other. The fundaments of partial democracy were laid down as if accidentally by the Parliament Act and were simultaneously denied to women. Britain was heading for self-destruction by ineptitude, and the social structure was preserved only by the First World War and only long enough for it to rot slowly into a new spring. A second war was needed before we achieved even our present version of democracy.

But in the meantime Britain was prosperous, and danced very prettily, as those who remember can remember with gratitude. Clerks smoked cigars and Barrie wrote *What Every Woman Knows*. To musicians the coal strike or the dock strike meant only exasperation, difficulty in getting to dates outside London and smaller audiences when they got there. They also meant that the Dome of St Paul's was seen ten miles away as none had seen it since before the Industrial Revolution.

The Aranyis all danced as prettily as anyone else. It so happened that they were friends with both political parties, the conservative Balfours and the liberal Asquiths. In which two *milieux* they made other people dance.

The Balfours were devoted to music. Arthur Balfour, even

An Advantage of High Society

when leader of the opposition and still more when displaced by Bonar Law, went to many concerts. At the Wigmore Hall once, where the sisters disliked the music stands and brought their own, Jelly in turning a page with the tip of her bow knocked the stand over. She went to the piano and read over Titi's shoulder, but the stand rocked off the platform and all but beheaded the ex-Prime Minister.

But it was chiefly his brother Gerald who was their friend. Gerald Balfour was a man of many interests; handsome, distinguished-looking; as little fitted for politics as Arthur and much less attracted by them. He had been president of 'The Apostles', that famous, eclectic society or club, to which Tennyson, a member, wrote in *In Memoriam* references which only the initiated fully understand.[1] Rupert Brooke also, I think, was a member. The sisters never met Brooke, but saw him often at concerts, especially those of the Classical Concerts Society.

Their connection with the Balfours was again Onkel Jo. Every year the Gerald Balfours gave a 'Joachim Party' to keep the memory alive.[2] Similarly with the Liddells, after the first war. Mrs Liddell had been Joachim's pupil. The three sons became like brothers to the Aranyis, and the whole family and connection helped them after the war. The boys played the violin and the piano and often joined in duets. 'A tremendous thing to be allowed to play it with you' wrote Guy to Jelly about the Brahms *Sonata in D minor*.[3]

The Saxton Nobles of Newcastle also remained friends. In 1911, when Madame von Aranyi returned to Hungary, they took the sisters to their house at Ardkinglas in Argyll and showed them the Highland Games at Inveraray. In this their first visit to Scotland they felt immediately at home. The Saxton Nobles seem also to have provided Adila with a Scottish ghost. Everyone, including the servants, went out; but Adila wished to practise, and was doing so in the gun room near the front door. Outside she saw a very lovely girl arriving on horseback and crossing the flower beds as if these did not exist. Then, oddly for a visitor, she turned and rode away. She wore her hair long on her shoulders, unusual

The Sisters d'Aranyi

in 1911. Adila's description, when the family returned, bore no resemblance to anybody in the neighbourhood; and if she had been a wandering stranger, it is peculiar that she did not dismount, or at least call out to see if anyone were at home. Also there were no hoofprints on flower beds nor tramplings of flowers.

Passed to you for comment.

On another visit to Scotland, in the early part of 1914, they stayed at Heriot Row with Alexander Maitland and his wife Rosalind, pianist and friend of Tovey, who that year had become Reid Professor of Music at Edinburgh. The Maitlands had a magnificent collection of modern paintings from Renoir to Modigliani, bought partly to give pleasure to their friends but also with one eye on the gaps in the Scottish National Gallery, which now possesses it.[4] At their house the Aranyis met D. Y. Cameron, who had just painted a highland landscape which Rosalind Maitland recognized. 'But' she said 'why did you put that loch in? There's no loch there.' 'Have you never been there in February?' Cameron retaliated, 'There is then.'

Adila and Jelly were enchanted by their first sight of Edinburgh, where they gave a concert with Mrs Maitland's orchestra. They played the Bach *Double Concerto,* and Jelly Mozart's *Concerto in G major.* They were to play there many, many times in a quarter of a century.

Adila was much taken with another of Tovey's pupils, Robin King, who though not a professional was a fine pianist. When he came back from the First World War incurably paralysed down the right side, Jelly bought and sent him all the works for left hand only that she had ever heard of. But it is doubtful if he ever played again. Certainly never in public.

In England among other people there were the poet Robert Trevelyan and his violinist wife Elizabeth. They had built a house at Leith Hill, which meant that the sisters met Vaughan Williams.

At Crabbet Park they met Belloc and Maurice Baring, of diverse but persuasive literary powers, and both Catholics. All the sisters remained nominally Catholic, but though religious not actively so; and in later life both Adila and Jelly preferred the

An Advantage of High Society

Anglican form. At Crabbet Park when the weather was fine everyone bathed in the lake, or played tennis, often 'rag tennis'. Belloc joined in, wearing a black frock coat, and two pairs of socks in place of tennis shoes.[5]

Such were the kind of friends they made and left behind when they returned to Hungary in January 1912, by way of Klagenfurt where they gave another concert. Titi (called Hortense) played the Schumann *D minor Sonata* with Adila.

The following winter they toured Switzerland, mainly in the neighbourhood of Zurich. This was a success, but Adila had not made the arrangements, and their Swiss agent refused to pay up. Taksony had to be summoned from Budapest to compel him to do so. Zurich remained in the gentle sisters' memory for the brutality of a troop of soldiers. A man wanted to cross the road between detachments. The troopers knocked him down.

In 1913 Adila gave a recital in Rome, but no details seem to have survived.

Even musically they had brought with them a piece of England. On their way to Switzerland they performed under Fritz Busch at Aix-la-Chapelle. Here Jelly played for the first time a *Conzertstück* which Arthur Somervell had written for her. It was the first work anyone had written for her, and she was doubly pleased that the composer came to Aachen to hear it. Pleased, but anxious to do it justice. 'Performers feel humble,' she says 'when playing in the presence of the composer. But for most composers it is a delight to hear their works for the first time. Even Ravel told me that it was "the finest moment in his life", though after that he forgot all about it.' And Ravel was less emotional than Arthur Somervell.

Jelly played the *Conzertstück* in London the next year with an orchestra collected by her 'Cleg' Kelly. At this full concert Adila played the Beethoven *Concerto*, and the two sisters again combined in what one wit said must now be called 'Bach's Double Concerto for 2 Aranyis.'

Madame d'Aranyi again came with them to Britain. She was as welcome as they in people's houses, but also served as musical conscience at rehearsals. 'Play it like that' she once said, 'and the audience will start whistling.'

Their financial position was easier. By 1912 they were supporting themselves. In February 1913 they all four stayed as paying guests with the Streets of Inverness Terrace. Street was an architect, son of the designer of the Law Courts, and his wife was a painter. They also had a fine collection of pictures, including Turner and Rossetti, most of which was destroyed during the Second War in a Baedeker raid on Bath. One of their daughters was a pianist.

The Aranyis never imagined, as they settled in to this house, that they had arrived for the last time together on British soil and would not see Hungary again together except for a month and a half in 1921.

Despite the war scare of the previous year, again they plunged straight into British music. The highlight of this season for Jelly was her first public appearance with Casals. For fifteen years now audiences had got past the quiet, dry-looking, scholarly face of Casals, and knew that from him they would get not only technical mastery, thanks to the new method of 'cello-playing he had worked out, but also a depth of feeling and insight such as no other 'cellist had. This, no matter what he played, but especially in Bach, many of whose works he rescued from oblivion. At this Classical Concert Kelly and Jelly played the Brahms *G major Sonata,* Kelly the Mendelssohn *Variations Sérieuses,* Casals an unaccompanied Bach *Suite,* and then the three joined in the Schubert *Trio in B♭.*[6]

Jelly's playing was attracting the notice of fellow musicians. 'Much you have' Leonard Borwick wrote to her in unconscious imitation of the Macbeth witches, 'more you have acquired; and more still you will attain to.... And it is a deep pleasure to me to watch your sure and steady progress onward and upward.'[7] With Adila he organized a Trio to perform in private houses.[8]

It may have been true in 1909, as Jelly says, that 'being Joachim's great-nieces drew the attention of interested people and made our first successes more easily won than in the case of

An Advantage of High Society

equally gifted but less fortunately placed musicians'. But the fact is that there were few, if any, equally gifted musicians beginning at that time, at least in the Britain of the violin. And by now that novelty had worn off; just as the novelty of Eileen Joyce being a 'young New Zealand pianist' had worn off (years later) long before critics and announcers stopped using the phrase. The sisters d'Aranyi were now conquering in their own right.

Conquest had little effect on any of their characters. Jelly continued to gurgle at untoward events in public. At Oxford in 1909 she had gurgled at Ernest Walker. Many readers may remember that charming bearded figure with his almost human cats, his inability to recognize his best friends in the street, and his high-pitched voice at Balliol Sunday Concerts announcing 'Th-the n-next p-p-piece is a W-w-w-waltz by Bva-a-amsss.'

Similarly at Oxford just before the war she got the giggles during an underground concert for the Ladies' Musical Club. The three sisters turned over for each other, so that it was easier for all to stay on the platform. While Adila was playing, her high heel caught in a hole in the boards and broke off, to Jelly's unmodifiable mirth.[9]

This irreverence continues in her memories. Ernest Walker wrote a set of *Waltzes for two Violins* for her and Adila, who played them in Oxford Town Hall. Dr Walker was very excited, and Jelly could see nothing of the hall full of faces and wicker chairs, except his ears, getting redder and redder with emotion, 'like two roses'.

They felt themselves secure enough financially that year to take a small cottage for the summer at Three Bridges, not far from Crabbet Park, and also rented a house in Lansdowne Crescent. Their social life flowed on. At a fancy dress ball on the roof of Selfridge's (to inaugurate the new building) Adila went dressed as a Hungarian Peasant, Titi as a Turkish Girl, and Jelly as a 'Savage'. To this came a civil servant who had just published his first book on political economy: Ralph Hawtrey, in his middle thirties, another member of the Apostles. Hawtrey and Titi took an immediate interest in one another.

The Sisters d'Aranyi

At the same ball a Swedish diplomat took a similar interest in Jelly. He was rich, noble, distinguished, and had translated Epictetus. He took her to the British Museum, where man and girl could be seen unchaperoned; and one day he proposed to her in a garden. Jelly returned his interest, or thought she did; and accepted him. They were more or less engaged, until his mother wrote that he had no business to get married, being gravely in the grip of tuberculosis—and indeed he did later have to go to a sanatorium. The match was broken off, but he remained inconsolable, and for a long time went on sending her Parma violets 'anonymously'; even when she was as far away as Edinburgh. Jelly seems to have got over the break more easily than he: at any rate she says little about it.

Jelly did not lack suitors. Or should one say, swains? Another, the year before, had been the handsome young tenor Steuart Wilson. His letters exist still, written with a light self-consciousness, as when inviting himself to tea he trusts she will not stab him with a hat-pin for boring her. In this letter he refers to his forthcoming first public concert.[10] He says he is not nervous as a rule, but hopes it will go all right. After the war he was our favourite singer of English *lieder*, especially in settings of A. E. Housman.

Society folk, however, could be disconcerting. The Asquiths were very different from the Balfours, not only in politics. Herbert Asquith himself was tone deaf and reacted violently when Jelly put music on a level with poetry, which he adored. He once greeted her, when she arrived for a visit with her violin in its case, 'Have you brought that coffin thing?'[11]

She was staying at The Wharf when he had a birthday, which she celebrated by playing outside his bedroom door in the morning. He thought the tune was *Christians Awake!* And he had been seen, when addressing a big meeting in the Central Hall, Westminster, with a white-clad women's-choir behind him, to leap to his feet at their first notes, thinking it was the National Anthem.

But Jelly found him, as a man, 'most just'.[12]

The Wharf was noisy with an anticipation of the 'bright young

An Advantage of High Society

things', so noisy in chatter and music-making that Jelly could hardly write to her mother. '*Je suis un peu fatiguée car nous couchons jamais avant l heures du matin, et je m'endors très tard—ça fait que je suis vert tout le matin—mais j'ai mangé comme dix loups pour le petit déjeuner.*'[13] (Jelly could no more write good French than she could spell the good English she spoke.) But she liked their fun and (literally) games. Parlour games of an intelligent kind were already the rage, and the Aranyis loved them: great men, analogies, I have a cat, and rebuses,[14] and all those taught in the *Week-End Book* in the 1920s. After all, Napoleon liked playing blind man's buff.[15] And in the evening of their days the sisters still played scrabble.[16] But when the house-parties came to their ends, there was always the fear that one would go back to London in a party, which would mean a first-class railway fare, and they still had little money for luxuries.[17]

Anthony, Margot's son, then a small boy, had a real feeling for music; at Winchester he composed, and at Oxford played the piano well. He never forgot Jelly, and years later when she had broken an arm and he heard of it, he came straight round with a huge wreath of roses, which, because there was no one to open the door, he left on the handle. '*Puffin est le meilleur garçon du monde*' she wrote to her mother in 1915, '*à part de son intelligence incroyable.*'

Although Lady Asquith says in her *Autobiography*[18] that at the age of seventeen she used to practise the violin before breakfast every morning, she could make the oddest comments on music. Once Adila played at a private party in a Brahms *Piano Trio,* and Margot Asquith asked why they had 'hurried' the passage marked *animato*. She was well-known for saying and doing eccentric things, and in 1919 having to leave a fashionable gathering while Jelly was still playing, she turned in going out and gave a full court curtsey, at which everyone laughed. Jelly, who was out of sorts anyway, felt humiliated and indignant.[19]

Nevertheless Jelly is the first to balance, and overbalance, such spontaneous lack of dignity with her real goodness and warmth of heart. The two women became intimate, sharing their full hearts in a world that did not seem always to want them: for Jelly had love troubles, and Mrs Asquith disliked the unemotionality, the very goodness and fidelity of some connections. 'They protect no one who is ridiculous, and love detecting the absurd. Poor darlings.'[20]

The sisters were frequent guests at Downing Street, where their contributions could be anything but serious. After one luncheon party two of them sat at the piano and burlesqued military marches in a four-handed duet.

Though they took little interest in politics, they were sometimes astonished by the ignorance of those who did. In 1910, at the time when Lloyd George's Budget introduced the principle of old age pensions, (first forerunner of the welfare state) and Grey precipitated a constitutional crisis which affected two kings and split the nation into angry halves over the prospect of the creation of hundreds of political peers, Asquith gave a lunch at No 10 to a party which included Lloyd George himself, Jelly, and her favourite political personage, Edward Grey. A prominent aristocratic lady, later to be authoress of a book on India, begged Lloyd George to tell her what old age pensions were all about.

Margot Asquith had a special fondness for Jelly ever since she had heard her playing at Winchester. In 1917 she invited her for Christmas, and sent her five pounds for expenses, knowing how difficult she was finding finances. But she often asked her to The Wharf, where she had a big barn in the garden, her personal place for writing and sometimes sleeping at night. Jelly says that Asquith before leaving for town used to go out to hear portions of her autobiography written the night before or in the early morning. This conflicts with Lady Asquith's own statement that her husband did not see the text before it was published. But as the text stops at 1906 (it was not published until 1920), maybe it was some more contemporary instalments or some other work which Asquith went out for to hear. Be that as it may, the Aranyis' friendship with this family stood them in very good stead when the clouds assembled over Europe. Yet Jelly often returned from

An Advantage of High Society

The Wharf with relief at getting home, particularly if Adila were away and she could have her mother all to herself. She did not by any means like, still less approve of, all the guests at the Asquiths'.[21]

In the three years before the war she got fonder and fonder of Kelly; but he was much abroad, in Germany: and in 1912 he made a tour of Australia, prior to his full London début with three recitals and an orchestral concert. In February 1914 Frances Dakyns and Jelly went to see him at the Queen Anne Street flat he was then sharing with Leonard Borwick. On the landing there was a step which Jelly neither expected nor saw. She sprained her ankle rather badly, and they took a taxi back to the Aranyis' house. During the flurry of carrying Jelly in, her mother gave the driver a sovereign. He did not come back with the change, but made straight off in the cab, which contained all their music.

This damage to an ankle was partly, if not largely, the cause of their staying in Britain during the war. Sprained ankles were major injuries to young ladies, and Jelly's went on troubling her. She was advised to take a sea-cure at Knokke-Zout in Belgium.

They went, all four. But the clouds over Europe were now crackling and rumbling. The maids in the hotel went about in tears. A tall, thickset German, son of Admiral von Tirpitz, played Chopin's *Funeral March* on the hotel piano. The Aranyis decided to make for their Hungarian home as speedily as they could, and went into Ostend to buy tickets.

It was too late. The clerk at the *guichet* could book them only as far as Frankfurt, from where they would have to find their own way in whatever trains were running and would accept them. Europe was already mobilizing.

'Ve veel return to Eengland' Adila announced: and nobody dissented. Anything would be better than going through Germany, and nothing worse than being blocked there. In any case to all four, Britain was better than any other country.

They managed to get on the Channel steamer and off at Dover. In those days British subjects entered Britain by one entrance; and the rest of the world by another, showing its passports. No

The Sisters d'Aranyi

British government thought or dreamed of giving a British subject a passport, which was a thing for Russian serfs. (My father once saw a patriot Irishman who refused to enter Britain as a Briton and was refused admission as anything else because he had no passport.)

Adila, knowing this, steered her party boldly in through the British entrance. Enemy aliens they were about to become, but they were safer in the land they felt at home in, and much less nationally confused than they might have been had the trains been running to Budapest. Whatever Britain's fate might prove to be.

Taksony, of course, was at his post in Hungary, and stayed there.

8

Enemy Aliens

The life of an alien in that war could be embarrassing: the life of an enemy alien intolerable. It was so for Alfredo Campoli during the Second World War. After Italy's entry against us, a BBC engineer made a public scandal for personal, and in his case understandable, reasons by refusing to balance for an Italian. Campoli had been resident in London since 1911, but had never bothered to naturalize himself. He was interned. Later in the War a programme about Paganini required a violinist of such skill and speed that only Campoli was thought suitable. He was sent for, played without credits and returned to the Isle of Man.

At the outbreak of the First World War we had heard so much about German spies from Baden-Powell and others, that a natural spy scare became spy mania. Two Swiss brothers, language masters at Rugby and Harrow, were overheard speaking French one Saturday afternoon in a punt on the Thames. The listener ran for the police, who detained them on suspicion.

Spies there certainly were; but not so many as there might have been, it was said, if a German diplomat had not had the curious habit of going to get his hair cut every month in the East End of London. On the declaration of War the police seized the barber, and with him a handlist of most of the German spies in London if not in Britain. But all aliens were suspect, and had to report regularly to the police.

The Aranyis were staying with the Asquiths when the police

came to investigate them; and it was the Prime Minister himself who motored them to the police station at Didcot. Although he did not make himself personally responsible for them, but sat in the car outside, I have no doubt that the constable on duty recognized the car, and some part in this valuable gesture was probably taken by Margot Asquith.

On arriving back in England the four ladies made for Broadstairs—not a very prudent choice after landing illegally: for Broadstairs is within easy reach of the Calais-Dunkirk coast and the movements of shipping are easy to watch. However nobody troubled them. They counted their money. They had two hundred golden sovereigns. Not much, for enemy aliens were unlikely to find engagements. But then everybody thought the First World War would be over by Christmas, as some did in the Second one.

As it happened, when this sum had dwindled to anxiety point, Adila lost fifteen pounds of it. Then they went about London with eyes alert for coins dropped on pavements.

They stayed at a flat in Beaufort Gardens, Chelsea, where before long they learned what to expect from public hysteria. Sitting in the garden on a soft summer evening (there were many such in August 1914), they heard a crowd assembling and booing and yelling in the street. At first they thought their tribulations had begun. But it was Sir Eyre Crowe the mob was after, on the opposite corner. He had been Under-Secretary for Foreign Affairs for the previous two years, had a German baron's daughter for mother, and a German wife.[1]

Nor was it long before they learned that even in music their nationality was likely to be an obstruction. The 'cellist Felix Salmond was invited to play in the Schubert $B\flat$ Trio with Jelly. 'I would rather play with a viper than with Jelly d'Aranyi' he declared with dogmatic patriotism. But when the war was over, they became good friends, often playing together in chamber concerts, and making a recording of this very work with Myra Hess, whose first recording it was.[2]

As we have seen, nobody had better soil than the Aranyis for

Enemy Aliens

cultivating national dislike of the two big teutonic nations, without need of the press to sow, grow, manure and arrange it in daily vases. But even this could go against them. There were three Misses Price, who lived in the Judge's Lodgings at Oxford. Alice, who had learned the violin as an amateur under a German teacher, loved the Germans. Before the war she could not understand the sisters' dislike of them; and when war was declared, would, consistently if imprudently, have nothing to do with the Aranyis.

Another day a police inspector called at Beaufort Mansions. The sisters had agreed to adopt the French form of their surname, with *d'*; while their mother was known officially on calling-cards as 'Madame Adrienne Aranyi von Hunyadvár'. The inspector found this alteration interesting, and wished to know their motives. It was not motives, but words and sounds that were the difficulty. A serious misunderstanding was about to put them in custody for the duration, when Frances Dakyns, who happened to be in the house, cleared matters up in such clear English from such a clear English face, that the inspector went away satisfied. Why he did not proceed on the subject of their nationality, discover their illegal entry, and intern them, nobody knows. A proper inference might be that friends in high places quietly submitted that they were not undesirable persons. But there was no hope of passing for other than foreigners, if any of them opened a mouth in public. Titi was shy; Jelly was only beginning; Adila's English was a disaster.

Adila, unlike Jelly who has a fine precision in a wide English vocabulary, made laughable mistakes in English to the end of her life. She once described a man as 'self-scented', and when everyone was amused, said she tried to avoid the word 'centred' anyway. She pronounced 'worm' as 'v-o-o-o-r-r-m' until corrected: after which it became 'wum'.

They got used to this. A tactful assistant in Derry and Tom's asked Madame d'Aranyi if she were French, because of her accent. 'No' she said 'I am an enemy alien.'

There was one household where enemy aliens were welcome as such: in Bedford Square. The Morrells were passionate paci-

The Sisters d'Aranyi

fists and loathed the war, and therefore by wolf-pack logic were loathed back as being 'pro-German'. The Aranyis often went to their Thursdays, and frequently to Garsington, where they stayed in the village. There they met famous writers of the past or the future from Henry James to Lytton Strachey and Virginia Stephen; and people like Duncan Grant and Boris Anrep. Not only pacifists went there: soldiers did. Jelly remembers Robert Graves and Siegfried Sassoon 'in Lancer's uniform with a little black tag on the back of the shoulders'. Friends from this circle invited them for visits, like Roger Fry in 1917 to the beautifully filled house at Guildford which he had designed and built as a home and rest-home for his ill-starred wife.[3] The sisters' very remote cousin Bertrand liked their vigour in a society which for him was too civilized; but his invitations got sadder and sadder. 'If affection were not very rare' he wrote in 1916, 'the war would have stopped long ago.'[4]

The Aranyis did suffer unpleasantnesses, but they were protected and welcomed by such friends as these, and others especially the Bighams. Robert Bigham was the son of a Law Lord, and his wife Nora loved getting together the interesting and the eminent in the arts or in society. A very nice kind of lion-hunter. Jelly often stayed with them, walking round to their house in Cheyne Walk, and she likes recalling some of the people she met there. Sargent, for instance, (the American painter, not the conductor who was still a young church organist at Melton Mowbray) who irritated her by ending every other sentence with 'Don't you know?': Ysaye the fine violinist whom Joachim is said to have discovered playing in a café,[5] now a refugee from occupied Belgium: the 'rather insignificant little figure' of Bernard Berenson, who when returning with Jelly from a visit to friends outside London mystified and amused her by turning gold and bowing thrice to the new moon: Mrs Pat Campbell, who not long before had created Eliza Doolittle in Shaw's *Pygmalion*.[6]

Though the Aranyis could play the social game as well as anyone, none of them was impressed by notabilities as such: nor could they stand pompousness or pedantry. During the war

Enemy Aliens

Jelly sat at a dinner table next to Professor Tonks, and said, simply and not insincerely, what an honour and pleasure this was. Tonks, in a literal mood, retorted 'How do you know?' Jelly could not bear rudeness, but she could quickly punish it. 'Well,' she said quietly 'I've been told about the honour. About the pleasure, I'm not so sure.'

Adila could be impenitently outspoken. Also later in the war, having fallen out with Adolf Busch (not because he was German) she was sitting in the Queen's Hall wearing a red widow's-peak hat and thundering out what she thought of him, when someone warned her that Busch's wife was in the row in front. 'I don't care' Adila went on without moderating volume, 'I'll say it to his face.'

And once she went round to the Artists' Room after a recital, crying 'Darling! Never play again with that *awful* pianist!' without thinking that of course the pianist would be there. Nor could she understand his coolness to her from then on.[7]

Her bluntness often sounded more hostile than it was, because of the deep pool of her voice under the torrent of her personality. But, diphtheria or not, the truth was the truth to her: and many fellow musicians at rehearsal were given corrections and counsel they could hardly resent, for these were right.

Also, she could make fun of the absurd in herself. She had always been a good mimic since the days she paced along like one of her uncles, one shoulder higher than the other. Once at dinner with the Somervells she burlesqued her own manner, bulging with cushions, as a cabaret star. 'Geef me some porrt-vine to gargle vid, please, vidout vich I cannot sing.' She could not gargle: she gulped the port: she was sick.

This social life went on during the war. One had to give up coupons for small portions of meat in shops and restaurants, but there were still pretty dresses, society weddings, even balls (for charity). Reading the memoirs of the time one is shocked, because one had forgotten, how social life did go on, even when one's loved ones were in special danger, at the Dardanelles, or in a Big Push. Very few behaved like a sister of my mother, who refused

The Sisters d'Aranyi

to go to a theatre or a concert for fear her husband would have been killed in France while she was at an entertainment.

Underneath the social life the Aranyis, Hungarian or not, suffered like the British. The loneliness of youth that survives when youth is being butchered, is poignant in the letters Aldous Huxley wrote from Balliol.

They had met his brother Julian at a Balliol Concert in 1909. When Jelly wrote in 1958 to congratulate Julian Huxley on his knighthood, he replied that he well remembered rushing after her down Hall stairs at the end of the concert, because she was running and there were excavations in Garden Quad she might tumble into. 'Why were you running?' I ask Jelly. 'I always ran when I was excited' Jelly explains. It had been her sixteenth birthday.

Also, stimulated by places, she had been playing in Balliol Hall.

Aldous was nearer Jelly's age, being one year older than she. Already at the outbreak of war he had been mourning the death of his middle brother Trev, whom he admired and loved, 'the noblest and best of men',[8] sitting in the room they had shared in the house in Westbourne Square, reading before the fire, and thinking of the happy evenings they had sat there and the hours they had hoped to have again. 'It's a selfish grief perhaps, but oh Jelly, you know what he was to me.'

As the war went on, with offensives, retreats, offensives, trench-murder and gas-attacks, Aldous found himself lonely at Oxford, unable to serve, reading English literature, irritated by the Oxford clocks all chiming together out of tune and by the noise of hymns from Chapel, near his rooms: while one by one his friends were taken from him. 'Very soon, I believe, there won't be any young people left in the world:—half of them being killed, & that doesn't make the rest feel any younger—or so I find. It's one's duty to stay young as long as possible.'[9]

'You ought to see Balliol now—' he wrote.[10] 'It's too curious. There are only about sixty undergraduates up, and the whole of the Front Quad is filled with soldiers: there are 250 of them there, sleeping four or five in a room—& a lot in my old room: I'm only hoping they won't smash my pictures & spoil my books—' 'Still', he goes on with surprising tolerance 'if they do, one will just have not to mind.'

He complains how dull Anglo-Saxon is, 'all good books of sermons and moral remarks. But occasionally there is good poetry, very sad and strange stuff, all about disappointment & sorrow.' He agrees with Jelly that *Oliver Twist* is depressing, and finds that his clock has ticked him into Wednesday morning. 'One day older! How very unpleasant!'

This passionate sense of the duty to be young became a philosophy. 'These long casualty lists of the last weeks have been perfectly dreadful—such a lot of names I knew. This war impresses on me more than ever the fact that friendship, love, whatever you like to call it, is the only reality. When one is young & one's mind is in a perpetual state of change & chaos it seems to remain as the one stable & reliable thing. It simply is truth in the highest form we can attain to. You never knew my mother—I wish you had because she was a very wonderful woman. Trev was most like her. I have just been reading again what she wrote to me just before she died. The last words of her letter were "Don't be too critical of other people & 'Love much' "—and I have come to see more and more how wise that advice was. It's a warning against a rather conceited & selfish fault of my own & it's a whole philosophy of life.'

This letter, written in the autumn term of 1915, when Aldous Huxley had returned to College, is perhaps the most affectionate and intimate of all he wrote to Jelly. He had been sending her 'silly little poems' from time to time, and encloses a very pretty one here, which is worth printing in full:

August 1915—The Old Home
In this wood—how the hazels have grown!—
I left a treasure all my own
Of childish kisses, laughter & pain:—
Left till I might come back again
To take from the familiar earth
My hoarded secret & count its worth.

The Sisters d'Aranyi

> I came: & the spider-work of the years
> All the time-spun gossamers
> Dewed with each succeeding spring,
> And the covering leaves of death on death—
> All scattered. Clean & fair & bright
> As ever it was, before my sight
> The treasure lay: and nothing missed.
> So having handled all & kissed
> I laid them back—adding one new
> And precious memory of you.

He had warned her that he was 'not a poet—except perhaps in a certain didactically flippant manner, particularly irritating to the high-minded. I am destined to write some long work of satiric & philosophic tendencies—poetry only doubtfully—but quite entertaining.'

Philosophy enters frequently into these letters, Leibnitz *versus* Spinoza, Bergson *On Laughter* of which Jelly has at last found a copy; and literature they had each read, or not read, the Russian novelists, Baudelaire, Mallarmé. Aldous Huxley was fascinated by French poetry, and wrote some himself, and sent her a sonnet in French, inspired by the long evenings and peaceful scenery of Connel Ferry, where he was passing a short wartime holiday. 'It looks as though the amount of good and evil were about the same in the world. I think the good will probably win in the end—though not necessarily, unless the most persistent and tremendous efforts are made—I don't think one is justified in taking a holiday, under the belief that everything is necessarily falling out for the best ... I think we shall ultimately work all the disorder into a single principle, which will be an Absolute—but which at present exists only potentially & at the nature of which we can only dimly guess.'

This idea of a Godhead that grows in power according to the efforts of mankind toward good was very popular among young people and young schoolmasters during and after that war, especially among scientists who had thrown over formal religion. Jelly, however, had more defined ideas, for she believed

Enemy Aliens

in personal prayer. But philosophy does not occupy all their letters. Aldous Huxley could be flippant, and he nearly always ends with self-conscious hopes that he has not bored her. In lighter mood he could even make gentle fun of his own loneliness. The following is an example, with the small crosses he often used in place of full stops.

> *Dear Jelly*
> You're not a very
> good correspondent—
> nor am I—but
> two wrongs don't make
> a right—
> However it would be
> nice to know how,
> when & where you
> were$_x$
> Oxford's very hot &
> stuffy—typical
> Summer Oxford, without
> the best part$_x$
> When all my friends
> are dead I shall
> become a hermit,
> and live in a cave—
> & perhaps you will
> come occasionally, &
> feed me with buns
> thro' the bars of my
> gate. It would be
> a charming life—!
>   *Yours*
>   Aldous

Jelly, whom he regarded as 'a bit of a genius', filled his cravings for friendship. If there were deeper feelings, he does not reveal or hint at them. At the beginning he was anxious if he did not hear from her, fearing something might have happened to 'my dear alien enemy'. He is grieved when she sprains her ankle (an accident to which Jelly was prone), and doesn't approve of her 'eating nothing'. He often writes at midnight beside his fire, as if Jelly represented something of his lost brother, and on such occasions could sign himself 'Yours affectionately'. But the friendship was in the mind: they met seldom, though he was constantly asking when he could call if he were to be 'in Town'. The gap between letter and letter lengthens, though he continues to write from Repton and Eton when schoolmastering.

Nor were Jelly's deeper feelings involved. Her secret heart, I fancy, was at that time with Cleg Kelly.

9

Wartime Music

The war did not end by Christmas, nor by all too many Christmases. The stock of golden sovereigns sank. Yet the sisters had much to give when war, as wars tragically do, stimulated in the middle classes an enlarged appetite for the arts. The outlook of the sisters was not particularly bright, but not so dark as it might have been. Adila took pupils.

The attempt to ban German music was half-hearted: and in any case a great number of classical European composers were not Germans but Austrians, and Austrians were regarded in Britain as nicer than Germans. The Aranyis were not really even Austrians. Besides, their reputation had grown .The Music in Wartime Committee, when it was formed under Sir Hubert Parry, did not disapprove of them. Fifth Columns had not yet been invented.

Kelly seems to have organized one more Chamber Music Concert with Casals, Jelly and himself. They may have repeated the Brahms. Certainly Jelly played the unaccompanied Bach *Sonata in A minor* and was very nervous. Then, after Kelly volunteered for military, or rather naval, service, this trio gave way to another. The fifty-four-year-old Fanny Davies took a fancy to the new young violinist. In November 1914 she formed an ensemble with herself, Suggia and Jelly in it. Rehearsals in her studio off High Street, Kensington were haphazard and incomplete, for they had no idea if Suggia could arrive even for the concert.

Fanny Davies found a spiritual contact with Jelly and planned

The Sisters d'Aranyi

a series of sonata recitals, taking the financial risk herself and paying Jelly a fee. 'If you would really care to,' she wrote 'I am delighted. For perhaps it might be given to me to be able to help you to bring your nice soul out! and it is such a nice one. I do feel it is a rare thing to find a young artist who really sees beyond the notes and marks.... Shall we try, and see what our combined efforts can bring out, and whether we can make people feel nicer because they share it. (A large order, Jelly dear!)' She suggests Brahms, Beethoven and Schumann. 'They have much to say.'[1]

Seeing beyond the notes and marks is to be open, receptive, to meaning and to the personality of the composer: and the background of this older woman, pupil of Madame Schumann, friend of Brahms, and an exquisite, strong and sincere pianist, encouraged Jelly. Not that she ever had much use for tradition in itself. 'Tradition!' she wrote in an intermittent and short-lived diary of these years 'what crimes are committed in thy name!'[2]

Suggia joined them for two such recitals, playing a Mendelssohn sonata in the first, between Beethoven and Brahms Trios; and Jelly played a Bach sonata in the second, between Schubert and Chaikovsky.*

The concerts paid well enough, delighting all three, to justify a third, at which Jelly and Fanny Davies played the Bach *B minor* because it followed so well after a Schubert Trio. An agent took the financial responsibility for this—sure sign of success—and added dates outside London. Suggia could not, or would not, go to Northampton, so Edith Hanson took her place. For those readers who take delight in visuality and colour: at this Jelly wore a black velvet gown with silk fringes and a soft ermine sash waist-high, which fell full-length at the back.

*That at least was the lay-out: but Suggia arrived saying she was ill, insisting on an announcement from the platform, and proposing that Fanny Davies and Jelly open the concert. Jelly had hoped to work herself in with the Trio, but she dutifully started to practise the Bach. Suggia made a sign. 'Don't play, Jelly' she said, 'I want to hear how the audience reacts.'

She was always unpredictable. Just as she was about to begin another recital, she recognized Alexandre Fachiri in the audience, and called out to ask him if by any chance he had a mute with him, as she had forgotten to bring hers. Nobody knew sometimes whether she was being genuine or not.

Wartime Music

The end of this promising partnership is obscure. The last letter Jelly had from her effusive, affectionate friend ran:

'May 17th 1915. *Dear little Jelly,* All right. I am glad you have written so frankly, as I should be the last person to do anything against your wishes. *Yours affectionately,*

Fanny Davies.'

In a sense the sisterhood too had by then broken up. On April 24th, 1915 Titi married her Civil Servant, who later became very eminent both at the Treasury and as an economist. After a short while in the Hawtrey home they made their own in Elm Park Gardens, Chelsea. But Titi's health, which had never been good, could not stand the strain of both domestic cares and a musical career, and her public appearances were few.

From time to time she did accompany her sisters, as during the 1919-20 session of London University, where they gave a concert in the Botanical Theatre: and even as late as 1930 they all played at Repton School, where the Joachim Stradivarius had another happy escape: for Rosamund Fisher, the Headmaster's wife, who had seen them to the station, noticed it in its case on a platform seat as the train was just moving out.

But Titi's health steadily got worse. She spent months in nursing homes, and in 1953 she died, three years before her husband was knighted. Sir Ralph lives on, with the distinction of an Honorary Fellowship of Trinity, Cambridge, at the age of eighty.

Adila was married in November of that same year. She was walking along Knightsbridge near Harrods in the early part of the war, when she had a strong sense, indeed a conviction, that she was meeting the man she would marry, a thing she had never conceived of. So compelling it was, that she turned round to see what kind of man it was.

Not long after, she was to play in a string quartet, whose 'cellist was a member of the Oxford and Cambridge Music Club. He caught a cold, could not come, and sent a substitute. When the substitute appeared, Adila recognized the man in Knightsbridge.

He rang her up later and won her heart's beginnings by saying he liked her voice. He also sent her chocolates.

Alexandre Fachiri, then twenty-eight, was of Greek extraction, but having been born in New York was an American citizen. His father was director-representative of Rally Brothers. He himself was a graduate of New College, Oxford,[3] and so good a 'cellist that he replaced Philip Somers-Cox in E. H. Fellowes' ensemble and for some time swithered between the law and music as a profession. The Bar won; and his dark, striking figure was pointed out to me by another student in the Inner Temple Library as the great authority on international law. He wore a big cloak.

By nature he was planned for neither profession, being shy and timid. But he became Secretary to the Master of the Rolls, in fact to three of them, and argued cases both in the Law Courts and at The Hague.

That he overcame his timidity, which had almost prevented him from accepting his first public appointment, was due to Adila. She teased him by calling him reproachfully 'Little Monkey' when he turned shy: which made him squirm. Little by little however, she used the phrase affectionately, and this gave him confidence, and changed him.

They were devoted to each other. In August 1919, when they were staying at a country house, Alexandre wrote to Jelly that their hostess hardly dared tell the servants that this couple wished to share a room, 'because it is unknown here for husband and wife to be friends.' And many years later, when Jelly was in America, Adila arranged for her husband to sleep in Jelly's room, because she had to go out of town for an engagement, and he might 'burn up' all alone in their big one.[4]

He had an inner quietness such as some people have to whom animals, especially cats, are attracted. In Alexandre's case it was birds that came to him, wild birds in parks without decoy of crumbs or whistlings. On his shoulder at meals stood his turquoise budgerigar, bred by Nina Balfour's son Archie. This he took to his Chambers, and even on holiday. It was called 'Floppy' because it never got used to its clipped wings and fell into the soup

Wartime Music

or even into the fire, from which it was rescued safe but brown or sooty-black. He and Floppy were inseparable, and when the little bird died, the whole family mourned, and Jelly wept in the train to Bournemouth where she played very badly.

During the war he and Adila lived at his mother's house in Hans Road. Jelly and her mother went to live with the Hawtreys; not a long walk from each other; which made Chelsea precious to them, because the Hawtreys were kind to them all.

That only chamber music was possible in wartime was much to Adila's taste. The sisters formed various temporary string- or piano-quartets to play at private houses: the Saxton Nobles', the Booths, the celebrated Wertheimers', those of Mrs Gooch and Mrs St John Hornby, the Bighams' and others; in Cromwell Road, Knightsbridge, Chelsea, Campden Hill, Mayfair. Some were friends: some became friends. The idea sprang from a Classical Concert at the Aeolian Hall in December 1915, when Leonard Borwick, Rebecca Clarke, and Percy Such joined them for the Dvořák *Piano Quintet*, and Haydn's *Quartet in F* (op. 77 no. 2) was given. Rebecca Clarke, still under thirty, was composer as well as viola player, and Percy Such, though only thirty-three, had studied ensemble under Joachim and had played the 'cello on occasion in the Joachim Quartet.

The following Classical Concert was given by Adila, Jelly, two singers, Leon Goossens and Ernest Walker.[5] It was devoted to Bach. Jelly played the *Second Suite* in A minor and with Adila the *Double Concerto*. Leon Goossens, later to be considered the finest oboist in the world, was at that time only nineteen. He had already volunteered, and was on active service for the rest of the war. In this way the Aranyis were gathered into the group of young musicians who talked the same musical language.

The new ensemble continued for a while. In February and March 1916 it gave four concerts at Kent House, Knightsbridge. (Details are given in the additional notes.)[6] But that year Rebecca Clarke went to America, and her place was taken by Raymond Jeremy. Four more concerts were given in different houses, and then Jeremy went to the war. His place was taken by no less a

The Sisters d'Aranyi

player than Lionel Tertis, regarded by us as the best viola-player in history until perhaps the advent of William Primrose. Although nineteenth-century composers like Brahms had begun to make fuller use of the viola, this instrument remained the charwoman of the household, because of its reedy tone and alleged unwieldiness. Tertis not only varied the tone but also achieved a dexterity not always achieved by competent violinists. If he had not existed at the time he did, many solo works for viola would not have existed either.

When Percy Such went, his place was taken by Arthur Williams, who had been caught, like many others, in Germany by the sudden outbreak of the war. Like them he was interned in Ruhleben, a ghastly detention camp whose horrors have been hushed for those who knew the Nazis but in the First War appalled the world. Some prisoners survived: very few got out. Arthur Williams did get out, but lived in constant pain. He became Professor of the 'cello at Aberystwyth.

This new version of the quartet again played in private houses, sometimes for war charities.[7] Among the familiar Mozarts, Schuberts or Beethovens, Adila performed a *Concerto* by the French violinist Jean-Baptiste Viotti, or Tertis played solo. They gave the Brahms *Piano Quintet in F minor* with a pianist not recorded, but Jelly is sure it was not Titi.

At one of these, Tertis, Jelly and Williams performed the *String Trio* that Kelly had written. Kelly had been among the band of young enthusiasts on Churchill's raid on Antwerp in September 1914,* and was in the Dardanelles with Rupert Brooke and other doomed members of the Royal Naval Division. From there he had gone to France, and was killed in action at Beaucourt-sur-Ancre in November 1916.

Adila still bore her maiden name on programmes, but that summer she appeared for the first time as Adila Fachiri, by which name she was known to my generation. This was at two recitals by herself and Jelly at the Bruces' and the Booths'. On one of these programmes were found several items which they were

*Lady Violet Bonham Carter, *op. cit.* p. 340.

Wartime Music

often to play together: Purcell's *Golden Sonata*, the Bach *Double Sonata in G,* and Spohr's unaccompanied *Duo in A minor.* The other recital was lighter, except for the Saint-Saens *B minor Concerto,* the Lekeu *Sonata,* and Jelly in the *Sonata* of Debussy, which for a time she thought decadent, though she knew she played it well. Again no pianist is mentioned, and again Jelly is sure it was not Titi.

Jelly now branched off by herself on a progress round schools, public or other. The start of this tour was due to George Leigh-Mallory, the mountain-climber, of whom more hereafter. He had known, adored and teased Jelly for years. He lived near Godalming, and suggested to his friend Edward Rendall, schoolmaster and musician, that it might be a good thing for Charterhouse if she played there. Rendall not only agreed to arrange this, but passed the idea on to his brother, the great headmaster of Winchester, who invited her there.

At Charterhouse in the Hall one September Saturday of 1917, the programme was a lightish one, of those short show pieces which Jelly used to call 'ear-ticklers': Schumann's *Garden Melody,* a *Spanish Dance* by Sarasate, arrangements by Kreisler of Porpora's *Minuet,* Couperin's *La Précieuse,* Cartier's *La Chasse;* and with these a Paganini *Capriccio* and *En Bateau* by Debussy. For even a slow piece can be a show piece in the hands of a virtuoso, and Jelly's hands made more than mere show. But she also played three of the Brahms-Joachim *Hungarian Dances* and Bach's unaccompanied *Chaconne.* This is the first mention in my records of her playing this latter work, which when she was maturer lay among her most stirring and comprehensive performances.

The Winchester concert was different. Jelly went with Arthur Williams and stayed with the Maitlands at Hillbrow. The concert took place in Wolvesey Palace. Rosalind Maitland accompanied her in some 'ear-ticklers' and played with the other two in the early *Trio in C minor* of Beethoven and Schubert's in *B flat.* This was on another Saturday, and on the Sunday afternoon Anthony Asquith came up the hill to fetch Jelly and her mother to tea

The Sisters d'Aranyi

with the headmaster. In the evening Jelly played more intimately in his drawing-room to selected boys and masters.

Such was the beginning of many college recitals and drawing-room music-makings and of a life-long friendship which with Dr Rendall as with many confirmed bachelors always hovered in the heart over deeper feelings. Jelly and her mother found him a man of the widest warmth who could also be vague and sometimes clumsy. Not on this but another occasion he introduced Jelly's mother as *Mademoiselle* d'Aranyi to the Bishop, and then stepped on her dress, so that a piece tore off.

Jelly kept all his letters, as she kept nearly everything, and there are over four-score of them: from this year 1917 at Winchester until 1924 when he retired, from Batley Priory where he retired to, and from Bulawayo, Wagga-Wagga, Sydney, Vancouver and other places on his triumphal educational tour of the Commonwealth, they are full of memories of the times when she had made his drawing-room 'sing'. In 1947, when he was eighty-five, he was still writing to her, and sent her, for Christmas, a short poem printed in red and black, enclosing a small bird's feather. Somebody once described him as a man 'never afraid to give himself away with both hands'.[8] No wonder he and Jelly liked each other.

Meanwhile the quartet went on. Raymond Jeremy returned for four afternoon concerts in private houses in March 1918, at the second of which Lionel Tertis rejoined it in the Brahms and Mozart *String Quintets with second viola in G major* and *G minor*. Which must have been quite an experience for its hearers.

And so, with these occasional concerts and teaching, the Aranyis were able to earn a little money, apart from two husbands' earnings.

And so too at last the war ended. 'Armistice with Hungary!' Jelly wrote in her fragmentary diary on November 4th, 'Hungary free!... But I am homesick—that I am. If only I could be in Budapest to rejoice, to take part in all this! To fall in love with all of them!'

At the end of the month she was at Sherborne ('And well I played! And to have Adila all to myself; it was like a dream! My

Wartime Music

beloved little sister.') and never forgot coming back to London's street lamps gay again without their maskings.

Her wave of rapture carried her on Boxing Day to see President Wilson arriving, 'a lovely London winter day with a hazy red sun. So went hundreds of thousands to cheer him. Oh just the things I adore the most. A big crowd; every individual enthusiastic, and so their nicest feelings coming up.' President Wilson had long formulated a plan for the dismemberment of the Austro-Hungarian Empire.

But the ends of wars are never all joy. The actual Armistice 'still darkens the sky. And the dearest to me, not coming back—never—yet Peace.' In this confusion of feelings she was by no means alone.

A week later she notes: 'and how dull, uninspired my playing was today—good god I would have asked my money back, had I been to such a dull concert. I begin to be alarmed about myself —am I going to degenerate into an empty-headed second-rate violinist?' She was now twenty-five: but no violinist is proof against playing badly when full peace comes back to a personally empty world.

Kelly and the Aranyis had been seeing, making music with, or writing to, each other since 1910. From time to time Kelly would recommend pieces he had come across, Schubert *Duos* for violin and piano to Jelly, the four Dvořák *Romantischstücke* to Adila. But when he first went to the war, Jelly heard of him mainly through Leonard Borwick, who being forty-six was over military age.

'We have heard from Mr Kelly' Borwick wrote in June 1915 'since his wounds in a letter written June 9. He talks of it as "an obliging little wound that will give him a short holiday in Egypt" —a bullet in the right heel that has made a little rent about two inches long and half an inch deep. I know you will like to know the exact extent of the damage. He writes in very good spirits.'

The obliging little wound bled music. During this spell in the Alexandria Hospital Kelly composed the *Elegy for Strings and*

The Sisters d'Aranyi

Harp in memory of Rupert Brooke, at whose burial on Skyros he had been one of the shore party.

Jelly had adapted for violin his *Flute Serenade*[9], and in giving his permission, though thinking it might be very difficult for the violin ('that, in your case, is not a consideration'), he wrote to her that he had a violin sonata for her in place of the work for violin and orchestra she had asked for. 'I began composing it about three and a half months ago and I have now about half of it written down,' and he hoped to finish it in January. 'It is all there in my head but not yet on paper. You must not expect shell and rifle fire in it! It is rather a contrast to all that, being somewhat idyllic.' He had meant to keep this as a surprise, but thought it deceitful not to mention it as he was writing.

After the Dardanelles he was in England for a while before going to France. In May, he sent Jelly the parts of his *String Trio* which Goodwin and Tabb were about to publish. In this letter he says he had hoped to see her at the Bonham Carters to say goodbye, but is now too busy packing.[10] Such was their farewell.

In a longish letter in August, he describes the trenches. 'The heavy shells send up a mixture of earth and explosions of gas that look like a monstrous cactus. The scream of the howitzers would be the despair of Richard Strauss—though it would be amusing if he tried to write a battle symphonic poem.' He himself had toyed with the idea of a *1914 Overture, à la 1812*, 'with Tipperary overcoming Ein Fester Burg but these sort of works aren't really in my line.'

He refers to a part-singing group of soldiers he has got together called the Minnie-singers (from *minnenwurfer*). 'They can't sing and the noises they make would make one wince in normal existence. Life can be very dirty and uncomfortable, especially when crawling down the narrow entrances into deep dugouts—but one enjoys the contrast like nothing in peacetime.'[11]

In his last letter, on September 23, 1915, he says he has no time for reading, and has been carrying Plato's *Republic* about with him to no purpose. Borwick provides further news of Kelly's

Wartime Music

musics that month. 'Making settings of a better class of music for the regimental band.'

On November 20th, Borwick said in a letter to Jelly: 'We had good last news of Mr Kelly about three weeks ago, though he was in an uncomfortable region. He actually sent over a little composition.'

Last news indeed. Kelly had been killed five days before Borwick wrote.

There seems to have been no word of love between him and Jelly. He signs himself 'Yours Sincerely'. Perhaps the war would have had to end before there could be any. But of all the men who touched Jelly's heart Kelly went deepest. For years she was happy when she had merely dreamed he was alive. His photograph stands on the Bechstein grand at Bellosguardo.

PART II

Jelly d'Aranyi

10

Drawing Flames

The war, as is recorded by Percy Scholes in *The Mirror of Music*,[1] had damaged orchestral music, but the Promenade Concerts survived. Composers not on active service, and those, the majority, who were, continued at work, however hampered. Recitals had raised big sums for war charities. Sir Henry Wood had opened the door of the Queen's Hall Orchestra to women, and never closed it; and other orchestras opened theirs. Music had received more public interest than it had previously for a long period, and works by 'enemy' composers soon trickled back into programmes. Scholes chooses two 'enthusiastically received performances' of Schönberg's *String Sextet* in December 1919 as the turning point. The Bechstein Hall, of which Neville Lytton had wittily deplored in pre-war years the 'spaghetti frieze', wondering when music-lovers would appreciate line proportion as they did musical proportion, and which had been closed because enemy property, re-opened as the Wigmore Hall.

The three sisters and their mother had survived. As a family, though in two households, they were as united as ever, continually in one another's houses: separately Adila and Jelly had begun to make a small but growing public each of her own. It will be convenient at this point to treat them separately, bringing them together when they stood together on the platform.

Jelly's first concert after the war, in January 1919, was only a continuation of her work in schools. She went to St Leonard's

The Sisters d'Aranyi

School in St Andrews. She had just recovered from 'Spanish 'Flu', a severe attack of that grave epidemic in which many died. She was told that violent nose-bleeding had saved her life. But she played well: and so did Adila in her first post-war appearance. She played with Titi, who looked pretty; and they were a success.

Jelly's first London recital was in the Wigmore Hall on February 10, 1919. The sisters had not yet found a constant, perfect accompanist, but chose George Reeves because they thought he was the best. Jelly played a *Sonata* by Fauré, a *Suite* by Locatelli (a minor eighteenth-century composer-virtuoso)*, Joachim's *Romance in C*, three of the Paganini *Capricci*, and two Hungarian pieces. The takings were £43 16s., and Adila was very proud of her.[2]

In a way these concerts were an official entry into post-war music, a thing all three of them had been somewhat dreading, 'a hall full of enemies.'[3] But the enemies had gone.

George Reeves again accompanied her in her next recital, only six months later, sign that people had taken notice. At this Jelly reminded the world of its war losses by introducing to it her version of Kelly's *Serenade*.[4]

What struck the audience was the vigour of her playing. Indeed one person at a big supper afterwards was heard likening her to Suzanne Lenglen the tennis star, already famous for her skill, agility and temperament. But this likeness may also have been due to the head ornament which Jelly was wearing across her head, as Lenglen wore a head scarf.

Three months later she returned to the same hall in place of Adila who was ill. She played first the *Concerto in E minor* by Pietro Nardini, eighteenth-century follower of Tartini, which according to a later Birmingham critic did not move far outside the Italian conventions of its century, but in her hands sounded the most exquisite poetry.[5] And then (the reason for the recital) Elgar's *Violin Sonata* in the same key.

This had been written only the year before, in 1919. It was

*Groves' *Dictionary* does not list any Suite by Locatelli. It may have been another name for a Sonata.

Drawing Flames

dedicated to an old lady of whom Elgar was very fond: but four days after the dedication and before the last, elegiac, movement was written, the old lady died.[6] It was therefore a work in which Elgar's emotions were specially involved. But although W. H. Reed and Landon Ronald had co-operated with him during composition, Lady Elgar noted that when he returned from their rehearsal in the Aeolian Hall, he was depressed, not liking his music, and had to be persuaded to attend its first performance.

Very different was his attitude in the Wigmore Hall. Elgar was astonished to find Jelly fully as good as her sister, for whom he had a high regard. In fact a critic in the *Westminster Gazette* said that this was a performance enjoyed by no one more than the composer. He wrote a message of thanks on a torn programme of a vocal concert. Later he was to address Jelly as 'My darling Tenth Muse.'

The *Westminster Gazette* was fervent. 'When will the musical public awake to the fact that in Miss Jelly d'Aranyi we have in our midst one of the very greatest of living women violinists—perhaps the greatest of all? ... She is standing head and shoulders above nearly all her contemporaries, even those possessed of the highest names.'[7] And referring to the *Chaconne* from Bach's *Suite* (or *Sonata* or *Partita*) *in D minor*, it said: 'Someone once said of Joachim in his younger days that he seemed to draw flames from his instrument, and listening on Saturday one could understand precisely what was meant by that remark.'

It could be held that Jelly re-created this *Chaconne* for her time, and it is good to find praise for her in it so early. It had been regarded* as too difficult for ordinary performers on the modern violin, because the instrument Bach wrote for had a flatter bridge and looser bow. When the nineteenth-century Norwegian violinist Ole Bull tried to adapt his, he is said to have lost sonority but gained grace. Jelly was able to recapture the beauty and spiritual depth under the technical difficulties on a modern instrument without losing either breadth of tone or ease of execution.

*The opinion of Herbert Thomson in *The Yorkshire Post*, October 21, 1931 after a concert at Bradford.

The Sisters d'Aranyi

The only performer who rivalled her in this was Lionel Tertis, who had the audacious dexterity of making it sound easy on the more cumbersome viola.*

Elgar wished to see more of this fascinating new performer. He invited her to Hampstead on February 29th next year to play his *Sonata* again with Ethel Hobday, and also one by Brahms. This was the last concert that Lady Elgar heard in Severn House. She died a month later.

The visit gave little pleasure to Jelly. 'I went to Elgar's and played there for a lot of early Victorian antiquities; I felt chilled to the bone at first, and wanted to kick everybody and thing during I (*sic*) played Brahms and at tea.' Nor could she take the snobbish side of Elgar, whom she had first met in the next chair at a dinner party. As conversation Elgar asked if it irked her to be introduced as 'Miss d'Aranyi the Violinist', because when he was younger, he went on, he greatly disliked being introduced as 'Mr Elgar the Composer.' ' "Mr Elgar, Gentleman" ' he said 'would have been enough.'[8]

A year or so later she could not take him at all. He conceived a 'violent affection' for her, showered her with compliments of the kind that shrivelled her, and lunched her more than once at the Pall Mall Restaurant. She went unwillingly, with a total lack of liking, though he could be charming, she says, despite his 'gorgeous top hat, rather tight-fitting overcoat and spats.' But she did not think him a great composer and felt it absurd that he had been given the O.M.

Things came to a head one day when he suggested taking a taxi and going to Richmond Park. 'Surely that isn't the place to go in midwinter' Jelly thought 'for a *viellard* and me!' So she suggested instead the British Museum, where 'the old gentleman' (Elgar was about sixty-three) 'exhibited no sort of knowledge whatever except that he could read inscriptions.' After that he invited her home to tea. This Jelly refused, but consented to go to his house for a book he wanted to give her. And there a little

---

*The feat was called 'staggering' by Percy Scholes, *op. cit.* p. 399.

Drawing Flames

scene took place which ended in Jelly ensconced in a taxi, 'cursing old men.'

She never wished to play his *Violin Concerto,* and never did. When he asked her why, she said it was "too English" for any but an English-born performer to do it justice: Sammons, for example, who played it beautifully. 'Of course' she adds gently 'Elgar's music wasn't really English. Vaughan Williams' ' (with a gleam in her eye) 'was'.

For many years now Ethel Hobday appears as Jelly's favourite pianist. As Ethel Sharpe she had had her début in 1891 at the Princess Hall and won a silver medal. She was much liked in chamber music with or without her husband Alfred Hobday, who had on occasion played viola in the Joachim Quartet.[9] When she was the age Jelly now was, she had been a friend of Brahms in Vienna, three years before he died. Brahms could never pronounce properly the english '*th*', and everyone laughed when his attempts at her first name sounded like the German for 'donkey.'

As an accompanist, or partner, she was discretion itself, but could take her place as co-artist with mastery, especially part-playing in Bach. Her sense of rhythm was very near Jelly's. She was twenty-one years older than Jelly, and so a handy chaperon as well: for though the war had broken many conventions and taboos, Jelly was unmarried and attractive, and behaved as she had been brought up. Ethel Hobday was Irish—'very Irish' Jelly repeats, remembering her wit on journeys. Remembering also, perhaps, how often she was attacked by accompanist's-disease and left the music in trains. She left all of it once in an American train, lost for ever.

One expression of her face remains particularly vivid in Jelly's mind. In 1930 that magnificent old singer and musician Sir George Henschel, who with his first wife founded the Song Recital as an art form in about 1880,[10] gave a concert in his eightieth year, which Jelly opened with the Bach *Concerto in E.* His voice, if it had an elderly timbre in it, was as sweet and true as it had been fifty years before; and the aged veteran was so joyous that his weapons had not rusted that Ethel Hobday burst into

The Sisters d'Aranyi

the Artists' Room of the Arts Club in the interval, with eyes like blue saucers, crying in her peaty brogue 'Sir George kissed me on the lips!'

One of their early recitals in the Wigmore Hall was when Editha Knocker conducted her string orchestra with Jelly in the Bach *Concerto in G minor*. She was a violinist and teacher from the North of England who had settled in London. With Ethel Hobday Jelly played, besides the Mozart *Sonata in D* (K.7), two new works in manuscript.

The first was dedicated to her by Ernest Walker of Balliol, where she had just given its first performance: *Variations on a Theme of Joachim*. This theme begins with the notes Gis-E-La (German G sharp, Italian A,) and was enclosed in a letter written to Gisela von Arnim. More an academic exercise than an inspired work, but quite fun for a violinist.

The second consisted of two *English Dances* by Edward Rendall. The tunes had been found in a manuscript book once belonging to an old fiddler at Great Rollright, the Cotswold village with the archaeological stones and long folk traditions, where the Rendalls' father had been Rector. Rendall called them *Anonymous Air* and *Miss Johnson and Holiday*. If the word *and* is a mistake for the word *on* (and it appears consistently in notices and programmes), I fancy the fiddler made the mistake. *The Referee* thought these dances should be published. They never were, but Jelly repeated them when Haslemere resumed, and elsewhere.

Shortly after the war there were several memorial concerts to the young men who had been destroyed before their talents had had a chance. One was Kelly, who was thirty-three when he volunteered. On May 2, 1919 at the Wigmore Hall such a concert was given by the Small Queen's Hall Orchestra under Frank Bridge: Muriel Foster sang the song *Aghadra* which Kelly had written in 1903, and a group of lyrics by Blake, Byron and Shelley, set from 1910 to 1914. Leonard Borwick played his own arrangement of a *Prelude for Organ* which Kelly had composed in H.M.T. *Grandtully Castle* off Rhodes in March 1915, the *Idyll* and the *Caprice* from the *Cycle of Lyrics* (1907-8) and *Five*

Drawing Flames

Monographs for Piano. The *Serenade for Flute* (with accompaniment of Harp, Horn, and String Orchestra) was played by Louis Fleury; and the *Elegy for String Orchestra and Harp* (In Memoriam Rupert Brooke) was repeated at the end of the concert by request.

Jelly did not take part, but she was there, like all Kelly's surviving friends. She had dreamed of him the night before, and found pain in the pleasure of the concert,[11] recalling the times when she had found the Bechstein Hall filled because his eager face was in the audience, and so empty when it was not.

The *Elegy* had already had its first public performance: in Rugby School Speech Room on the afternoon of Tuesday, March 28th, when Bridge conducted it at a Memorial Concert to Rupert Brooke.[12] Sydney H. Nicholson, another Old Rugbeian, conducted the School Orchestra and Concert Chorus with the baritone J. F. Hubbard, in his own setting of three of the 1914 *Sonnets*, whose rapturous tunes still ring in the heads of old men who were boys there. Less so do the gentle, simple and wise words of Walter de la Mare, who read a paper on *Rupert Brooke and the Intellectual Imagination*. Few were heard beyond the first few rows.

The *Elegy* with its inscription from a Callimachus poem (the one so softly and nostalgically done into English by W. J. Cory) recaptured something of that wistful, pagan burial on Skyros with a faint breeze beginning to stir the olive leaves under a beclouded half-moon.[13] If it were revived as a musical counterpart to a Georgian Poem, I think the nightingales would still sing.

Jelly was hurt that the organizers of the Wigmore Hall concert had not asked her to play the *Violin Sonata,* and indeed it does seem a strange omission, especially as it was Leonard Borwick who with her had given its first performance in December at a Classical Concert (still so called, though the range no longer stopped at Brahms). She played it again with Tovey at another Kelly Memorial, in Balliol Hall, when Tovey played also the *Studies and Monographs.* Kelly's sister Maisie sang three of his songs, and

The Sisters d'Aranyi

Robert Murchie played the *Flute Serenade*. Jelly had as second accompanist in three *Hungarian Dances* Tom Spring-Rice, who by then had succeeded his uncle as Lord Monteagle.

Kelly's name did not slip at once into oblivion. In June 1920, Jelly, Lionel Tertis and Arthur Williams played the *String Trio*, which had been first played at Kelly's home Bisham Hall by T. F. Morris, Frank Bridge and Ivor James in another June, the last before the war. For years Jelly included the *Jig*, and as late as 1933 at Lausanne her arrangement of the *Flute Serenade*: in which same year Lord Monteagle in a concert with a young tenor at Limerick played 'some of the dances in Cleg's *Youth Pageant* which makes an excellent concert piece.'[14] But alas! by 1933 the world was more concerned with its actual troubles than with past musical losses, and when Jelly played the *Serenade* at a Hallé Concert, it was dismissed as 'an amiable but unimportant serenade by F. S. Kelly, a young Australian who was killed in the war.'[15]

At the beginning of 1920 Jelly was a young woman with a divided soul. Always younger than her age, she was psychologically still adolescent. She had conceived a passion for a young man who showed no sign of returning it, and being with him was that torment of joy and misery which we have all known. This set up what she called an 'oriental languor', which her mother's understanding did much to dissolve.[16] Her music was not improved by it, however, at a Chappell Popular Concert, which she hated anyway, feeling she had played down to her public, a thing Onkel Jo would never have done. Nor did she feel any better at Charterhouse, from where she and her mother returned very unhappy.

Press opinions should have reassured her. Edwin Evans discovered her 'generous flow of temperamental expression' warming up the 'classical tendencies' of Schumann; the *Daily Telegraph* liked her 'full-blooded vitality in Brahms'; while the *Daily Express* critic called her striking tone in shorter pieces 'rich, full and penetrating with a delicious bite like good Italian wine.'

But even the greatest event of her musical life so far was

Drawing Flames

made miserable: the first time she played the Beethoven *Violin Concerto* with an orchestra. This was at Edinburgh on February 16th with the Scottish Orchestra conducted by Landon Ronald, its director for four years. Jelly knew she had played well, but thought she would one day play better. It was not her music that dissatisfied her. She was exhilarated and proud of her responsibility, and had a great reception. But alas! the perfidious young man was not to be seen in the Usher Hall or after and she spent the night crying in the dark till her cheeks burned from her tears.

There was no doubt that people wanted to hear her. 'Again, again and again engagements pouring in', she wrote in her desultory diary, pleased that she had never pushed herself into having five appearances in the Queen's Hall in one season. Or into anything else. The current season was full enough. Her reception was rapturous.

'A progress from good music to good fiddling' *The Times* commented, as she moved from Brahms and Bach to Sarasate, which last almost convinced the critic that she was right to play it. The Brahms, he said, was so well understood that an inattentive listener might think nothing was happening: and of a Mozart *Concerto* 'Here was the true childlike spirit of Mozart.' He crowned these accurate compliments with the astonishing query about Joachim's cadenza in the Mozart: 'Why did she not play her own?'[17]

Jelly cheered up. 'What a spoilt creature I am', she confided to the night hours in April 1920, 'it is quite an honour to have the greatest success in London now, always. Life is fun. Fun to dress up in that gorgeous old crinoline Mama made for me*, fun to play, fun to be so loved by the public and afterwards to talk, talk and talk with Mama', for the Fachiris were away.

It was she who was invited to play at a dinner in honour of Albert Coates, then conducting the Beecham Opera. This was difficult fun, however, playing among the tables. So was her first

---

*Of a dark red Indian material, above which she wore a long necklace of oxidized silver and beads.

outright Sonata Recital, with Ethel Hobday in the Wigmore Hall. She had not yet the feel of a Sonata Recital.

A Sonata Recital is not unlike reading poems in evening dress to a large crowding public. One sonata can be fitted into a varied programme without special effort: but three or four of them with nothing else require an atmosphere which anything like false solemnity, a static 'personal' style, or glibness, will ruin. Jelly did not have these failings: at each of her sonata recitals one entered at once into the several minds of three masters. But she did not yet know how easy this would be for her. As yet she preferred playing sonatas to a chosen few.[18]

At this recital they played the powerful Beethoven in C minor, which was Jelly's favourite except the big one in G;[19] Mozart's in B♭ (no 15) and the César Franck. Jelly was not nervous, *'mais je n'etais pas dans mon assiette.'* It was the first time she played the César Franck, which she had learned in four days.*

Such concerts acknowledged her abilities in the classics. But Jelly also wished to be with the music of her time. She was pleased in the summer in 1920 to be invited to take part in Stravinsky.

Stravinsky had written *L'Histoire du Soldat* in 1918, to earn some money in Switzerland, where he had fled from Russia. It had only one performance on an intended strolling-player tour, owing to the same outbreak of 'Spanish 'Flu' from which Jelly's nose saved her. Its second performance was not till 1923 at Weimar, and only in 1927 did London see it on the stage, at the Arts Theatre. The concert performance in the Wigmore Hall on July 20, 1920, fragmentary though it was (but the fragments were many) seems to have been ignored by some musicologists.

Ernest Ansermet, who did more than any other musician to foster Stravinsky, first gave a lecture (rather too long) to an audience of Society and musicians. Then he conducted the Philhar-

---

*It astonishes us in these days how little time was needed to get a programme printed in those. But maybe this explains why in so many, keys and opus numbers are printed wrong.

Drawing Flames

monic String Quartet and an assortment of instrumental virtuosi including Jelly as solo violin. Olga Haley, a mezzo-soprano devoted to contemporary music, sang *Pributki*; there were pieces for string quartet; and Haydn Draper played wartime works on the clarinet.

Stravinsky was becoming known, liked and admired by half musical London, as he was misunderstood and ridiculed by the other. When Jelly first saw her part, she thought it was 'desperate'; but if it was a joke, it was a good joke, and she studied it with as much attention and curiosity as she studied Bach. In the result she became 'mad with enthusiasm' for it.[20]

But she was not at ease. Adila kept telling her that her violin was bad, dead. After the party where Mrs Asquith made her tactles curtsey, Adila said so again. Jelly wept tears of rage but she knew Adila was right. She borrowed a Bergonzi from a collector. She could not bear this newcomer. She was faithful to her Balestrieri. She felt like a mother who sends her child for the first time to school and houses a changeling. Then she gave the new instrument a knock, and hardly dared to touch it for fear of further damage, muttering to herself about collectors who thought violins must never go out into life.

This doubled the difficulty of studying Stravinsky: but she persevered, and got to know the Bergonzi well enough to take it out to a party in Sir William Rothenstein's studio in Holland Park, where she met Tagore, of whom I will write later; and next day to another party; at both of which it behaved beautifully. When the Stravinsky concert was over, she went to *The Beggar's Opera* at Hammersmith, which she was too tired to enjoy.

It had been a stimulating season: another concert in Edinburgh, which the Liddells came specially up from London for; orgies of private music with Tovey, and many dates outside London. But she had not yet found communion with all publics. Trips out of London she dreaded, and returned by the first available train. Yet even from these she learned. Not being nervous, she could criticize herself in front of a new locality: chords and trills she had been practising went well, other passages not so well; she found her left thumb sticky, which must be looked into.

Crowded success can strain the spiritual sinews. She knew she was now a celebrity, but like many celebrities she liked fame's outside, not its inside. Partly because of the *affaire du coeur*, she wanted to be wanted for herself and not for her music. Heart to heart talks with Mrs Asquith at The Wharf did not help. Nor even the arrival of water-colours and woodcuts made of her by an artist from sketches during a recital. A holiday with her mother in Paris was right for several reasons.

All three families had wished to go to Budapest; but the Foreign Office refused permission to Jelly and her mother, I do not know why. Being still Hungarian citizens, now that the war was over they presumably were not under British control. However, Sir Ian Malcolm was adamant, and only the others went.

France had compensations. To land at Dieppe for Jelly was to hear her mother's tongue spoken all round her after six years. 'Paris was Heaven', she says, tilting her head in recaught rapture. The last time in Paris had not been all heaven. In 1912 they had gone there from the warm South and found it chilled, dripping and drenched. In that year of the floods, they had passed by the Ritz and seen in the basement chefs cooking in topboots which splashed water. They had taken unknown lodgings in the rue du Seine; not good rooms, with a view of sodden roofs and shut windows. Next day they moved to the Hôtel Métropolitain in the rue Cambon, and 'life began.'

On this visit too Life began, in two senses; and by a strange spiral of it, again in the rue du Seine, where Tom Spring-Rice had a flat. He had followed Kelly and Tovey as Nettleship Scholar at Balliol. He was a good pianist, and could easily have sacrificed his social position to a career in music.

There are these spirals in our lives; and both Adila and Jelly experienced them, as most people do. No situation exactly repeats itself—ever: for the very fact of being a second time creates a new situation. But events, sometimes years apart, can resemble each other so closely, that their differences stab, or stimulate. The

Drawing Flames

same place with a different companion, a sunset over a differing hill, words said, seasons, two series of mishaps or pleasures that recall each other, even anniversaries, these serve to show us how far we ourselves have changed, or not changed. It is as if we were riding in a gyrating car, and can look over the side at ourselves above the self-same point, and see ourselves soaring above ourselves or swimming under. Which serves also to show us more clearly than usual that other people are organically part of our consciousness, and therefore of our character.

The difference between Jelly wretched in the rue du Seine and Jelly not wretched in the rue du Seine has very little importance in itself. But it serves to introduce a principle which a biographer (and a reader) would do well to notice.

On Tom Spring-Rice's piano lay a present from Adila, left on her way through. It was a pair of shoes: but they were 'tango' shoes, of black satin with red heels: and they 'made' Jelly's holiday. So did Tom Spring-Rice.

The spiral completed, the new London season welcomed Jelly to her first Prom, which was broadcast, and to her first broadcast in her own right, which was of a Mozart *Concerto* with Adrian Boult conducting the City of Birmingham Orchestra from Daventry Experimental Station.[21]

The Prom might have been a disaster. Jelly tells me that there were no orchestral rehearsals with soloists until the BBC took the Proms over (in 1927). The work was Lalo's *Symphonie Espagnole*, which Jelly had never played in public and which she had rehearsed with only an amateur pianist. At 6.30 that evening she had a temperature of over 101°, and took so many aspirins that she could hardly hear the orchestra. Titi, who had nursed her into the Queen's Hall, was blocked outside the Artists' Room by a brusque and overbearing giant commissionaire. For misery it was equalled only by the Edinburgh Beethoven.

And yet Jelly's playing that night was never forgotten by Henry Wood. 'What a personality and what a born violinist!' he wrote in his autobiography.* 'The audience was completely carried

*My Life in Music, London, 1938-1946. p. 305.

The Sisters d'Aranyi

away by her fire and dash. Yet when a concerto demands it, she can be the classical of the classical.'

After that Lord Mayor's Show came a line of dustcarts. She gave two recitals with the pianist Siloti at Sheffield and Nottingham. She thought little of their *Kreutzer Sonata*. The only time that their playing seemed to face in the same direction was in *ppp*; which both took much more quietly than most artists. But Nottingham was the better of the two dates, despite another coal strike and a half-empty hall. Jelly had an ovation, and was mobbed on the way out.

Siloti was a difficult, self-centred artist, for whom Jelly had to interpret. He kept asking if they had understood.'*Dites-leur qu'ils sont des cochons! Est-ce que vous avez dit qu'ils sont des cochons, Jelly?*'

She tried to enlarge her repertoire. For Chislehurst in November she prepared a Dohnanyi *Violin Sonata*. At Winchester the Purcell *Air in D minor,* which she played more often than any of his other Airs; the Beethoven *Sonata in F*; some new short pieces.[22] This concert was an ordeal, as she had a local lady at short notice to accompany her. According to a College[23] commentator, the piano was a horror. According to Jelly, the lady was worse.

In any case the image of Tom Spring-Rice had not yet grown more necessary to her than that of the young man who had troubled her at Edinburgh. On another spiral, she and her mother walked up the hill to the house where they had stayed with the Maitlands on their first visit. They recalled how oddly happy they had been there in the worst days of the war when they were full of sorrow and anxiety too.

Nevertheless they stayed a day or two with Dr Rendall, and Anthony Asquith and his friends helped to restore their spirits with their wit and culture, and Dr Rendall gave a lantern lecture which opened Jelly's eyes to Renaissance Art.

In London Jelly continued to experiment. A first performance of a *Berceuse* by a Hungarian named Antallfy made little impression. Her playing of the Corelli-Kreisler *Variations* made a

Drawing Flames

little more. Malipiero's *Canto della Lontanezza* meant nothing. Visits to Haslemere and Oxford brought no light, except that in Oxford Town Hall she showed her mastery over Paganini's demoniac *Le Streghe*.

Revisiting thorny ground in Edinburgh and The Wharf reawoke her loneliness, and concerts at Cardiff and Sidmouth, though her music was pure and people loved it, did not cure her soul. Not even an encounter at Sherborne School with a boy who asked to kiss her in the dark. Touched though she was, and sweet though he was, it was not that way, in her personal life, that she called being wanted being wanted.[24]

Paris again was a stimulant but not a cure. She went to the Salle des Agriculteurs in January 1921 for her first solo recital there. She played Mozart, Nardini, Sarasate, and the unaccompanied *Chaconne*. Paris fell at her feet. She had 'flowers from everyone'. The Marquis Jacques de Broglie in an accompanying *billet* declared himself *'trop timide pour parler, trop ému pour me taire. Vous êtes un grand, grand artiste, et votre talent m'a émerveillé.'*

Jelly's head was not turned by flattery or fêting. To her credit: for she had been brought up in the belief that she was ugly; and sudden admiration easily turns a modest head.

Not so Jelly's. In her joy of other people Jelly may often have had her head turned: 'so often' she says 'that now it has come back to its original direction'. But never over matters of music. The reverent attitude of Onkel Jo became part of both sisters, and their mother's gentle moderation of excesses lasted long after their childhood, indeed for as long as they lived.

Jelly and her mother did go back to Hungary for their first visit since the war and their first sight of Taksony after years of correspondence (for a time through Holland). The Foreign Office gave permission, and they went by way of Nuremburg. But Hungary was broken. Many of their friends and relatives were ruined. Some were outspokenly bitter. One old aunt even exaggerated her wretchedness by deliberately putting out dirty tablecloths.

The Sisters d'Aranyi

Besides, it was in Hungary that Madame d'Aranyi first complained of the internal pains that were to lead her into her last illness. Jelly and her father took her to a nursing home, and when she seemed to have recovered, could not bear to think of her returning to her old home, but went instead to a good hotel with Adila and Alexandre, who had just arrived from Britain, and with Titi and her husband, who came later.

Jelly and her mother had brought for expenses forty pounds of their savings, which they gave to Taksony for safekeeping. He had hardly put them in his pocket, when this was picked: for in the chaos and depression of post-war Hungary petty thefts were common, and several British visitors had the same treatment, despite warnings.

It was not a happy holiday, except for Jelly in one respect. She went up one morning to the Bartóks' house on a residential hill. Béla Bartók was at last beginning to win some respect in his own country, and was, if not well off, at least as well off as he was ever to be.

They played together. If Elgar was bowled over, Bartók was bowled out. He was completely taken aback by Jelly's personality and inspired playing. When they played again at the house of a friend, his impression was confirmed. The little girl he had known had become a musician and a woman of exceptional ability and charm.

Hungary was having a railway strike at the time, and the Aranyi families had to return to Britain by taking steamer up the Danube to Vienna. Béla Bartók came to see them off, an impressive figure in a big extravagant cape. (Béla always liked to be different.)

As he stood on the quay he said to Jelly drily, 'I've started a sonata for you'.

11

Béla Bartók

Having reached a position where she could do so without drawing undue attention to herself, Jelly brought out as many pieces new to the public as she could, to draw attention to them. In Glasgow the pianist Philip Halstead had arrived at his sixtieth concert of chamber music in the Arts Institute or the McLellan Galleries; and for this Jelly chose among more usual items Richard Strauss's *Violin Sonata in E♭* (op. 18). It was interesting rather than impressive, for Strauss was not a master of chamber music.

A few weeks later in Glasgow Jelly had a shock. She had arrived to play, as she thought, one of the Mozart *Concerti* with the Scottish Orchestra. The posters said Mendelssohn. Quick enquiries showed that this was in fact what she had to play. She had studied the Mendelssohn *Concerto* with Hubay in Budapest, but had never played it in public. Some thirteen years passed through her head as she conned and bowed and memorized the work in her bedroom at the St Enoch's Hotel, where she and her mother were staying. She was a phenomenally quick study, and this was not the first nor the last time that she had to prepare an important work in a hurry. For, despite the report in the *Musical Times* next month that she had played Mozart, it was truly the Mendelssohn that she played. I don't doubt that this performance did not reach the flawlessness of later ones: but very likely she already made the slow movement much less sugary than most violinists do.[1] Being neither sentimental nor super-

The Sisters d'Aranyi

cilious, in her maturity she took it honestly without spinning a thick *vibrato*, so that out came the original natural honey of which the composer might have made a better product.

The position she had reached meant also that the London press could take exception not to her playing but to her programme.[2] 'Two violin pieces by M. Szymanowsky, of the clever and capricious order, made an instant appeal at Wigmore Hall last night, chiefly because Mlle Jelly d'Aranyi played them. Neither *La Fontaine d'Aréthuse* nor *Tarantelle* would have counted for much without Mlle d'Aranyi's surpassing technique, her abandon and her living expression.' Though how any performer can give living expression to a work that does not live is a subject more profound than the hasty choice of words by a hurried critic. What is more revealing is that at this concert she played Vivaldi's *Concerto in A minor*.

The same critic found that Jelly's performance of it was 'apt, with refined quality and vital phrasing.' Vivaldi was then all but unknown to us, except as a composer who was born a little before Bach, and whom Bach held in high enough regard to copy out from manuscript, and on occasion re-set a work or so of his. Even as late as 1950 a popular encyclopaedia of music dismissed him in the words 'His fame rests on his violin concertos, which were arranged by Bach for the clavier and organ.' It is only in the last decade that his true stature has been discerned in Britain.

The version Jelly played was edited by a Hungarian violinist, Tivadar Nachez, who lived in London in the nineteenth century.

By now it must be coming clear, quite apart from Jelly's astonishing technique, how widely she could give the right sound to the written ideas of many types of composer. Her secret was that of all good (and not many) actors, orators, preachers, readers, announcers, compères, comedians and even lovers. Granted the equipment derived partly from nature, partly from practice and partly from concentration, she opened a different part of herself to each different quality of music. Her now recognized 'personality' was in fact absence of personality, or withdrawal of it; or perhaps a personality so big and open that the person could be cleared

Béla Bartók

out of the way. So the music, because of the composer, was open to life in various forms, which flowed through unobstructed.

In this way when she played Bach, it was the living Bach one heard: yet only she could pass him across in this way. Because of inner honesty she could receive and give what composers had received and given when marshalling the notes.

This versatility, or receptivity, was noticed in both sisters at two separate recitals in the winter of 1921. They took precedence, a critic said, among living violinists 'with that all-round faculty that will bring out all that a mercurial modern work contains and at the next moment play Bach.'[3]

They had both become aware of their impact. It made neither conceited. But that did not mean that Jelly, for one, was a mere wax disc to receive impressions and dutifully vibrate them back. Trained to good music, she could bite at bad. When Felix Weingartner returned to London for his first visit after the war, Jelly was asked to play one of his *Violin Sonotas* with him at a festivity in his honour in the Suffolk Street Galleries, (thereby seeming to one journalist as if she knew everything ever written for the violin). At the end Weingartner made a formal compliment on her playing. But Jelly had found no merits at all in the work, and the performance had been torture. 'You can't judge my playing' she snapped 'having heard me only in this.'

Again, when rehearsing the Bach *'Concerto with Figured Bass'*, she heard the oddest noises coming from the Queen's Hall organ. 'What on earth is that?' she asked up over her violin at Sir Henry Wood. 'The figured bass' he said. Jelly continued to play. '*Dis*figured bass' she muttered, and never knew if Wood had done the arrangement himself. She did not care. It was bad.

As early as 1920 she wrote in her diary at Leicester on a rainy February night: 'Fun to astonish a new audience. This is conceit. But it's a fact.' It was perhaps less conceit than the smile of a contented master when his good work is praised for the right reasons. And Jelly was by now a master. She was in control, and knew when she had worked well. She also knew when to stop. At a Hallé Concert in Burton-on-Trent, after she had played the Mendels-

The Sisters d'Aranyi

sohn *Concerto* and *The Lark Ascending,* the audience wanted more. She had no more to give, on the plane she had just left. There was the usual tussle: but she won. 'Very frankly she acknowledged the help of Sir Hamilton Harty and Mr Barker, the principal violin. In fact she impulsively shook hands with everyone within range. But play an encore she would not.'[4]

A concert hall had become her private garden, in which her friends met great and magical guests. She herself was less important, though nobody was ever unaware of her physical presence on the platform. Neville Cardus describes her, again with the Hallé Orchestra, in 1931 playing the Brahms *Concerto*. During the *adagio* he noticed 'the devoutness of her aspect, with her cheek as if giving warmth to her fiddle, her bowing gracious and solicitous—to look at her was to see with the ears and hear with the eyes.... When the orchestra takes over, she savours the scene, and every delicious touch of orchestration. She looks dotingly on this instrumentalist and that.'[5]

Devout she may have looked, but her love for the Brahms *Concerto* was no idolatry. Both at the Centenary Concert of the London Bach Choir, when its new director conducted, and in Gloucester Cathedral at a Three Choirs Festival, her treatment of this work was too discerning for some traditionalists. 'Full of devilment,' said one 'which was good for the repressed Brahms. One feels Brahms would have officially disapproved of his concerto as given by Miss d'Aranyi, and that secretly he would have loved her for it.'[6]

Both she and Adila had known from an early age while playing, that they had something unusual in them. Jelly rejects the word 'genius'. She prefers 'sacred fire', with an emphasis on the 'sacred'. She sees this metaphorically as a kind of nebula, which has to come down and condense. 'If it is only here,' she gestures at the body 'you never do anything. And if one doesn't have it from the beginning, one can never get it. But one goes on improving to the very end.'

With much of this one must agree, even if by not quarrelling over definitions of metaphors. But with the nebula image I for

Béla Bartók

one cannot agree: for the time is now near when I first heard and saw her playing, and my own impressions, always consistent, were quite other.

She tucked her violin under her chin (always laying under the wood the pad that her mother had made for her), and stood with eyes expressionless, the bow held downward a little distant from her thigh, waiting. As soon as she raised the bow, a kind of sternness or nobility came into her face, no matter what the work was to be: and with this, an expectancy, an eagerness. The eyes lit up, and then either concentrated as if seeing more than hearing, or burst into dark flame.

But this flame never gave the impression of descending from above. Quite the contrary. We were always aware of her body, supple, young and exquisitely set off by her clothes. Her body was part of her playing. So were her feet. As if the music already existed inside the earth and would rise up and through her. She was not nebula-flask but tree, almost visibly branching in sound.

Even the silence after a last bar was music. I remember at Balliol a final upward thrust of the bow, which seemed so much part of a triumphing eruption that one would not have been surprised if the bow had rocketed out of her hand and exploded under the roof of Hall in a shower of stars. Even her grace notes and nuances seemed leaves, derived from a chemistry of solid earth.

But a very human tree. She was often just gay with us. She led us gently through green pastures and nimbly and knowledgeably through hedges. She made us part of Beethoven or Bach. She could make us feel great. She never, as some clever soloists do, made us feel cheap.

Such was the musical figure whom Béla Bartók re-met when he came to Britain in 1922. He was not unknown here. *Kossuth* had been performed by Richter at Manchester in 1903, the year it was written: in the summer of 1914 Frank Liebich had played piano works by him and Kodaly in London: and the same year Wood gave at a Promenade Concert his *First Suite for Orches-*

The Sisters d'Aranyi

tra, written in 1905.[7] But his welcome as composer and pianist astonished him, both at Aberystwyth ('*où il écoute ardemment le rumeur des vagues océanes*')[8] and in London.

Bartók, according to his own classification, was then in his second period, of 'radical homophony'[9]. But his *First Violin Sonata* looks toward his future and is among his most interesting works. On November 9, 1921 he wrote to Jelly from Budapest to say that the first two movements were completed, and that his wife Marta was copying them out. The news that he felt able to compose again after two years of teaching and spiritual despair had been taken by her as the best birthday present he could have given her. It appears that Jelly during a meal at the Gellert Hotel had asked him if he would write something for the violin, adding flippantly that if need be she would mesmerise him into it.

He had the themes in his head next day, and would have told her at the Danube steamer, if he had been more sure of himself after so long a silence. While writing it, he kept imagining with what *élan* she would play the *allegro* first movement, how beautiful her *cantilena* would be in the *adagio*, and with what *fuoco barbaro* she would play the exotic dance rhythms in the third movement.

He had written it entirely for her, he said, and if she couldn't or didn't want to play it, then he would never play it. Calvocoressi had not yet been successful in arranging a London visit for Bartók, but could Jelly and he not have a tour of Hungarian cities next autumn? He multiplied queries to make her answer, and said she could reply in English, French, German, Italian, Slovak, Czech, Rumanian, ('I do not speak all these languages, most of them I can only read'): or could Jelly not come to Frankfurt am Main at the end of January, when two of his stage works were to be performed?

Two other letters show the financial circumstances of these two musicians. For a time Bartók was not sure that such a tour would be feasible, as it was not likely that the Hungarian towns could pay enough; and what he meant by 'enough' is seen when he tries to get Jelly to play at Frankfurt. 'I must know whether

Béla Bartók

you want a fixed sum, or reimbursement of travelling and hotel expenses? ... I of course understand that you do not want a deficit from the concert.'

Meanwhile for Christmas he went to the Puszta, the Hungarian steppes, from where he wrote to Jelly about the violin part. He had had the help of a guinea-pig violinist, who said that this could be played but was very difficult, especially some four-string arpeggios in the first movement. He asked Jelly to study it in the piano score, and if they were much too difficult, he would write-in *ad lib.* alternatives. If any discrepancies, stick to the piano score.

This is a charming letter. Jelly seems to have asked him about sunsets on the steppes. He replies: 'This is somewhat difficult, since the sun here has gone down for some years now and has no intention, for the time, of rising.' Admiral Horthy had set up his authoritarian government in July 1919, and Bartók was an ostracized left-winger.

But he gives her country-news. Their well still produces water (28°) in midwinter. On a count's estate where his brother-in-law is steward, a bullock put into a stable had grown so much in a few months that part of the wall had to be knocked down to get him out. Frogs and beautiful water-beetles are splashing about.

Jelly's engagement book was filling for months ahead, and Frankfurt had to be abandoned. Adila and Calvocoressi and Jelly tried to arrange a visit of Bartók to England. This had to be postponed, because though the Frankfurt date was put off until the following winter, he had now received an invitation to Paris in April and could not afford two journeys abroad. Could Jelly not come to Paris? Back from his holidays, he ends this letter: 'I cannot now write either of bullocks or frogs. This Budapest is an insufferable town, nothing of this kind is here, unless in the form of human beasts, and there are too many of them. It is too hard to see them, I do not want to write about them.'[10]

Calvocoressi could not manage a concert of only modern works, and did not co-operate very freely with the Aranyis over a mixed one. But in the end Bartók's visit was made possible by dates be-

The Sisters d'Aranyi

fore Paris. He wrote asking Titi to find him a boarding house near the Aranyis, where his daily overall expenses would not be more than two pounds. But I imagine he stayed with the Fachiris.

A private concert was given on a Tuesday in March 1922 at 18 Hyde Park Terrace, the home of the Hungarian *chargé d'affaires* de Hédry, and his wife. Both sisters took part, with Bartók at the piano throughout. After the new *Sonata* came one of the Spohr *Duos*; Bartók played some of his piano works, including the *Allegro Barbaro*, and Adila and he closed with the warlike Beethoven *in C minor*. This brought Bartók a fee of thirty pounds. A much intrigued Stravinsky was present.

Then Jelly and he were invited to give another private concert in Sydney Place on the 31st, at which after the new work and piano soli by Bartók, Jelly and he played the *Kreutzer Sonata*.

The first public performance came on the Friday after this at the Aeolian Hall. Then the BBC wanted to broadcast the new work, but Bartók doubted if the microphone would take the correct acoustics, so they gave the Beethoven instead.

The forceful barbaric last movement gave Jelly great joy to play. 'Rhythm' according to one of her adages 'is the soul of music.'

Then Bartók returned by Paris to Hungary, where he wrote another sonata for Jelly. As *No 1* had nominally had the key signature of C♯ minor, so *No 2* was nominally in C major: but tonality had by now all but gone. 'Tonality is a stake to which the goat is tied' Pierre Citron wrote prettily of these works, 'but the rope is a long one and the goat skittish. The goats, rather; for each of the instruments goes very free in relation to the other.' Bartók had nerved himself for the *First Sonata* by stipulating with himself that each instrument should have a separate theme.[11]

Bartók preferred *No 2*, which he played frequently in later years with other pupils of Hubay: Szigeti, Tsekely, Waldbauer. But Calvocoressi says that when he played it with Szigeti it sounded less tense than with Jelly.

This had its first performance on May 7, 1923 at the Contemporary Music Centre, established by the British Music Society after the war. Both sonatas were given. Edwin Evans called the

Béla Bartók

music 'purposeful expressionism' and praised Jelly's 'amazing sensibility to its shades of emotion which pass in quick succession.'[12] *The Pall Mall Gazette,* saying both performers were beyond praise, hailed Jelly's exceptional sensibility for new works.[13]

This time Bartók took back with him a large supply of bananas, which were scarce in Hungary. He loved fruits, exotic or otherwise, and before dinner often went to inspect and help himself to several from the fruit bowl.[14] But between the two sonatas the relations between Jelly and him had changed.

Jelly may have found Bartók gauche; Balkan peasants found him kind and patient; but he was a passionate man also, and did unexpected things. Just as in 1908 he had been in love with the Hungarian violinist Stéfi Geyer, wrote a concerto for her* and then suddenly and clandestinely married one of his piano pupils, announcing to his parents that she would stay to lunch because she was his wife, so now he fell in love with Jelly and promptly married another pianist. (Oddest of spirals.)

He did not get on with his wife well, despite the domestic scene adumbrated a page or two back. Divorce was easy in Hungary; but Jelly could not consider marrying him. Where Adila went, there was bustle; where Jelly went, there was fun: but Bartók had no sense of humour. That alone put him out of court. Once in Paris he was so impressed by the luxury of the Hôtel Majestic where he was staying, that he announced he had a telephone in his chamber. He hated being laughed at even by the Aranyis, and could not understand being laughed with. When his mistake in English was explained to him, only a slight relaxation of sober cheek showed any reaction.

Jelly had feelings for him no more tender than those of an old friend and a great musician: but he took his rejection badly. By habit an abstemious man, he drank too much at lunch next day. This upset Jelly. 'It is good and great' she wrote in her diary 'that I should have inspired that gorgeous sonata—but apparently

---

*Unperformed for fifty years, according to a letter signed N. C. Hamilton in *The Observer,* August 18, 1963.

The Sisters d'Aranyi

a woman can't inspire the soul of a man without doing great harm. It is sad, too sad, that I should make this great man suffer.'

She may have felt a little guilty. She had loved playing with him in Budapest the previous October, and had said so: but, as she had to keep reminding herself somewhat naïvely, it was all in front of his wife. Like many born flirts, Jelly had no idea that she singed people's cheeks by the mere speed of her wings.

She really did love playing music with Bartók. 'He had such *rhythm!*' she says, and on the word her hands fold into fists for the forcefulness. And certainly when Bartók played, especially in his *Allegro Barbaro*, holding his hands sometimes perpendicularly to the keys,[15] the piano could become an instrument of rhythmic percussion as much as Manuel de Falla made of it a super-guitar.

In their relations as artists there was no strain. They played *No 1* at Geneva. They flung *No 2* at London again in December 1923. Edwin Evans, who curiously thought little of Bartók as a pianist, wrote of Jelly that in the last year she had developed not only breadth of expression, but a depth of insight that ranked her among the elect of interpretative artists. Of the *Second Sonata* he now said that he had heard other readings which provided an excuse for those who were not receptive to it; but as played by her it 'triumphed over its own sparseness of conciliating blandishments.'[16] They also gave the *Kreutzer Sonata*: and an anonymous writer in *Truth* said his memory had gone back thirty years to the time when Joachim opened a recital with this.[17]

But here their duo ended. It was a loss to musical history that it did not go on.

Another visit to Paris by Jelly in 1922 has little programme interest other than that her *rondo* in Mozart's *Haffner Serenade* showed a union of clarity and speed which French critics found unequalled. It is more interesting for a rare close-up of Madame d'Aranyi. In the Artists' Room at the Salle des Agriculteurs a delightful Frenchman introduced himself as a friend of Robert Trevelyan, and could not have found a better passport. His name was Félix Gicquel, a thick-set man of about forty-five with dark eyes.

Béla Bartók

Madame d'Aranyi was so drawn to him on sight that when he invited them out to dinner and a theatre, she accepted at once. Jelly and her mother had one more night in Paris, and he fetched them from the flat on Île St Louis which Princess Bibesco had lent them; and Madame d'Aranyi for once stopped putting her children before herself. There was such an immediate liking, a happy rapport, between her and M. Gicquel that over dinner Jelly simply sat back and listened to her mother, who had not blossomed out like this for years.

M. Gicquel planned to come to London the following June, and Jelly's mother kept on referring to '*ce cher homme*'. But it was that very winter that she had a serious exploratory operation; and when she had recovered from it, she told Jelly she had dreamed of going to Heaven and meeting Félix Gicquel there. Jelly, who by then had been warned that there was no hope for her mother, had not the heart to tell her that in the meantime they had heard of M. Gicquel's death.

Her mother had these premonitions. In November she went with Jelly to Bromley, where Gwynne Kimpton* invited many famous artists. In the taxi on the way from the Central Hall to the station, she suddenly burst into unexplained tears. For some time she refused to account for them; but after the operation, when she thought she was getting better, she said she had been convinced that this was the last time she would hear Jelly playing in public. As indeed it proved to be.

Jelly had no thoughts of Bartók or anyone else through the next months. But her anxiety and grief for her mother did not affect her playing. Adrian Boult invited Adila and her to a Bach Friday afternoon in the Aeolian Hall, a very pretty event: the *Double Concerto*, the *Concerto in E major*, the unaccompanied *Adagio and Fugue*, and the unaccompanied *Chaconne*. Appearances by Jelly at Bradford and Sidmouth and at the Wigmore Hall were made in deepening shadow, but her notices were as excited as ever. 'Words cannot tell the rush, the hover, the quiver of it all',

---

*Pioneer, among other things, of children's concerts, and conductor of the British Women's Symphony Orchestra, which she founded in 1922.[18]

was *The Times'* comment on her Bach unaccompanied *Suite*.

She played with Ethel Hobday a *Sonata in E minor* by Eugene Goossens at the Chelsea Music Club; but the shadow stops her from remembering this event very clearly. She went to Danesfield, a country house near Henley-on-Thames, and played Nardini and Beethoven and Schubert and a piece called *Le Nil* by Xavier Leroux, a Frenchman who wrote operas. She played this with the Russian pianist Tatiana Makushina, but cannot recall either it, or who asked her to play it, or why. All she recalls is the music room, an exact copy of a hall in Versailles, and a strange sensation during the Beethoven *Romance in G*, that she was no longer there playing but was somewhere else, and returned to find herself, with some surprise, still playing.

On one occasion only did Jelly show any sign of impending disaster. That was on the evening of the day when she heard that her mother's tumour was malignant. A friend wrote his sympathy after the concert she had to give, saying he had seen from her hands when they were not on her violin how anxious she was, and he was 'glad to be so far back that she could not see in his eyes the tears she was too brave to shed'.[19]

It was a miserable Christmas, and the disease took its usual, relentless course thereafter, sometimes relaxing only to tighten with crueller strength. Madame d'Aranyi died on June 10th, 1923.

Dr Rendall, in his last year at Winchester, wrote sadly of the 'mother of motherless Jelly' and how much they would miss her gentle, lovable personality at Winchester. During her final weeks he had had prayers said for her in Chapel: 'a friend of the School asks for your prayers for her mother.' . . . 'I am letting the boys know; but I think they know already.'

12

Ravel: Vaughan Williams: Szymanowsky

When a cutting is parted permanently from a stem, the spur makes independent roots or dies. It was good that when Adila and Jelly returned to musical life in the autumn of 1923, both cuttings should be in the same pot: the *Bach D minor Concerto*. This was like starting the same curve on another level, and if Jelly might have been seen dabbing her eyes with her back to the audience after the slow movement,[1] the personal situation of neither affected the playing. Jelly's loss was made easier, as Adila's was, by the warmth and the number of the welcomes she got from the public. There was no doubt now that she was a musical event in demand all over the country.[2]

In December 1923, Marie Hall could not appear for the Chaikovski Concerto in Manchester, and Sir Hamilton Harty asked Jelly to substitute. She was practising it anyway for another numb occasion, a return to Bromley. This was not her first appearance in Manchester, for Adila and she had been there the previous year with Juliette Folville, but it was her first with the Hallé. She played this concerto fairly frequently afterwards, but not in London till 1935, at the Palladium.[3] The second movement of it she made into a 'tender devotional song with birdlike passages, and the audience hardly breathed'.[4]

At the Philharmonic Concerts she first appeared on February

21, 1924, playing Mozart (K. 211, in D) under Eugene Goossens. 'Deliciously played by that great artist' said the *Westminster Gazette*. But the great artist must have felt lonely, and even lightweight, playing this fresh young work in a programme that contained Rimsky-Korsakov's *Sinfonietta on Russian Themes*, the *Siegfried Idyll*, the *Firebird Suite*, and Holst's new *Fugal Concerto* with Leon Goossens, which was the hit of the evening.

She recalls having played the same concerto under Beecham a year or two later. Beecham as usual was conducting from memory, and as not seldom occurred, brought in an entry wrong. If Jelly had not known the work thoroughly, it would have collapsed.

The public on that occasion had come to roar at Jelly, armed with floral tributes. 'Not half a dozen double-basses would have contained those roses and tulips and carnations, and several journeys had to be made to collect them' the *Evening Standard* recorded. 'But these floral tributes must really be left to revue first nights. They are out of place in a concert hall.'

Many people would agree with this, including Beecham himself. I have read that he was once presented with an enormous round wreath, which being too big to put on his shoulders and too clumsy to carry, he bowled off the platform like a schoolboy's hoop.

Of course the admiration and affection behind such offerings touched the tender Jelly, but they could be embarrassing, and sometimes crude. At Geneva in 1938 some gigantic men bore onto the platform flowers bundled up in thick closed white paper. 'It might have been the laundry coming back.'

The new curve continued into other familiar places. In a week she gave two concerts with the Orpheus Choir. She loved St Andrew's Hall for its acoustics, perfect even from the back of the pillared tunnel of a gallery. Of all British concert halls she liked best for playing in this and the Liverpool Philharmonic both of which have since been burned down. Discussing acoustics with Asquith, she found that he also preferred these two halls for speaking in.

In her visits to small towns and musical societies now, generally

Ravel: Vaughan Williams: Szymanowsky

with Ethel Hobday, she found herself met by a greater respect, a more informed enthusiasm: from Sutton, Surrey, where Lionel Tertis lived, to be-coronetted Red Heath, home of Lord Ebury near Rickmansworth. Sometimes we find her playing the Elgar *Sonata*, sometimes Mozart, sometimes César Franck. At one time or another she played nearly all the Mozart sonatas. Kelly's *Jig* persists. At Llandudno on Good Friday, giving the Chaikovsky *Concerto* with orchestra, she puts in a sixteenth-century *Alman* arranged by Harold Craxton; and about this time gets fond of a *Scherzando* by the Belgian violinist Marsick, who had been head of the Athens Conservatoire. Her mother and she had heard Thibaud playing this, and agreed that Jelly should do the same. Once in Brussels the composer's son came round after a concert, and she was able to tell him how delicious she thought it. (Another *Scherzando* which she played later was unclaimed by its father.)

If at this time this piece had a sentimental value for her as well as a musical, it should be remembered that minor music, if unpretentious, can be perfect; indeed it is more likely to be so than gigantic works which are false.

All these developments were leading up to the creation of another new work, which you may call major or minor according to your measure, but which could not have existed without her, and with which her name seems most likely at present to endure in the history of European concerts.

Maurice Ravel had first met Jelly in the Ritz at Paris through their mutual friend Mrs Stoep. When he heard her playing of the first Bartók *Sonata* in London, he asked if she would not do his *Sonate en Duo pour Violon et Violoncello*, written the year before and already played by André Mangeot and May Mukle. She did this with the Dutch 'cellist Hans Kindler in July 1922 at Lady Rothermere's house in St John's Wood. It was a concert entirely devoted to Ravel, who was there. He played some of his piano works, Madame Alvar sang some of his songs, the Allied Quartet played his quartet for strings, and were joined by Gwendolen Mason, Louis Fleury and Charles Draper for the

The Sisters d'Aranyi

Introduction and Allegro for Harp, Flute, Clarinet and String Quartet.

Ravel was engaged on *L'Enfant et les Sortilèges*, due to be produced at Monte Carlo by the end of 1924; but he put this aside to write a work for Jelly.[5] According to M. D. Calvocoressi, this was to be in the style of a Hungarian rhapsody with plenty of opportunity for the virtuoso.[6] It was called *Tzigane*; and Madeleine Goss says it is seldom played because few have the superlative technique to do it justice.[7] Jelly does not agree. Part of technique is familiarity, and today 'everyone plays it'. But Ravel himself wrote to her on March 13th: '*Certains passages peuvent être d'un effect brillant à condition qu'il soit possible de les exécuter, ce dont je ne suis pas toujours certain.*'

Ravel himself never had the technique to encompass the piano version of the accompaniment, and Henri Gil-Marchex was entrusted with it for the first performance. He had been called at that time 'the chief hope of the younger school of French pianism.'[8] The violin part, described by a jocular North-American critic later as 'being filled with double-stops and such things that fill the nightmares of virtuosos,'[9] came into Jelly's hands only three and a half days before she had to play it.

There have been several mis-statements about *Tzigane*, which may be corrected here. The first is the time available to Jelly for study, which was as above and not two days.[10] Secondly, *The Complete Book of Twentieth Century Music* and some authors of books on Ravel say that *Tzigane* was originally written for violin and luthéal, an organ-like attachment to the piano. Jelly however states for certain that it was scored for ordinary piano. 'Later,' she says 'in the orchestral version there was a little instrument of the kind, but you could hardly hear it.'

Rollo Myers relates: 'When Miss d'Aranyi passed her copy to the composer in the hope that he would inscribe thereon some complimentary dedication, she was disappointed to read the words *A Jelly d'Aranyi—Maurice Ravel*.

' "Is that all?" she asked.

' "Yes, that's all" replied Ravel, "but it's for posterity".'

Ravel: Vaughan Williams: Szymanowsky

Listening back in time, and perhaps a little hurt at this uncharacteristic *prima donna* talk being imputed to her, Jelly says 'I didn't expect anything. So I couldn't have been disappointed.' Ravel gave her another piece of music which she prizes: a copy of *Hommage à Gabriel Fauré*, signed by himself and the other musicians who had taken part in this. I read to her another page in the same book.[11] 'It's said here that Ravel performed at that concert in red carpet slippers. Is that true?'

'I don't remember it. And I think it's unlikely. He was always very *soigné*—rather a dandy.' Lastly, *Tzigane* was billed as having its first performance in England. This was also its first performance in the world. The concert itself lasted over two hours, and was expensive: tickets cost one guinea, 12s. or 5s. 9d.[12]

The Times could make nothing of *Tzigane*. Either it was a parody of all the Liszt-Hubay-Brahms-Joachim school of Hungarian music and fell into the class of *La Valse,* or it was an attempt to get away from the limited sphere of what Ravel had hitherto done and put some needed blood into his work. 'But in neither case does it greatly matter.' The public wrenched open this closed judgment on Ravel. To the concert-goer *Tzigane* mattered a lot. It still does, when it gets a good chance of being heard.

The Times, however, did have the grace to notice Jelly's 'amazing assurance', and in fact she made the work even more brilliant than it had been written. In November 1924 when she went to Paris for a performance of the orchestral version under Pierné, she was running through it in Ravel's presence, and at one point made what she calls a '*glissando* with trills.' Ravel turned to a friend and said '*Je ne sais pas ce qu'elle fait, mais il me plaît.*'

There seems to have been some mix-up about the very first performance with orchestra. There exist letters from the Société Indépendente of Paris and Jelly during July, August and September about Ravel's wish that she should come to Paris for this. There are complaints that Jelly does not reply (she was always a poor correspondent), although Ravel himself pleaded with her in several letters to do so, reminding her that the work was dedicated to her. The Society says that the Hall they had booked for a certain date is no longer available. Jelly asks at last for October 17th and for a second concert in Paris if possible. Both these proved false hopes, and in the last letter they have engaged another violinist.

The little dapper figure with the big well-groomed head had a quick, well-timed wit. Jelly was annoyed by a crowd of gushers who surrounded him after one of his concerts in London, calling him affectedly *Cher Maître*. She addressed him as *Monsieur Maître*. His reply was *Oui, Mademoiselle Maîtresse?*

Though he attended rehearsals in Paris he did not feel well enough to attend the performance on November 30th. In public he felt nervous, already the beginning of that agoraphobia which later made him seek side streets and byelanes when going about a city. Itself, perhaps, a symptom of the cerebral tumour that made his death so tragic. But every now and then he could appear in public, as he did in 1928 in North America. So too in London at Mrs André's house in Grosvenor Street. He still could not manage *Tzigane*, so he and Jelly rehearsed a sonata in the Aeolian Hall and moved to Kettner's for lunch.

At Kettner's (favourite restaurant then and since for musicians) Jelly happened to use a d'Aranyi family phrase for anyone who spoke French execrably: *'Elle parle comme une vache espagnole.'* Ravel corrected her: *'comme une Basque espagnole.'* His mother was Basque.

It was Jelly who got Ravel the recital at Mrs André's, who was an amateur pianist and also gave wonderful parties. Jelly had suggested that she and Adila should play for nothing while Ravel should have a fee of fifty guineas, a very big sum in those days. Her pleased hostess gave Jelly a gold cross.

There is a word picture of Jelly in 1928 playing *Tzigane* in Antwerp. 'Matt complexion and very dark hair was all that a tiresome shadow allowed us to see of her face. But dressed in a princess of a gown, of a sumptuous, frivolous red, well modelled, bodice very long, left foot set back, drawing herself up somewhat *garçonnement* from a waist flexible in the extreme, she was like a flaming, slightly malevolent apparition. She undulated, poised herself, then again let her body rise up on the music itself, so to speak.... And the bow went its diabolic way.'[13]

She liked playing Ravel, and often gave his *Violin Sonata* with Myra Hess from 1927 on. This 'ravished' Scott Goddard.[14] But as a character she thought little of Ravel: a lonely, empty-living man devoted only to his mother. 'He believed in nothing' she says, 'a sad pessimist'.

Pessimist herself Jelly never was; and she believed in much. Her mind and sprit lay as open to her listeners as it lay to the music: which gave her a rare sense of occasion and locality. At Winchester in 1924 Rendall had established his 'War Cloister'; but it would not be complete till Jelly had consecrated it musically. This, in the last month of his long and great reign.

Writing in August for the last time in his half-emptied study, he felt how spoilt beyond belief he had been by all his friends and not least by Jelly. He recalled her music in his drawing-room, 'when a pack of ideal boys, full of "grace", sat on the floor and listened with all their *Eyes* and all their hearts to you and Beethoven.... And then you took it to the Cloister, and music interpreted our deepest and highest belief in that palace, or rather temple, of sacrifice. What a wonderful climax in the last month of my Winchester life. You' ('and your dear mother' written above the line) 'will always be tightly bound up with the soul of the Winchester I love.'

Eleven years later from Batley Priory he sent her a long quotation from J. de A. Frith's book on Winchester, which describes that moonlit evening 'when Jelly d'Aranyi played the violin as only she can play it, with Dr Rendall standing alone, wrapped in his cloak.'

If *Tzigane* had been written by Vivaldi, the result might have borne some resemblance to the next work written for Jelly: Vaughan Williams' *Concerto Accademico* which had its first performance at a Gerald Cooper Concert on November 6th, 1925. with a string orchestra conducted by Anthony Bernard.[15] For years Vaughan Williams used to send Jelly little fond notes of praise or thanks or interest in her welfare, usually signed 'Your devoted Uncle Ralph'. He did so even when she was in the USA in 1929; 'I wish I cd. have been there to hear and see you—I know you played beautifully and looked lovely—what dress did you wear? It is a great sorrow to me that I have not seen you for more than a year—& I get older every year....' The latest dated one is October 18th, 1957.

Frank Howes says[16] that the new work was called *Accademico* originally 'as an act of defiance against all the Big-bow-wow concertos from Beethoven to Sibelius viâ Mendelssohn, Max Bruch, Brahms and Chaikovsky. It is all that these things are not—it derives straight from the eighteenth-century concertos of Handel and Bach.' On the other hand A. E. F. Dickinson in his long learned treatise[17] regards it as a *'jeu d'esprit*, a mock reference to the earlier type, on a "What was good enough for the eighteenth century is good enough for me" plea.' At the same time it is full of consecutive fifths, simultaneous chords a semitone apart, and other such twentieth-century delights, plus plenty of violin agility. A work, in short, which Jelly could see at first reading was all she responded to.

She brought to it also 'the right rhapsodical style, which is just the quality the composer cannot put down on paper—': 'that hairbreadth poise between dash and style which is her peculiar distinction' as another writer put it. In spite of this the critics were lukewarm; some were puzzled. Many critics tend to be puzzled when a new work is not exactly what they expected it to be: others, hostile, can say they are disappointed because it is. Most musicians now agree that this is not one of the major works of a (to me, at least) major composer. But it was not meant to be. The souls of creative artists do not have to wear their haloes always while working. It is excellent of its kind, which is rare; and I wish it could be heard more often—with something like that 'hairbreadth poise'.

Jelly played it in many places; including Edinburgh, Chicago, and she thinks perhaps Geneva. It was one of the last things she played in the grim August of 1939, with Wood at the Queen's

Ravel: Vaughan Williams: Szymanowsky

Hall. It never quite took on; but she several times put into programmes with piano accompaniment the dreamy middle movement which people liked best.

At Paris in 1921 she had met another contemporary composer, Karol Szymanowsky, who sent her flowers because she had performed a little piece of his, and then introduced himself. A tall man with a pleasing round face, full of charm but not aware of it. Since the beginning of the First War he had been experimenting with atonality, though he never held the same attention in Britain for his work as did Stravinsky or Bartók. Some think he still does not hold enough; and at that time he was certainly Poland's leading international composer.

He became a friend of the family. In 1934, when he arrived for dinner at the Fachiris' house, Adila had not finished dressing, so Jelly came forward to greet him as he descended the steps into the music room. Jelly speaks French well, but this time her tongue slipped. Instead of saying 'What an honour' she heard her voice saying with conviction '*Quel Horreur!*' Szymanowsky after the first shock merely answered gently '*C'est si terrible? Est-ce vrai?*'

Jelly played several of his short pieces, but nothing of weight except the *Violin Concerto* (at that time his only one) op. 35, which had been written in 1917 but not performed until 1924, by Oziminsky. Jelly gave it its first British hearing with the L.S.O. in 1930. She had six weeks to study it, quite a long time for her, and did so mostly in Battersea Park, since she preferred to memorize away from instruments.

In performance, however, she had a fright. Malcolm Sargent suddenly ducked over his desk in his idiomatic way, and Jelly thought her memorizing must have gone wrong. But she went on playing; and soon Sargent surfaced again.

Ernest Newman was in the Queen's Hall that evening, and said to his neighbour 'She won't play this without music.' But she did; 'as if' wrote somebody who may well have been Newman himself, 'she had been steeped in it and nothing else for years. One cannot sufficiently honour an artist who becomes so wholly

The Sisters d'Aranyi

absorbed in the service of a work which she may never, perhaps, play again.'

But that was another side of Jelly, consistent with all the other sides. She had no interest in a career for herself and little in a career for the music she played. Passing or not, repeated or not, her job was to be the open moment of the opened music, whatever it was.

2 Adila in Budapest

3 Adila in London

4 Jelly as a child

5   The Music Room at Netherton Grove. (Left to right: Alfred Hobday, Adila, Alexandre Fachiri, Gaspar Cassadó, Jelly)

6   The effect of the sisters' playing: friends listening at Netherton Grove. (Adila's daughter Adrienne in foreground)

7 Musicians off duty. Myra Hess and Jelly burlesquing each other. (Note the early BBC Microphone)

8 A study of Jelly playing inscribed to Adrienne

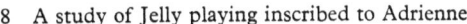

9 and 10 Two studies of Jelly playing

11 Last years at Bellosguardo

13

Variations on Various Themes

On Wednesday, October 15, 1924 Jelly put on a specially fine gold dress to go to the Queen's Hall. The orchestra wore white ties. The goldfish and the fountain were sent downstairs. Royalty was coming.

Royalty came, Queen Mary in a blue and silver gown with a soft blue feather collar and a flowery embroidered cloak of dark turquoise. Royalty was received by the Earl of Shaftesbury, who presented Robert Newman, manager of the Proms since 1895. Wood's daughter Tanya handed to Royalty pink carnations. Royalty then took its seat in the extreme left-hand corner of the Grand Circle, where it got a distorted balance of sound but could be seen.

It was the first time Royalty had been seen at a Prom, and possibly at any serious music since Georgian times, though some people recalled that King Edward VII had once gone to a Sunday Concert.

Elgar, as Master of the King's Music, conducted *Cockaigne*, doubly suitable as being sub-titled '*In London Town*' and having been dedicated to 'my friends the members of British orchestras.' Also it had been written in the excitement of King Edward's Coronation, with Pomps and Circumstances to follow. Frank Bridge conducted his *Sea Suite* because the King had been a sailor. Jelly played two movements from the Beethoven *Violin Concerto*. Eric Marshall sang *O Star of Eve* and Leila Morgan, a leading soprano, sang Granville Bantock. The orchestra gave

The Sisters d'Aranyi

Coppélia, and the *Prodigal Son* of André Wormser (both French) and Wood's own *Fantasy on Sea Songs*. In the interval the artists were presented.

All except Jelly, who knew nothing about such festivities and had gone in the interval to sit with Dr Rendall in the body of the Hall.

On the evidence of the *Westminster Gazette* Jelly was the musical success of this extraordinary programme, even in two-thirds of a work. She was recalled (presumably at a sign from the monarch—for these manners still prevailed) and remembers a smile of genuine approval from the King. She was then recalled seven times by the public.

Mercifully the King had early lit a cigarette, so that the Promenade audience could, as usual, put up its filter of haze. But the tension was so great that some ten or twelve people, who had been queuing since early morning, were carried out in faints.

If Jelly missed meeting Royalty on that occasion she came to know part of it well later on. She became a close friend of the Bowes-Lyons and was no stranger at Glamis. When Princess Elizabeth was two years old, her mother asked if she could bring her to Jelly's room to hear her playing. The little girl had heard only military music, and when she saw Jelly with a violin asked 'Where's your band?' So Jelly became the Lady Without a Band in that quarter from then on.

Jelly's shrewd eyes noticed that the future Queen at a children's party years later beat everybody at 'Hunt the Thimble' because she watched the other players' eyes. She also noticed, later still, that with Jelly there her mother tried to draw her into talk about music.

In the course of her life she met other members of the Family. In June 1927[1] she played at the London School of Economics when the Prince of Wales opened the Founders' Room on the fifth floor (with a pre-war Bechstein Grand bought to make this a place for music as well as quietude).

But her real friends were Princess Helena Victoria and her sister Marie Louise, whom the Aranyis had known almost from

Variations on Various Themes

childhood. These came once to an Aeolian Hall concert in 1926 given by Adila and Jelly, 'with Lady Londonderry in a velvet cloak of petunia and purple' sitting between the Princesses.[2] These two ladies, grand-daughters of Queen Victoria, were often at the Fachiris' house in Netherton Grove, because they loved music; and the voice of Adila or Jelly was frequently heard in protest or argument beginning 'But Ma'am darling!'

Neither Adila nor Jelly had any social ambitions. These ladies liked them and music, and they returned the liking. Jelly indeed could have reservations about Royalty. She met the deposed King of Greece at a dinner party, and found him pathetic: 'poor, really poor ... and then all that curtseying and Majestying is such a mockery.'[3] Princess Olga of Yugoslavia, however, formed great liking and admiration for both sisters when they went to live in Italy, and was distressed when they died.

Liking and admiration were continued by ordinary people. Not the eve of a General Election in 1924, when half England rejoiced in an extension of democracy and the other half groaned at the imminence of mob rule, could keep crowds away from the Bach *Double Concerto* when the Norwich Festival was resumed after thirteen years.[4] Not even torrential rain dispersed the Queen's Hall queue the following month when Jelly played the Brahms *Concerto,* even if Jelly (in a parisian mauve silk dress trimmed with ostrich feather) and Sir Henry Wood (who admired the integrity of her musicianship, but was in one of his rigid-tempo moods)[5] were not wholly of one mind throughout.

As a rule Jelly played the Brahms in her own unconfoundable way, the first movement warmer than any other performance of it, and the last dancing 'with reckless gaiety and brilliance' into usually terrific applause. Neville Cardus recalls how she tossed back her head and flashed the vivacity of her nature into the Hungarian rhythms of the last movement.[6] In 1926 she gave it for the first time in twenty-five years at Sheffield since Kreisler with Weingartner.[7] For she was now of the innermost circle. The Manchester season of 1925 had as visiting artists Cortot, Casals, Suggia and Moiseiwitsch, but the local correspondent of the

The Sisters d'Aranyi

Musical Times said the greatest personal triumph had been Jelly's in Mozart and Ravel. The attitude of the orchestra to interpreter as distinct from mere virtuoso, 'an almost infallible guide to quality,' is the finest compliment it can bestow: and here the Hallé was fervent.[8]

Adila at this time, I would venture, was not far behind Jelly, and their *Double Concerto* had justly become the eclectic delight of musical Britain. The scene in a Queen's Hall double recital in September 1931 was described in the *Evening News*.[9] 'Neither in Queen's Hall nor anywhere else have I heard anything like the roar of cheering which broke out after the last concerto. Sir Henry Wood came down from his dais, sat down by the *célesta* and applauded like the rest of us, until Miss d'Aranyi dressed in pale yellow, and her sister in dark brown, came across, grabbed him by the hands and forced him to join in their acknowledgements.' Five hundred people had been turned away from the box office, and the queue reached up Great Portland Street.

The fact that either sister had played a particular work scores of times never meant that they played it as if they had. They were not like a world-famous pianist, a friend of mine, who was so bored with his craftsman fingers that he never practised; with the result that his performance had the imperfection of standardised perfection.

Kreisler, it is true, seldom practised, but for a different reason: 'I should hate to become stilted.' Thibauld told Jelly in Paris, shortly before he was killed in 1953, when she was adjudicating a *Concours du Violon*, that he and Kreisler shared a flat when they were young. They were preparing a new season after a holiday. '*Mais il faut étudier, Fritz!*' Thibaud insisted. Kreisler took out his violin and played the *Devil's Trill* as if he had just finished a run-through. 'He did his tra-tra-tra-tra perfectly' Thibaud said, 'I was flabbergasted.'

The sisters d'Aranyi worked for hours every day. 'How I love playing the violin' Adila said, grabbing it to practise.[10] And Jelly was no less assiduous. It was partly because of this, that she could approach each next performance of a work as the first one, even

Variations on Various Themes

if one London Sunday she was doing the same work twice in public. The first time was spoilt by the knowledge that it would all have to be done again in the evening.[11]

Grace is the result of effortlessness, which comes usually through previous exercise. This, a subconscious mechanism to her conscious receptivity in performance, enabled her to make even of 'ear-ticklers' something nobody else could. Marsick's trifling *Scherzando*, for example. When she played this at Rochdale in 1925 for the umpteenth time, Neville Cardus wrote that by the time she had finished it 'Marsick stood in the eyes of the gods as a man who in his own way had achieved a perfection proportionately not less than that achieved by Brahms in his weightier way.'[12]

So for Jelly there was no likelihood of glory gleaming after glory in a dull night of routine. On the contrary she could make a glory of the routine.

One of her most gleaming performances was in *The Lark Ascending*. Vaughan Williams wrote this for Marie Dare,[13] but after her retirement people associated it with Jelly, so much so, that her brother-in-law Sir Ralph Hawtrey considered her performance of it in Westminster Abbey the peak of her career.[14] This was in 1940, with the Queen present, in aid of the Red Cross. She first played it with its composer at Dorking in 1926. Vaughan Williams and she were spiritually very close, and he got much joy from her fresh informality, especially when she was rehearsing the Mendelssohn *Concerto* with his strings, and he and she had fun singing the wind parts as a duet. For some curious reason the *Musical Times*, forgetting the fame of Marie Dare, called this performance at Leith Hill its first ever.[15] Jelly had only had ten days to learn it, and practised it in the train from Norwich. She liked to practise in trains. She secured a compartment to herself, as first-class passengers frequently could in those days. If the ticket inspector called, she entertained him with *Sadko*.

However, she did not always play with equal inspiration. On at least one occasion the lark seemed oversized and too near the

The Sisters d'Aranyi

ground, as a critic put it.[16] But this was with piano accompaniment; and maybe not even Ethel Hobday's fingers could make the musical landscape swell on hammered wires. *The Lark Ascending* is essentially an orchestral piece, and without the heaving malese of the coloured counties wings find it hard to rise.

She had her share of mishaps. Ethel Hobday and she went to a date in Belfast a day early to rest and rehearse. Ethel Hobday went out of their hotel, and shortly returned looking as if Sir Henry Wood had suddenly died. Jelly asked if perhaps the concert had been the day before. 'No' said Ethel Hobday 'it's just started.' The principal violin had taken Jelly's place. When she went to apologize, Wood growled 'You're always doing this!' But it was the fault of the agents who had sent the tickets.

In November 1928, the night when a 105-mile-an-hour wind swept Britain, so many trees were down across the roads round Sidmouth that she and Ethel Hobday could not get to their appointment next day in a girls' school at Exmouth, and only just managed to make Exeter for a train back to London, where Jelly had a Queen's Hall concert. There she was so bemused by exhaustion that she started the Vitali *Chaconne* without waiting for the piano's introductory bars.

The same night the Spanish pianist Iturbi was playing. His steamer had tossed about for many hours in the Channel, and he arrived a nervous wreck. A doctor gave him a sedative, which made him burst into tears: after which he recovered and played well.

At Santander once there were two intervals of twenty minutes. During one, the lights failed and were restored. Jelly was about to begin the next part of the concert when they failed again. Forgetting that the public was expecting the soft harmonies of her agent's sentimental Spanish piece, Jelly startled them by striking up in the dark *Tzigane,* which opens with five minutes of unaccompanied fiddling. The lights came back before she reached the *tutti.*

Violins can behave badly in humid weather, and Jelly's did. Strings break. Traffic noises can drown even the last movement

Variations on Various Themes

of the César Franck *Sonata*. The college yell of a Welsh University can alarm. But Jelly got used to everything, and 'gurgled'. At Burgos one of the piano pedals fell off, and music was suspended till someone fixed it on. They had asked for a turner-over, and a commissionaire came on the platform in a uniform worthy of a Mexican general. He hummed his own tunes all the way through.

Once Jelly played in public to the accompaniment of a pianola.

These things seldom put her off. Her 'gurgle' was really a mixture of bubble and giggle. A caper on the rising thin end of suppressed laughter. It was not always enough. At Repton she and Myra Hess went out for air on a staircase leading down from the School Hall. Jelly threw her shawl over her head to keep her shoulders from chilling. It caught on something, and she looked up, met by the fierce red stare of a bison's head fixed to the wall. They both got the giggles, and Jelly had hardly stopped laughing when it was time to return to the platform. Myra waited, her finger poised on the opening note—and came down on the wrong one. This finished Jelly, who gave way to uncontrollable and unheeding mirth.[17]

A similar thing happened at Aberdeen, when Jelly muttered '*Bravo!*' to Adila and both found it hard to go on playing. But the audience heard only music.

This interference of the physical incident on the general musical occasion need not have ill effects. It can have good ones: according to the freedom of the artist. Jelly, Felix Salmond and Myra Hess were playing the Brahms *Trio in C major,* when Salmond broke a string in the first movement and left the platform. The other two went on improvising, and gradually slid on a common association of musical ideas into the Brahms *Violin Sonata in A major*. After a while Jelly broke off and followed Salmond amid cheers and laughter, and Myra Hess went off the platform too, with a similar tribute of common adventure and thanks.[18]

Jelly played the Bach *Concerto in E* at Bromley in what amounted to a Memorial Concert to Gwynne Kimpton who had recently died. The audience stood at the opening for an *Elégie* by W. H. Reed. Jelly's response to the atmosphere was such that the concerto sounded as if each member of the orchestra at her own desk were Jelly's counterpart.[19]

If the reader will bear with me, I must say some words about this concerto. It was more Adila's than Jelly's, but I never heard Adila in it.

Jelly's purity in this work was unforgettable; and I mean, 'which cannot be forgotten'. Listening to a recording by another artist some days ago, I thought I could hear by contrast how Jelly played it. I asked her, without saying why, to let me hear it again. We have just finished playing it, and the impression is identical with what I heard more than thirty years ago. As soon as the threatening gravity of the strings is established in the slow movement, her violin enters, on the long sustained note, a kind of pinpoint that becomes a beam. So evenly slow in its development that in Barcelona Casals said afterwards he had wondered if the bow would be long enough.

This note has a pure innocence, unaware of the gravity around it, and continues so when it moves and expands. Gradually it is influenced by the prevailing anxiety, and in a sense contaminated by it. By the end the violin no longer has an innocent voice; but its purity remains, a tranquil protest founded on an inner strength.

Kogan, by contrast, suffers among and with the orchestra. He protests. In his pathos he is sure. His long notes assert his position, Jelly's her trust. Both are legitimate, being the expressions of different periods and localities. But I think Jelly is nearer to Bach, whose pathos was never sentimental nor, in the modern version of sentimentality, 'compassionate'.

Yet the odd thing is that Jelly tells me she was never quite happy in this concerto, possibly because E major is not a key very comfortable for the violin. However, she played it a lot.

The occasion with Casals was in his freakishly decorated Palau de la Musica Catalana in Barcelona. Ethel Hobday accompanied her, and Casals crept unobtrusively into a box to listen. That was on an Iberian tour in 1928, where they were trailed everywhere by

Variations on Various Themes

Krone's Circus, and even mistaken for members of it when they told a Burgos Cathedral guide that they were Hungarian and British. They played also the Mendelssohn and Mozart *A major* concerti with other works in over a dozen cities: including Valencia, where the rehearsal room was so thick with tobacco smoke that Ethel Hobday compared Jelly to Joan of Arc at the stake; and Pamplona, where Sarasate was born and was welcomed with brass band and bullfight at every return home. A work by Sarasate appeared in all these concerts.

An aunt of Jelly's, niece of Joachim, had known Sarasate. He played from the score and was apt to loose his place if his eye fell on a pretty ankle peeping from under a skirt.

In Barcelona they played also at one of Casals' concerts for the people, which his mother attended. Casals was proud because his public 'all wore their best clothes', which mostly they had hired. Exile from these people has been of all the confiscations made by Franco, the one Casals has felt most deeply in his long deprived years. (His sternly democratic convictions ruptured his friendship with Thibaud, though Thibaud would have given anything for an invitation to go and play music with Casals at Perpignan. They ruptured also for a time his friendships with Cortot and Cassadó, even denying that the latter had ever been his pupil. With these two he was later reconciled, but Thibaud was by then dead.)

Casals did for the 'cello, even more than Piatti, what Joachim did for the violin. He folded people into music by a mere descending C major scale at the opening of a Bach unaccompanied *sonata*: and Jelly says of him that he reached an altitude where music ceases to be earthly.[20]

He could not but admire the Aranyis. '*Ca me fait du bien*' he said to his wife while shaving, the morning after a recital in New York by Jelly and Myra Hess, '*d'entendre Jelly qui jouait le Schumann.*' This was a favourite phrase. Between the wars, playing in Britain, he had no objection to paying British taxes: '*Ça me fait du bien, de donner à votre gouvernement.*'

Suggia had left Casals and was now back in Portugal married

The Sisters d'Aranyi

to a famous radiologist, an influential person. When Jelly heard that Suggia was coming to her first concert in Lisbon, she was uneasy; for Suggia could be extremely kind or extremely unpleasant. However she proved helpful. She had obviously been speaking highly of Jelly, and led the applause in the Opera House. Jelly did not as a rule like playing in theatres, but here an apron stage had been built out, and the tone of her violin was 'like liquid gold'. But it gave her a shock to see Suggia in the stalls with her hair coiled over the ears in exact imitation of the way Jelly did hers at that time. In certain lights there was something of a facial resemblance between them, as both knew.

One must deplore the irrelevances that deprive the world of art masterpieces. The Tate Gallery will never have the portrait Augustus John wished to paint of Jelly playing, a companion piece to his astonishing portrait of Suggia.[21] He enjoyed going to concerts to study her movements, and even fixed a date one December morning for the first of four sittings. Jelly insisted on the mornings, thinking he would be drunk in the afternoons.

Now, although the Aranyis were famous by then, they still did not have much money, and Jelly's mother had made up for her a special dress of Hungarian material, embroidered with fringes. She also made a pair of red knickers to go with it. As Jelly was taking her position, she felt an ominous slackening round the waist, and the worst had happened. Fortunately John was at that moment called to the telephone, and before he returned she had them in her handbag.

She sat for three mornings, and John did sketches of her; but pressure of commissioned work made him postpone further studies till the spring, 'hoping to begin again when the light would be better'. But when he was free, she was not, and nothing more happened. I cannot trace the present whereabouts of the sketches, which he must have kept.

Sketches by Sir William Rothenstein have also disappeared. Jelly sat to him in July 1920 'all morning in a most tiring position.'[22] In his *Men and Memories* he described Jelly in his Campden Hill studio meeting Tagore and playing to him, piece after

Variations on Various Themes

piece. 'The expression of her face, the beautiful movements of her arms and hands as the sounds travelled wailing round the walls and roof of the studio, I tried more than once to record. Only Watts could have done her justice.'

W. B. Yeats also was there, and after he had intoned some of his poems, Tagore took his *vina* and recited some of his. Tagore became friendly with the Fachiris, met them frequently, and twice came to tea, he and a retinue. Jelly admired him as a writer, and liked him as a man; 'if perhaps a little vain?', she queries, eyes lightly apologetic. But she didn't like him when he said he had never met such a personality as hers, and felt she had made a wrong impression, as often, and 'now to an Indian saint!' She wished she could be convinced herself about this personality.[23]

The French painter Charles-Louis Geoffrey-Dechaume made two portraits of her, one cancelling the other, earlier rendering, on the same canvas. In the first picture Jelly had been little more than a child. The second was used by *The Times* when she died.

De Laszlo's portrait, already spoken of, arrived in time for Christmas 1928, when Jelly was abroad; and Adila, finding it 'quite glorious in the reality' started to imagine the best place to put it and the right frame to have. De Laszlo had painted it from a single sitting after his return from a holiday in Sutherland in August. It is good De Laszlo, but it shows a quiet, thoughtful, somewhat reserved Jelly, and not the vivid vivacious passionate person we knew on the platform, as John would have re-created her.

Jelly made four tours of Spain. During one she gave four concerts in Madrid in twenty-four hours, one being in the Royal Palace. As the Aranyis were leaving, an armed sentry spat in their direction—'a long Spanish spit'—which they later heard was political not personal, for the Monarchy was tottering and fell not long after. From one political side this was like the greeting a Myaskovsky work received in London from the other, when an opponent of Soviet Russia made in the gallery a noise described by Richard Capell as 'in excellent imitation of a euphonium.'[24]

Jelly had played at the Spanish court before, when it was on

The Sisters d'Aranyi

holiday at San Sebastian. Then she had been impressed by the King's mother, the Reina Cristina, a Bourbon, who seemed able to talk informedly to almost everybody about almost everything. That time the Queen had given Jelly a diamond brooch, which she lost later in the Savoy Hotel. This time she gave a bracelet, which Jelly still sometimes wears. But looking with a sinking heart at those rows of stiff faces in the Palace, she noticed a small boy sitting on the floor and gazing at her. She played for him alone.[25]

Afterwards she discovered he was deaf and dumb.

Spain was by no means her only foreign tour. She made several to Holland, Belgium and Northern and Southern Ireland. In the early twenties while still creating her reputation she had been startled to find Middlesbrough plastered with proclamations of 'An Angel playing the Violin'. Now, when at the top of it, in Ostend an enormous poster in red, white and pale indigo announced 'Monsieur Yelli d'Aranyi'.

While on tour in Holland she unexpectedly appeared back at Netherton Grove, knocking at the door, displaying a black eye and a bruise on her forehead, and saying 'I can't think how I'm alive'. She had been driving with friends after a concert in Amsterdam, when another car shot out on a cross-road and cannoned into theirs. She was able to go to Newcastle the next day, and then back to Holland: but the press got the news too late for the evening papers, and it was a horrified Adila who opened the door to her.[26]

At Brussels, playing *Tzigane* and the Beethoven *Violin Concerto* under Robert Ledent, she lost her passport. It was arranged through Alexandre that the British Foreign Office would re-admit her without one; but meantime it was found and sent to the Belgian foreign minister. *'Vous êtes un grand artiste'* he said, stern as a schoolmaster, *'avec la tête d'une linotte.'*

Everywhere Jelly went she was alert to people. In the course of either her third or fourth visit to Dublin, during the Second War, she was suffering from indigestion with the rich food, and envying the trouble-free life there, until she found that the son

Variations on Various Themes

of her hostess was fighting with the British Army. He was killed soon after.

Dublin was full of contradictions. She felt badly as she stood to begin the Beethoven *Concerto* and saw in her audience the Nazi Minister. Having filled the Theatre Royal to a record figure,[27] but hit by the poverty and misery, she told a friend that she wished to do something for someone. The friend, Mrs Yseult Cochrane, took her to the Legion of Mary.

The Legion of Mary had been founded after the First War by two or three Catholic civil servants, who bought an old granary and fitted it up as a hall, to which anyone could come in for free entertainment. They did: toughs and drunks. They made their own entertainment. They smashed the seats and tore down the curtains. After this an admission fee of 6d was charged. Alcoholics and down-and-outs paid and came, but not any more to destroy. The Legion of Mary is now world-wide.

Jelly played some short pieces. There was a good, indeed a moving audience, listening in a silence as tense as that of Casals' audience at Barcelona, one young man keeping his head in his hands as he followed Jelly back to the world of culture he had deserted for drink. 'An audience of picturesque vagabonds.' The women were rough and tipsy, and roamed about in the wild. There was no piano.

Jelly went back in 1945. One young man she thought rather eccentric in his fancy dress, his suit being made of newspapers. But it was not fancy dress. He had no clothes. And newspapers are easier to scrounge than rags, when not all have even rags.

She went on to the Catholic College of Maynooth. After lunch she asked to rest in the Artists' Room, which was filled with smoke because a cleaner, thinking the fire was out, had put the cinders in a bucket with some amateur costumes on top. The Irish press joined other people in comparing Jelly to Joan of Arc at the stake.

De Valera wished to see her, and the invitation reached Jelly in a big store where she was buying underclothes on Mrs W. B. Yeats's ration book. At first she thought the invitation was for 'the teashop at four o'clock.' But it was the Toiseach. 'Tall and stooping, with a brown Spanish appearance' is Jelly's description. Shortsighted, wearing very thick lenses. 'Nervous as a hunted animal,' Jelly goes on. Nor was his conversation of much interest. In ten minutes all he had to say was that he had himself at one time played the trombone in a band, and once because the music card fell out of its metal holder, he had to stop playing. Holst would have made more of such an incident.

At Belfast in 1936 she played Sir Hamilton Harty's *Violin Concerto*, first performed by Szigeti in 1909. Harty conducted, and Frederick Stone accompanied her in short pieces, one of them by Somervell. This had been written for Jelly to play to Adila's little daughter Adrienne. They did not know what to call it. 'Call it what you will' said Adrienne, and *What You Will* stuck. Arthur Somervell wrote several things for the Aranyis. Jelly and Ethel Hobday gave his *Violin Sonata* its first performance at the New Kensington Music Club in 1924 or '25.

By 1927 Jelly's views as an interpreter of the deepest music were of interest to the musical reading public; and A. H. Fox-Strangways, founder and editor of *Music and Letters,* asked her for an article for the Beethoven Centenary. These 3,000 words are among the most illuminating things I have read about the Beethoven *Violin Sonatas,* and show her devoted independence of intellect. He made a similar request about Schubert, whom Jelly loved, for the Schubert Centenary in 1928, and she tried, perhaps not quite so successfully, to show the impact of Schubert on contemporary ears.

In that year Ethel Smyth conducted the sprightly *Concerto for Violin and Horn,* she had written for Jelly and Aubrey Brain. Aubrey Brain was held the finest living player of the French Horn, until his son Dennis challenged his lead.* The concerto was not liked by all critics. One said the horn merged too much in tone into that of the orchestra.[28] But it was also thought to be the most attractive thing Ethel Smyth had so far written,[29] especially the

---

*Dennis Brain could make an extraordinary note on the horn. It sounded like a wheel revolving with a hole in the middle. I heard him doing this once in a work by Benjamin Britten.

Variations on Various Themes

backchat between horn and violin. The composer came, two months before, to sew the third movement into Jelly's piano score and violin part, because she believed in seeing to such details as three movements in one cover.*[30]

But it was an important concert for other reasons. Chappell's had just decided to disband their Queen's Hall Orchestra, and this would have been the last concert at least for the violins and double-basses, if the BBC had not assumed financial responsibility. Sir Henry had an ovation.

1930 saw yet another centenary, that of Joachim's birth, and again it was obvious that much of this agreeable burden would be on Jelly. She had already done a little in anticipation the year before. At Leeds she gave her first performance of the *Hungarian Concerto***. And in a long concert at the Norwich Festival (which contained the first concert performance in England of Vaughan Williams' *Job*)[31] she had played Max Bruch's *Concerto no 1. in G minor,* which was dedicated to Joachim. Among the d'Aranyi papers is a programme of a tour made by Joachim and Brahms in Hungary when the latter was about forty-nine or fifty. They played this concerto together. Jelly made it seem good music, a critic said, but he felt that Bruch did not understand the violin. She was happy in it, and shared her pleasure with the orchestra.[32]

There was a Celebration Concert in the Queen's Hall on June 28th, at which Adila, Jelly and Gabrielle, Joachim's granddaughter, performed. Gabrielle Joachim sang a scena from *Maria*, an opera founded on an unfinished Schiller drama, which Joachim wrote for his wife Amelia before their marriage folded up and led to a breach between Joachim and Brahms. Tovey conducted the New Symphony Orchestra with Jelly in the *Hun-*

---

*When this concerto was given at the Eastbourne Festival in November following, somebody told Ethel Smyth, as she was going on to the platform, that her petticoat was showing. She took her fur coat with her, draped it over the rostrum rail, and defied her public with the reason why.

**Jelly had played the 1st movement only at the Wigmore Hall in 1920.

garian Concerto and with Adila in the *adagio* from the *Concerto in G* and the *Variations on a Hungarian Theme*.

The portrait which G. F. Watts had painted of Joachim, and of which Roger Fry[33] said that it was one which took rank with the finest achievements of English art for all time, was placed under the stage, so that people in the interval could pass and pay their respects. Jelly, according to a friend, looked like 'an angel by an old master but with fur wings instead of feathery ones'. But the concert itself does not seem to have gone very smoothly.

In tribute to Joachim's friends Mendelssohn and Brahms, it was intended to open with the *Hebrides Overture* and close with the *Academic*: but there was no time to rehearse the latter. So Adila and Jelly played the slow movement from the Bach *Double Concerto*. Both of them taking the critical runs *staccato*.

Fault was found with Tovey's handling, and *The Times* was disappointed by the heaviness of the *Overture to a Gozzi Comedy* when 'play of fantastic humour' had been promised in Tovey's full programme notes. But the London press was always against Tovey; and one, ungushing, friend[34] said that Jelly had played 'as if the *Concerto* and you were the same' even if the orchestra did on occasion drown her. Jan Masaryk told her that she couldn't have been stopped from doing her best 'even if you had been accompanied on a zitter'.[35]

Jelly played this *Concerto* elsewhere, Lincoln's Inn, Liverpool, Folkestone, Edinburgh. At the last the elderly Dutch composer Julius Röntgen was present. He had been friend and biographer of Grieg, and had played the piano at Vienna with Brahms. Edinburgh University, through Tovey who admired him, had just given him an honorary degree, and he had in return conducted his specially written *University Symphony*.

He had met the Aranyis in 1911 at Northlands,[36] but he was now so impressed by Jelly's playing that he went home and wrote a *Concerto* for her. It was not the major work he had hoped, and the last movement in particular was so patently influenced by the *Hungarian Concerto* that Jelly had no wish to play it. She let the matter slide for some months, and then heard

Variations on Various Themes

he had died, asking for Joachim's *Concerto* on his deathbed. So he may have realized. But this did not help Jelly.

The *Hungarian Concerto* may not be one of the world's greatest violin jewels, but it is well scored, Hungarian-rhythmic to the point of rapture, and contains an 'inordinately difficult *cadenza*', which Jelly performed with 'surprising lucidity' according to a critic who heard her at Leeds.[37]

The more serious a soloist is, the greater his right to divert with a difficult and showy *cadenza,* as a fine actor playing Romeo has a right to divert in the dance, if he can dance. Jelly enjoyed a good *cadenza* perhaps more than a mere virtuoso can, who has been showing off all the time. She even arranged them. For the Beethoven *Concerto* with the New Symphony Orchestra and Harty 'kindly assisting' in 1931, she restored 'with as little alteration as possible' the two that Beethoven himself had written in the piano version of the first two movements. In the *Rondo* she used Joachim's, since Beethoven wrote none for that. Her lively programme note mentioned that the use of the *timpani* was Beethoven's own idea. (Another concert, incidentally, at which she played three concerti without fatigue or loss of tension.)

She might accept Groves' explanation of these interpolations as due to singers who took advantage of a held dominant so that the audience 'might have the impression of astonishment fresh in their minds to urge them to applaud.' But cascades of notes on a held dominant are as old as Bach and Vivaldi for instrumentalists. Modern composers, who do not write for *prima donnas,* continue to write them and serious artists to perform them. In 1928 Jelly asked Donald Tovey to write two for the Mozart *Concerto in G,* which he was to conduct for her at Edinburgh. He did this so well that Gioconda de Vito, who heard them, asked Jelly to get her copies when about to make her gramophone record of the work two years later.

In any case, though one can be pleased, diverted, delighted, stimulated, impressed, even made a little envious, during a *cadenza,* the standard of instrumentalism has nowadays risen so high that it is rare for any but a new concert-goer to be 'astonished'

The Sisters d'Aranyi

at personal skill. And if it is more than mere personal skill it is beginning to be music. The *cadenza* in the first movement of the Brahms *Concerto* ranged in Jelly's fingers from robust breadth of tone to an almost ethereal lightness.[39] But the pleasure this gave was implicit in the music already written, not stuck on to it.

'She is one of the few who can play *cadenzas* as an integral part of the work' wrote *The Times,* when she took a sick Szigeti's place in another Mozart *Concerto* under Beecham, 'and not merely as an opportunity for spreading a peacock's tail.'[40]

For a *cadenza* is not just a cloud of midges dancing; it has the shape of a cloud of midges among the curves and colours of musical painting. Each midge may seem to move by the skill of performing fingers or of whoever first drew it, usually a violinist. But the colours and curves are those of the composition, and sometimes add much by reminiscence of meaning.

This chapter, I hope, has had something of the character of a biographer's *cadenza*. In any case it is time to return to the tonic key, and to another fine performer of those days.

14

Myra Hess and America

Jelly played with many prominent, or promising, pianists. At the Leith Hill Festival of 1924 there was Arnold Goldsbrough, still a master at Westminster but already organist at St Annes, Soho, who had studied the double-bass under Claude Hobday, Ethel's brother-in-law. As a rule Jelly did not like organists at the piano: she found they tended to rely on imaginary stops instead of varying their tone as a pianist should enjoy doing. But this was not true of Bruce Hylton-Stewart, of St James's, Piccadilly, whom she liked playing with, and was glad to find free in 1935 in Holland on his way to Mannheim, and who could play for her at The Hague.[1]

Nor was it true of Herbert Sumsion of Gloucester Cathedral. He accompanied her on an occasion still vivid to her in colour. It was in Malmesbury Cathedral during the Second War, and Queen Mary was an unwilling and distastefully unoccupied evacuee not far away. She came, in powder-blue from head to foot, and sat in the Bishop's Chair, which in Jelly's memory glints with gold. Jelly herself wore red.

There was John Ireland, with whom she played his *Second Sonata* in Chelsea Town Hall for a charity. There was Iso Elinson, with whom she became great friends later in her life. There was of course Donald Tovey, with whom she played sometimes in London, often in Edinburgh. Especially there was the quiet Harold Samuel. Quiet, but no dry intellectual, either at the piano or away from it. He could be so good a comic that it was said he

The Sisters d'Aranyi

had started in music halls.[2] This could hardly have been true, since he made his début at the age of fifteen in St James's Hall and was a student at the R.C.M.—unless he earned a childhood living as a feed.* A favourite piece of his fooling was to sing comic songs at the piano, and then turn round facing his guests and play (and well) with his hands behind him. He had also a psychic side, with odd experiences in Ireland, extra-sensory perception at the death of his mother, and so on. He was very sensitive, as Jelly was; and when they met in the United States, both being established figures and accepted and fêted everywhere, they were so overcome by homesickness that they wept silently together along a New York street.

We used to consider that he had no equal in Bach; and Jelly often played Bach with him, notably the *Sonata in A* at a special concert in 1926, the fiftieth year of the London Bach Choir, at the Central Hall, Westminster. At a mixed concert to city men in the Goldsmiths' Hall in 1924, however, Bach gave way to Beethoven.

On the other hand there were men like Nicholas Orlov, famous pupil of Taneyev but no player of chamber music. Jelly gave a private concert with him before his London début in 1925. His line was 'most interesting little thrills', a miniaturist; but when he partnered someone with temperament like Jelly, he tended to thump and play coarsely. In 1928 at Birmingham he seemed reluctant to start Schubert, perhaps being peeved by the late arrival of a local bigwig.[3] Yet he was a generous-minded man, 'for ever praising everybody, including most pianists'.[4]

Apart from partner players, Jelly had varied pianists as accompanists other than Ethel Hobday. In London and outside the list contains George Reeves, Ivor Newton, Frederick Stone, Reginald Paul, John Wills. Often there were local ones. But none of these, notable, craftsmanlike as they were, was preferable to Ethel Hobday. Jelly never took a male accompanist abroad. For this an American agent reproached her. 'It's psychologically wrong to travel with an elderly woman,' he said. One can see his point of

* But see note[2].

Myra Hess and America

view. Two glamorous creatures scraping and pounding glorious music would bring in more money than one with a pounder who might look like an appendage. But it was not Jelly's view. Ethel Hobday was no appendage. In railway trains she was fun and in music she was exquisite. She also avoided complications. 'It would be physically worse to travel with a man,' Jelly retorted.

By far the most lasting, deep and fruitful partnership she made was when she started to give regular recitals with Myra Hess, news of whose death has unhappily arrived while this chapter is being written. As a pianist Myra Hess had a grand authority, an impressive and solid scholarship and a fine taste controlling hands superbly equipped. She was later to be held the finest woman exponent of Beethoven and among the best pianists of the world.

In parenthesis I must add that she was not at her best on the air. The absence of an audience, maybe, the anonymity, the vacuum-like studio, made her so nervous before the red light flickered, and her hands trembled so visibly and violently that they seemed unlikely to hit the right note. But on the concert platform she was magnificent.

The two women met during the first war at the house of mutual friends, whose music room was frequently used for private concerts. Jelly recalls that they 'eyed each other like dogs'.

Their first joint appearance seems to have been in a trio with Arthur Williams, which gave two concerts in March 1917 at Kent House. But they may have played at other private houses, for by October 1918 Myra Hess was writing in an already fond way to Jelly, having heard that she was thinking of playing to patients in the 'Face Hospital'. She suggests playing together, and in other hospitals too.

From this haphazard meeting grew an ensemble which to the younger generation was like the sun and the moon making music together, until some of us faithlessly deserted Myra Hess for Schnabel. The silvery quality of Jelly's violin blended beautifully with the golden tone of Myra Hess, so that Fox-Strangways in *The Times* compared them with watches: Myra Hess, top of the wrist-watch class, Jelly a gold repeater 'the best that money can buy'.[6]

Society hostesses heard of these treasures. One, very rich and an amateur pianist, offered five pounds the pair for an engagement.[7]

Each woman continued her separate career and came together now and then. Many programmes survive, but London concert halls by no means always date their notices fully, and it is hard to see any pattern. Sometimes there would be a sonata or two with solo works; often two, sandwiching these: as at Lincoln in 1924 when between Brahms *in D minor* and the César Franck, Myra Hess played piano pieces by Frank Bridge and O'Donnell and two Rachmaninov *Preludes*, and Jelly three Paganini *Capricci*. Sometimes they gave a solid wad of sonatas, as at Banbury: Brahms, Mozart, Beethoven and César Franck.[8]

César Franck had been 'discovered' by us in the twenties. We tried to hear all he ever wrote, and spent hours going to obscure churches to hear indifferent performers on organs. The *Violin Sonata* we thought the nearest thing to paradise we were ever likely to hear in modern music (for some reason Franck seemed very modern): and what those two did with it, only those who heard will believe. Especially in the last movement, when in that paradise every joy-bell was pealing.

The critics were slow to notice the new ensemble, being too much impressed by Jelly. They said of the Franck *Sonata* at the Queen's Hall in 1925 that Jelly had the same breadth as Suggia (by then very famous indeed), not noticing the width and concentration of Myra Hess.[9] Again at Derby a critic gave the credit for perfect balance and blending to Jelly, whereas, if any control is needed, it more often comes from the pianist.[10] Princess Helena Victoria attended this concert, and by a prudent and musicianly act of grace asked that the National Anthem should not be played. There would have been something incongruous in these two young craftswomen solemnly (and probably after anything but solemn rehearsal) striking up that four-square chant before the subtle unofficial graces of Mozart (in B♭, K 31).

Myra Hess and America

There was nothing solemn about either of them in their twenty-year long partnership, which exploded in high spirits and laughter and jokes, when together or when writing to each other: not even in their serious double-musicianship. Jelly called Myra Hess 'Pishkosh' from the Hungarian word for 'dirty', which Myra Hess could never spell[11] and made a mere squiggle of a signature right down the page. Myra Hess, as most of Jelly's friends, came to call her by the family's nickname of 'Sai' (pronounced *Shai*), but could also start a letter 'Darling gut-scraper'. A friend once photographed them on the tennis-court at Myra Hess's cottage,[12] holding rackets and making outrageous faces, Myra Hess as a fiddler, Jelly 'at the piano'.

They had real love and solicitude for each other: also for interpretation and ensemble: which they tried to make more and more *innerlich* (Myra Hess's word).[13] They discussed works away from their instruments, then put their decisions into practice at rehearsal. They had post-mortems in talk or by post, admitting mistakes in a good-humoured, indeed merry, manner, vowing to get rid of weaknesses. All this in bubbles of youthful high spirits. Nor was either jealous. Each enjoyed the other's scoring of double encores.

When first they started to play together, Jelly was about thirty, Myra Hess some three years older. By 1925, one enthusiast said, Jelly was universally accepted as the greatest woman violinist.[14] At first she seems to have been the less erratic of the two: for the piano-violin combination is among the most difficult to keep in perfect balance (possibly flute and piano are worse), and even in their prime they did not always maintain it all through an evening. A fact they soberly recognized afterwards.

In June 1927, playing Mozart,[15] Schubert, Brahms and Beethoven in the Wigmore Hall, they gave a slight sense of uneasiness, for example: whereas by October, at a Bach concert in Westminster, 'they exchanged smiles and almost danced to the music'.[16] Perhaps this was because between two Bach concerti came the Ravel *Violin Sonata* which contains one movement founded on the Blues.

The Sisters d'Aranyi

This had recently had its first performance by Hélène Jourdain-Morhange and the composer, who had written it for her: it had also been heard at a private concert in London that summer. As usual the London press had no use for Ravel. In the Blues the piano plays in G and the violin in A♭. Nothing to shock us now, but then rousing irritation and (for a reason I cannot understand) anger. 'The pianist' said *The Times* 'has little to do but peck out dry staccato rhythms.'[17] 'New and mechanical' said another paper when Jelly and Myra Hess gave it again in the 'pronouncedly obstreperous sonority'[18] of Chelsea Town Hall to the 500 members of the Chelsea Music Club. But the public liked it.

Max Mossel, the Dutch violinist turned impresario, spotted them and took them to Birmingham and Scotland in January 1926. This time Jelly outshone not only her companion, but Elizabeth Schumann herself, queen of soprani to us.[19] At Glasgow she had to give a double encore. But at Edinburgh (or Bridge of Allan—always a welcome for good music there) it was Myra Hess who had to give a double encore, first a Mozart piece, then her own arrangement of *Jesu, Joy of Man's Desiring,* another work which we of the twenties considered in her hands one of the most magical new discoveries of all keyboard music. And maybe we were not so far wrong.

This pair could also be 'popular' when tastes were getting sharply split between popular and 'highbrow'. At that time a group called the English Singers was re-discovering Elizabethan and Jacobean madrigals and part songs, as at the same time the theatre was re-discovering seventeenth-century drama. They were the idols of hundreds of amateur madrigal groups all over the country, making a historical link between the Glee Clubs of the nineteenth century and the Pop movement of today. Quite unaccompanied (this was unusual) they took their pitch from a pocket tuning-fork, and sat round a handsome period table, with their music lying on it, as singers in madrigal times had done. They turned the concert platform into an old-English home, without affectation or costume; sincerely, with the simplicity that only skill and good taste can achieve. But a difficult item to fit into a mixed concert.

This group was invited to a Chappell Popular Saturday Afternoon Concert in November 1925. Frederick Kiddle, the Queen's Hall organist, played light pieces. No place, one might have thought, for Jelly and Myra Hess in the César Franck *Sonata*. And yet they fitted perfectly, and gave a finish of executive brilliance to the afternoon.[20] Jelly had by then got over her dislike of Ballad Concerts and their like. In 1927 she and Myra Hess played Franck's *Variations Symphoniques* and *Tzigane* amid drawing-room ballads by vocalists.[21]

That they could also find a big public for the more intellectual sonatas was due, said a long article in the *Saturday Review*, to their ability to make their audience feel as if they were performing for him or her alone. This had already been said of Jelly. That it could be true of a duo set them apart from most other artists, and this article could compare them only with Elena Gerhardt, the purest contralto of our youth. In her *lieder* singing Gerhardt had much of the directness of Kathleen Ferrier.

So, whether the celtic haar of Debussy or a solid evening of Brahms, they could put music across to ever increasing crowds. Once when they played the Ravel *Sonata*, even the space on the platform was filled with listeners. By 1927, *The Times* at last notices the brilliant solidity of their ensemble. 'The impetuosity and energy of the violinist enlivens and is set off by the steadier charm of the piano ... whereby without any trace of antagonism they give more than one side of each case.'[22] And *The Observer* said[23] 'Such playing as Miss Hess-d'Aranyi gives ceases to be a struggle between one four-stringed instrument and one with 500 wires, becoming instead a consort of well-modulated sounds.' The *Sunday Times* went deeper: 'While they were playing Bach in A, it was to Bach himself we were listening rather than to two very able artists who had conceived twin views on the subject.'[24]

In other words, the twain of them by dual experience and intuition of balance could forget technique and open itself to a

The Sisters d'Aranyi

mutual music as cleanly as each did when performing by herself. They gave the lie to those old exquisites who held that violin and piano are incompatible. Compatibility depends on consciousness.

This belated recognition by the London press of what lovers of good music had known for years may have been due to the fact that the concert being reviewed was a farewell one to their thousands of admirers before they left to play in North America. It was not Myra Hess's first visit there, nor did they make a joint tour. They joined by appointment.

Jelly left Southampton with Ethel Hobday in ss. *Berengaria* on November 19th for New York, where she found such a forest of dates as bewildered her. She was also jolted by Felix Salmond, who was already there and who invited them to tea. Jelly wished to practise, so Ethel Hobday went, and returned with her blue Irish eyes wide open. 'Guess what he said! He said he was very sorry for you, facing a first appearance in New York, the most nerve-racking test in a musical artist's life!'

Nerve-racking Jelly did not find it, but she did suffer from time-strain. When at her tiredest, she heard the telephone ringing, and the voice of Szigeti, wooing and adulatory, saying what a sweet and wonderful friend she had always been. He had undertaken to play the Béla Bartók *Second Sonata* without a fee, but had since had a wonderful offer, with possibilities, for the same date. Seeing that Bartók had written the work for her, would she take his place?

Jelly refused. She could fit in no more. But Szigeti rang again, imploring her; so she agreed. The busiest public figure can get through the thickest jungle of dates, if they are chopped down one by one: and there always seems time to do another while you are at it, if there are enough of them.

The Bartók concert was not a success, even with the composer at the piano. The wonderful *Second Quartet*, a landmark in musical history to us in Europe, which had been available for a year or two in a German electric recording, was called 'cacophonous and curious purrings and whinings'.[25] But the U.S.A. never treated

Myra Hess and America

Bartók well; and it is only recently that amends are being made there to his spirit and name.

'Yelly' (as her American agent insisted on writing her name in publicity material) and Ethel Hobday gave their first American recital in the New York Town Hall on November 26, 1927. The programme was: the Tartini *Devil's Trill Sonata*, the Mozart *Concerto in D* (K. 218), the Bach unaccompanied *Chaconne*, *Tzigane*, Paganini's 23rd *Capriccio*, the *Nana* and the *Jota* from Manuel de Falla's *Spanish Suite*, in which Jelly twanged her *pizzicati* like a guitar, and a *Bagatelle in D* by Nicholas Gatty.

Gatty was an old friend of Vaughan Williams, who had sent him round to Jelly the previous March.[26] She thought he looked like a 'sick ghost', but she liked the violin pieces he brought, especially the *Bagatelle*, which one critic described as a 'cascade of lovely notes'.[27] She recorded it in the USA; and when his gramophone royalties started to come in, Gatty was surprised and grateful: for though he was in his fifties, these were the first he had ever had. He was known chiefly for his operas.

This was the basic programme for the tour, minor works being occasionally substituted. Also basic on the printed programme was a mention of the Baldwin piano, a breed hitherto unknown to Ethel Hobday.

They went to several schools, the Knox School, Cooperstown, where they introduced arrangements by Harold Craxton of two pieces by Baldassare Galuppi, eighteenth-century composer of comic operas on *libretti* of Goldoni; to Groton School (Jelly made four visits there in the next few years, a fact recorded with pride in her last programme); to St Mark's. Jelly played the Mozart *Concerto in B♭* (K. 207) with Arthur Turner and the Springfield Orchestra. On December 2nd, she played at No 26 Chestnut Street, Boston, a road Jelly thought could have been in Chelsea, and she loved Chelsea. Here with the American pianist Frank Sheridan she played the Brahms *Sonata in D minor* under a really immense chandelier that hung in a small room with a low ceiling. No sword of Damocles fell.

In New York there were two more important engagements:

The Sisters d'Aranyi

first, a Sunday Night Concert in the Metropolitan Opera House, primarily vocal, at which she gave Bruch's *Concerto no 1* with Giuseppe Bamboshek conducting the Metropolitan Orchestra. The second, the day after Christmas, was a joint recital presented by the Beethoven Association, with Harold Bauer, Myra Hess, Harold Samuel (somewhat invidious to invite three pianists on the same evening, as if they were competing), the 'cellist Maria Roemaet-Rosanov, and Jelly. At this Jelly and Myra Hess gave the first performance in America of the Ravel *Sonata*, thereby beating to it Szigeti and Ravel himself, who played it the following January.[28] This was the wonderful offer with possibilities that had caused Szigeti to plead a poisoned finger for the Bartók concert, maybe.

Jelly and Myra Hess then left for Havana. They left Key West in bitter winter weather and landed into an English spring. Or rather a Scottish August, for there were mosquitoes. Myra Hess went out to try her piano and came back with her face ruined. Jelly tried to comfort her. 'It's your left eye that's swollen, not your public one.' But Myra Hess was neither comforted nor, on this occasion, amused. Understandably.

The hall was a circus, I mean this literally. Separated from their playing area by a gauze curtain lurked a lion in a cage no bigger than a kennel. Jelly hoped it wouldn't roar. But it did, during Brahms in *A*. Jelly believes the keeper had prodded it because she had said the lion didn't like his quarters.

At that time Havana was a wild place, mad on horse racing and gambling. It was also a victim to the worst vices set up by American prohibitionism. The coarsest types came oversea for a booze-up. Once the violinist Zimbalist returned to America with his wife Anne Glück, the singer, who was caught at the American customs smuggling a bottle of whisky. Zimbalist was angry with her in public, but later willingly shared with her one of the dozen bottles of champagne she had also smuggled in under cover of the smaller offence. But Havana was one of the most beautiful ports Jelly ever saw.

Two more concerts at schools (typical of Jelly that for one, St

Myra Hess and America

Paul's, she changed almost the entire programme) and she and Ethel Hobday left for home, full of American honours, dollars and Christmas hospitality. Jelly in *Tzigane* had been the musical craze of the year.

When Myra Hess also came home, it was to a popularity of the duo so big, that the Wigmore Hall was too small, and like the Lener Quartet they had to move to the Queen's Hall.[29] Part of the London press took exception to chamber music in so large an auditorium, but this had been much fuller than usual for such concerts. Most of the printed praise was lyrical. 'The *pianos* are whispers, the *fortes* crashes; the several figures are dandled and stroked and smoothed and coaxed into a maximum of meaning' said *The Observer*,[30] and then, maybe nervous at having said too much, accused them of having 'lost the line'. The *Daily Telegraph* said there had been no such partnership since Busoni and Ysaye twenty years before.[31]

This was the Schubert Centenary year, and with Felix Salmond they recorded for Columbia the great *Trio in B♭*—still a delight, for all its primitive acoustics, to those lucky enough to possess a pressing. 'Damaging comparisons are being made' the *Musical Times* of July reviewed this record 'with the Casals-Cortot-Thibaud recording; but it gave me no impression of inferiority.'

The *B♭ Trio* had a special side-value for Adila and Jelly. Before Joachim's last illness Adila had been listening to her great-uncle rehearsing it. When he came to the part after the *pizzicato* at letter B of the finale, Joachim was annoyed. All his life, he said, he had spoilt this passage because there wasn't enough time to get his bow on the string after it. Adila shyly suggested playing the final *pizzicato* with the left hand and getting the bow ready with the right. Joachim called this a brain-wave, and nowadays everyone plays it so.[32]

Though Jelly had been homesick in America and never more than at a sumptuous Christmas dinner given by a Hungarian lady pianist married to a music publisher, she went back there with Myra Hess next winter. They gave another farewell concert be-

The Sisters d'Aranyi

fore leaving London, and a farewell broadcast too, as in the previous year. At the former the *Sunday Times* was not sure that it was good to have the piano open on the short support, a view one could discuss without end; for on the one hand notes boxed up give an unfair clarity to the violin, while on the other to let full volume out preoccupies a pianist with thoughts of balance.[33]

The Observer observed, as if this were news, that they were now making it a habit to perform together.[33]

As before, both curved their separate American orbits to coincide when required: but this time Jelly's accompanist was none other than Titi, whose health appeared, illusorily, to have taken a permanent turn for the better. She was billed as Emilia Hawtrey.

The basic programme was the César Franck *Sonata*, *Tzigane* again, the sentimental piece by Figuerido, Jelly's Basque agent in Spain already mentioned, and Hubay's *Czene de la Csardà* (Scenes in a Country Inn) 'a thing of almost hurtful poignancy'.[34]

Jelly never pushed Hungarian music by playing second-rate works just because of her own nationality: but something national was expected, and Hubay was useful. On her third visit to New York Town Hall she included in her solo recital his *Sarya Csereboyar*, a folk song, ('*The Yellow Cockchafer*'). If his violin pieces may not all have the elegant brilliance of Kreisler's, which were then the rage, they were fun to play, pleasant to hear, novelties to the public, and she owed Hubay much.

This time she spent Christmas in England first. The tour opened at Springfield, where she played the Mendelssohn *Concerto* under Arthur Turner. She joined Hans Kindler and the pianist Ossip Gabrilowitsch at Lycoming, the Turners' home, in the Beethoven *C minor Trio* and some sonatas. But the rehearsals were in Philadelphia, whence they motored. Jelly never got used to the North-American contempt for distances, in spite of her own vagueness in geography.

Her first day at Cincinnati, for example, was a whirl. She was met at the station and taken straight to rehearsal. Her ex-

Myra Hess and America

compatriot Fritz Reiner invited her to dinner, but this was in the country forty miles out. And so on.

At Cincinnati (as happened also at Chicago on another visit) the soloist had to step down to a separate and lower rostrum, from which neither orchestra nor baton could be seen. Curiously, this did not disturb the ensemble: the orchestra and she played in perfectly adjusted time just the same.[35] An interesting illustration of the old-fashioned practice whereby in a concerto, music was mere accompaniment to the soloist. Not so old-fashioned, either. In all too many *dernier cri* commercial recordings the soloist sounds too brightly and the inner notes of the orchestra cannot be heard at all. These are abstracts from concert performances.

Then Jelly joined Myra Hess in New York, playing Brahms, Mozart, Beethoven and César Franck.[36] Myra Hess had brought her own Steinway; but the programme in all Jelly's recitals in America drew attention to the inaccurate boast 'Miss d'Aranyi uses the Baldwin'.

The following day they were in Washington for 'Mrs Lawrence's thirty-fourth Musical Morning at eleven fifteen o'clock at the Mayflower' (hotel). They gave a mixed programme. 'The audience' Jelly says 'was all ambassadors and retinues.'

They did not get jointly to Boston. The agent refused to consider two artists at one time for box office reasons. The public might think neither was good enough to play separately.

But Jelly herself did go again, and loved the acoustics of the Symphony Hall. 'The first notes of *Tzigane* floated out, and I had to wait till the sound finished.' It was her favourite hall of all; and no wonder; since the Boston Symphony Hall was the first concert hall in the world to be built after careful study of acoustics, a science in which in 1900 original research had to be done for the purpose.'[37]

Jelly never got used, either, to American hotels and houses, the way they were overheated. 'You could get an electric spark by shaking hands, the air was so dry.' Especially if wearing silk.

The Sisters d'Aranyi

But there were graver dangers. Several times in American hotels the bridge of the Bergonzi showed signs of sinking. It actually started to do so before Jelly's second New York recital, on a Saturday morning about 11.30 with the recital to start at 3 p.m. Some doors away in the same street there was a violin-maker, to whom she took the instrument in despair. In the time there was nothing he could do. Even if he could have made her another bridge, this would have had to be played-in. He advised filling a bath with very hot water and hanging up the violin in the steam.

Jelly went back and did so, staring with terror at her by now beloved Bergonzi. The trick worked; the bridge returned to normal; and 'the sound, when I had re-tuned the loosed strings' she says 'was Heaven'.*

And then Segovia rang up from his hotel crying that the heat had cracked his guitar.

It may have been this dry, ferocious heat which ruined Casals' modern Labate 'cello, and less the climate to which Lilian Littlehale ascribes its permanent loss of tone.** Jelly thinks so too.

When our twain returned to London, it could fill the Queen's Hall whenever it wished, despite the *Sunday Times* continuing to call for a closed piano.[38] (But another critic found that Myra Hess with the melody played too softly for the violin as accompanist.)

They gave recitals in series. They gave all ten Beethoven *Sonatas* on three successive Saturdays. We heard the versatility of this

---

*For the interest of violinists I append a paragraph in a Norwich programme during the 1930 Festival, signed C. R. 'Jelly d'Aranyi always plays on a beautiful Carlo Bergonzi instrument (with a Joseph Guarnerius label) and she has an exceptionally fine Tourte bow. In place of the usual wire or whalebone lapping she uses a thick piece of rubber and also her violin is strung with a covered D and wire E string.'

In 1937 Ethel Hobday started a subscription to present Jelly with a Stradivarius. This reached £1,400, but a Strad in those days cost about £3,000. Jelly paid the difference herself, saying that she had bought the body of the Strad and her friends and admirers its soul. She gave the Bergonzi to her niece Adrienne on her fifteenth birthday. In 1965 Adrienne sold it to Isaac Stern, a fact giving as much pleasure to him as to Jelly, who called Stern her 'ideal violinist.'

**Pablo Casals*, revised edn., London 1949, p. 65.

pair, and varied music passing smooth through that versatility. In Beethoven they could be 'Olympian—if that were not too little human a word',[39] or serene, or sober. They could be elegantly formal in the Haydn-like op. 12, No. 2 *in A*. They released the melancholy strength of op. 30, No. 3. Or they could be robust or amusing when Mozart was these. One felt one was 'assisting at the pleasure-making of two personalities intensely alive.'

In 1935 Max Mossel, for Liverpool, founded a group to be called the New Trio Ensemble: Jelly, Myra Hess and Gaspar Cassadó. It was an admirable trio: 'where strings lie in the extreme of their compass with the pianoforte between them is a test of ensemble', an experienced judge pronounced. 'Their playing never allowed one to be conscious of the fact'.[40] But it did not last.

Neither did the partnership between pianist and violinist.

Meanwhile our sorrow is that there is no recording of what many placed among the most discerning and impressive performances of that time. Maybe the sounds of them are beaming round the universe behind the stars, to be recaptured when man has a macrophonic apparatus to register them on their curve. But the gramophone monopolies, as so often, declined to sell great performances to those who wished to buy in an everlasting market.

And now Myra Hess is dead.

The Truth About the Schumann Concerto

The Aranyi family had no interest in spiritualist séances. In Hungary people who had, they thought cranks or crazy. True, one of the priestly uncles had dabbled a little, but had given up under threat of excommunication. True also that Madame d'Aranyi had further premonitions beyond what we have told of. But second sight about deaths is not uncommon, as Scots folk know.

For such perception Jelly had no gift. Ten days after Kelly's death she did seem to hear, at the improbable time of two in the morning, sounds as from across water which might have been made by a beginner on the violin. The notes were not unlike the opening notes of his *Violin Sonata*, and Kelly never played the violin. But when a close friend said she had a 'message' for Jelly from Kelly in another world, she would have nothing to do with it.

What happened in 1933 is utterly different.

Among the leisure pastimes of that period was 'the glass game'. A tumbler is set upside down on a table in a circle of letters of the alphabet, often the little square cards used in 'word making and word taking' and games of that kind; but they can also be written by hand. Fingers are placed lightly by more than one person on its upturned bottom, and quite often, after a kind of indecision, some form of collective pressure slides the tumbler from letter to letter. It is a point of honour not to push deliberately, and in-

The Truth About the Schumann Concerto

deed this would be soon detected. 'Questions' are asked aloud and 'answers' if any written down. It is remarkable how frequently the letters group into words and with what speed the glass can sometimes move. Most people at some time or other have played this game.

In February or March 1933, Jelly was staying with friends at Eastbourne after a concert. In the evening they were asking 'questions' which Jelly thought silly, about the rise and fall of stocks. Suddenly the glass spelt out 'Adila is playing beautifully at this moment': which Jelly thought even sillier, because she had left Adila in London for an afternoon concert there and she never made mistakes about what people she loved were doing.

When however she telephoned to ask Adila how the concert had gone, she was staggered to hear that it had after all taken place at the time this 'signal' came through the silly questions.

Some four or five weeks later she decided to play the game again. A love affair had reached an end, and she needed some kind of comfort, support or guidance. Now still when in a crisis she missed the wise sympathy of her mother; and maybe there was a feeling at the back of her mind that there might be some truth in these 'messages', and if so, the spirit of her mother might help her. But she suggested it merely as a game.

Her companion was Anna Robertson, friend and assistant of Jelly and Adila, who was in a similar state of depression. They had tried some diversion by lunching in Soho but without success; and motoring home, Jelly asked Anna Robertson in.

For some time the glass stayed still. Three letters were missing from the circle. These supplied, the glass moved three times in a slow circle, then darted from letter to letter. It spelt out sentiments like 'we are glad you are here' —not at all in the style of Madame d'Aranyi.

'Do I know you?' Jelly asked aloud, feeling a fearful fool when there was nobody to know. The reply was that the person had left earth before Jelly was born, and wanted her to find and play a posthumous work for violin.

This was the year of the Brahms Centenary. Jelly had recently

The Sisters d'Aranyi

played the *Double Concerto for Violin and 'Cello* with Gaspar Cassadó and the Royal Philharmonic.* And if any dead composer had been in her mind it would have been Brahms. But when she asked if she might know who was speaking, and the letters got as far as ROBERTS, she thought that either her companion was playing a trick or her subconscious mind was doing so.

Instead the glass finished CHUMANN.

'Is it the *Fantasia*?' she asked. She had more than once played this work, which was dedicated to Joachim. But no, it was something never published. A violin concerto. 'It is in Germany. In a museum, we think.'

'Is it good?' asked Jelly: the first thing that came into her head. The reply was that it was 'not one of my best works, but much better than a good deal that is being written today.'**

Anna Robertson, who didn't much like this sort of pastime in any case, refused to do any more, but Jelly told Adila and tried to find out more about this work, of whose existence she had never heard.

She went to H. C. Colles, *The Times* music critic, who received her in his study with shelves of books behind him. He took down one of the dark blue volumes of Grove's *Dictionary of Music and Musicians*, the third edition of which he had himself supervised in 1928. After studying an article he said 'There's no such thing.'***

She asked Guy Liddell, who asked other likely people such as Edwin Fischer and Klingler. They knew nothing, but Klingler replied rather pompously that there would be no sense in looking for it, as it couldn't do Schumann justice.[1]

She asked her cousin Elizabeth, wife of Harold Joachim of Oxford, herself a grand-daughter of Onkel Jo, just as her husband

---

*'It was a unique performance' Jelly says with glee. 'It was *good*!'

**According to a later source it was said here that the work was for violin and piano, and 'probably in D minor.' Of this more later.

***There was a short reference in the Third edition; indeed the concerto was mentioned in the First Edition, of 1883, according to Edwin Evans, *Time and Tide*, Feb. 26th, 1938.

The Truth About the Schumann Concerto

was his grand-nephew. She said she knew nothing about such a thing. Jelly applied again to the glass. It said 'Robert Schumann. Remember what I told you. Museum Weimar.'

She tried Tovey. Tovey was more informative. He recalled, and analysed from memory, some manuscripts shown him by Eugénie Schumann (daughter) at Interlaken, which she was about to present to the Schumann Museum at Zwickau: but no violin concerto. About the 'messages' he called himself a 'scornful sceptic.'[2] But with his intimate knowledge of Joachim he did know that Schumann had written a *Violin Concerto* in 1853, which he thought was in D minor, though he did not know what had become of the manuscript.

It was generally thought, among those who did remember, that Joachim, Clara Schumann and Brahms, after long study and discussion and a private run-through by Joachim at the Leipzig Gewandhaus in 1867,[3] had sadly decided that it showed signs of Schumann's imminent mental breakdown in its lack of inventive control and of sustained inspiration; that Clara Schumann had asked Joachim to write a new *finale* and he refused; and that Joachim, after the deaths of Clara Schumann in 1896 and of Brahms in 1897, had deposited it somewhere with a proviso that it was not to be published or performed within a hundred years of Schumann's death in 1856. The three had concealed their feelings from Schumann, 'Oh!' he cried in a letter to Joachim 'if I could hear your rendering of my *D minor Concerto,* which Clara speaks of with such enthusiasm!'

But nobody knew where the manuscript lay, except presumably some uninterested and unknown guardian. In this sense only was it 'lost'—a word to be abused in what followed. The actual locator and first outsider to set eyes on it for many years now comes before us.

This was Baron Erik Palmstierna, Swedish Minister in London, a man in his early fifties. He had written books which according to his obituary in *The Times*[4] in 1959 were considered among the best guides to Swedish political history in the first part of the twentieth century. He had been very religious since his boyhood

The Sisters d'Aranyi

in the Swedish Navy, when he used to annotate his bible in the crow's nest. By all accounts a lovable person, and a close friend of the Fachiris. In fact it was at Adila's house in Florence after she retired that he was staying when he died of heart trouble.

Palmstierna was mildly interested in psychic matters, but had never been to a séance. Neither had Adila, though her resistance to the possibility of 'communication' had been lessened when a friend discovered by these means where to find the drowned body of her mother. He and she agreed to follow up the Schumann matter.

About a week later all four were staying on holiday at a hotel in Studland Bay, where in a private sitting-room they tried the 'glass game'. Transcripts of this and other sessions, from verbatim notes, were the basis of a book Palmstierna wrote later. I have seen copies. They bear every trace of having been typed out, not very well, at the time.

In July 1933[5] the glass intimated that Joachim was in touch. When asked if he could locate the manuscript, 'he' replied that it ought to be in the Museum of the Berlin Royal High School of Music, but he couldn't remember for certain. In reply to the question Why had Schumann said Weimar: 'He showed it to me there. *Mein Kind*, we do not know everything.'

Jelly wrote to the Director of this Museum but got no reply. At the end of the month the glass indicated Schumann's anxiety that something should be done. When they answered that they had written, they were told the addressee was away.

In August, Jelly and the Fachiris went for their usual summer holiday to Scotland, and Baron Palmstierna back to Sweden for his. He returned by train viâ Berlin, where he had some hours to wait for a connection. It occurred to him to go to the Royal High School (now the 'Royal' had been dropped) and look for himself. The Director was in fact still away, ill; and a young secretary produced what there was in the Library. They came on a folder marked with Schumann's name, but it contained only odds and ends of music by other composers. A bystander advised the Baron to try the Prussian State Library.

The Truth About the Schumann Concerto

Here too the Director, Herr Wolff, was away, on holiday. Palmstierna had some difficulty with his assistant. But in the end he was shown the manuscript of a violin *Concerto* by Schumann in piano score, but not in his hand, and marked Unfinished. On September 14th he telegraphed to the Aranyis that he had found the *Concerto*.[6] It was the wrong manuscript.

According to Professor Schünemann later, when he had succeeded to the Directorship, there were four relevant manuscripts: (1) a version by a copyist with headings and corrections by Schumann, (2) the piano score just mentioned, (3) the violin part, (4) a complete orchestral score with the piano part written-in on the lowest staves. These piano staves are not included in the published version. The layout is unusual: strings at the top, then woodwind, then brass.

Finding was one thing, getting permission for copies to be made and for performance was quite another, and took several years. The guardians absolutely refused public access of any kind till the ban should lapse in 1956. In England the glass kept urging patience, determination, and careful handling.

In the meantime Jelly gave the first performance for over a century and a half of a musical curiosity believed to be authentic: in November 1933 she played the so-called *Adelaide Concerto*, which Mozart wrote for, and under the eyes of, the eldest daughter of Louis XV, when he was ten.

Robert Casadesus had found the manuscript of this, written in two lines of music only (solo or *tutti* + bass), which had been kept by the family at Trieste ever since Madame Adélaide of France emigrated there in 1791 together with violin and bow, also preserved.[7] It was dated 1766, but at a place where scholars said that Mozart could not have been on the day given: and though Casadesus was challenged to prove its authenticity, he never did.

Willy Strecker, the head in Mainz of Schott and Son, the music publishers who printed the concerto, came over to London for Jelly's performance. She told him about the *Schumann Concerto* and what they were trying to do. At first he too was sceptical. 'Do you think that if such a thing existed, I would not have

The Sisters d'Aranyi

known?' But in the end he undertook to do what he could in Germany.

The glass was pleased at this, saying Strecker had the key; they should leave it to him and meantime have patience, 'a hard thing on earth'. It used German.*

Strecker applied to Professor Altmann at the Prussian State Library, but there was nothing to be done. The authorities were adamant. The Austrian pianist Würher, who had been in England, tried too. He reported that not even Professor Altmann was allowed to take the manuscript home with him.

The glass suggested getting in touch with Elizabeth Joachim and through her with Johannes, Onkel Jo's eldest son who lived in Göttingen. With their permission it might be possible to buy the manuscript. Johannes Joachim gave Jelly permission to have a copy made, provided she kept it to herself and never played it in public. But even this was refused by the authorities. The conditions on which the manuscript had become State property must not be altered, it seemed, even at the request of the man who laid them down.

For it now turned out that it was not Clara Schumann nor Joachim who had deposited the manuscript anywhere after Schumann's death.

Schumann's surviving daughter Eugénie, when she was eighty-six, issued two printed pages in which** she described an impressive scene at Frankfurt, when her mother came into the room and announced that she, Joachim and Brahms had taken the de-

---

*The glass seems to have moved, apart from on a table, on a most ethereal plane. Alexandre Fachiri once while writing down the words, called out that it was now just gibberish. It was in fact good Hungarian, purporting to come from the loved uncle who had died on Jelly's thirteenth birthday. Part was in English too, a tongue the uncle never understood. 'Here we have no languages. We can reach you in any language you know.'

**Eugénie Schumann, Über Das Letzte Werk Ihres Vaters Robert Schumann (no date, publisher nor printer). Most of this was published in The Times (January 15th, 1938) headed 'A Plain Statement'. It was answered by a whole column from Tovey, saying that the very same piety toward Schumann's good name which made publication imprudent when critics were trying to run down Schumann's entire work because of his mental condition at the end of his life, could now be invoked to do his name justice.

The Truth About the Schumann Concerto

cision against making the concerto public 'neither now nor ever (*nicht jetzt und überhaupt nicht*)'. She solemnly laid the manuscript in Joachim's hands, on this understanding; and he told the family afterward that he was preserving it with a note 'This must never be made public.'

After Joachim's death a quantity of music manuscripts was sold at a valuation, and the State Library took its choice, including the *Schumann Concerto*: which explains why there is no mention of the matter in Moser's *Life of Joachim*, which had been published in 1901.* Although this was a sale, Johannes, thinking he was carrying out his father's wishes, laid the embargo on publication within a hundred years of Schumann's death.

Eugénie Schumann was evidently sincere in thinking the ban was for ever; she said her information came from Joachim himself. But as Elizabeth Joachim wrote in a letter to *The Times*, either he thought he had made it for ever, or Miss Schumann had misheard.

Mrs Reginald McKenna, wife of the banker-politician and friend of Jelly, was in Berlin at the beginning of November 1934 on a visit to our Embassy. Palmstierna suggested that she examine the actual wording of the embargo, in case there might be some legal loophole. He also suggested, more ingenuously, that our Ambassador approach Hitler directly.[8]

She saw Dr Krüss, the General Director of the Library. He could do nothing about the ban, but he showed her a manuscript, it does not appear clearly which. She, who was a good musician, described it, but said there were several pages blank with numbered bars. When she pressed for photostats to be made for Jelly, Dr Krüss said that many manuscripts were entrusted to the Library under conditions, and to make one exception would be to cause complications later. Also once a copy had gone out of his hands, he could never be sure it would not be played or made

---

*Letter from Elizabeth Joachim to Alexandre Fachiri Oct. 21st (no year), quoting a letter just received from Johannes. In this he stated that one movement of the concerto was once played at a Schumannfeier rehearsal in Zwickau by a lady whose name he did not remember.

other use of. And from this bureaucratic platitude he refused to budge.*

There for the moment the question of performance stopped. But German musicologists, now that attention had been drawn to the manuscript, seem to have had all the scholarly access they wanted: for in December 1935, Hermann Springer published in French in *La Revue Musicale* an article headed *Les Péripéties du Concert pour Violon Inédit,* which quoted from Joachim's letter to Moser, gave the affecting cry of Schumann already told of, and was accompanied by a facsimile of the first page. Thus far at least the fruits of Jelly's diligence ripened for musicologists and violinists the world over.

The glass, however, renewed its pleas for action. In November 1936 it begged Jelly to take the matter very seriously: *'Sie müssen das Concerto erhalten.'* And *'Remember Schumann!'*

But by then it was too late. Professor Altmann had died; and Willy Strecker, meeting his successor in Unter den Linden the following month, was informed that the official decision had been revoked: but the first performance of the work which was to be published by Breitkopf and Hartel would be given in a version revised by Hindemith and played by the leading German violinist Georg Kulenkampf.[9] Further, 'that ghastly Nazi' as Jelly called him, wanted a twenty-five-year world monopoly.[10]

Shocked, Strecker telephoned to the Fachiri house as soon as he arrived in London. Jelly was in bed ill, and Adila came back from the telephone appalled. But after all, the decision conformed to Nazi idealogy. Schumann was a full-blooded Teuton and Joachim a full-blooded Jew. Consistent for Hitlerites that the world's first performance (for the unknown lady's may have had piano accompaniment) should be given by an 'Aryan'.

Eugénie Schumann tried hard to get the embargo renewed for ever, but gave up when her legal advisers persuaded her that in any case the concerto would be made public eventually. But

---

*Letter from Mrs Reginald McKenna to Jelly d'Aranyi, November 3rd, 1934. It should be noted that this corrects Edwin Evans's otherwise accurate account in *Time and Tide*, already quoted, which says such a copy was made.

The Truth About the Schumann Concerto

German bureaucracy was not to eat its bone in smugness. What struck Strecker to the heart was Breitkopf's announcement of forthcoming publication. Had it not been for the efforts made in and from England, the manuscript would still be lying unused and forgotten. It was he who had been fighting for the release of the 'imprisoned concerto' as one writer correctly called it:[11] and seeing that he and others had first been awakened and then prodded to liberate it by Jelly d'Aranyi, fairness itself, apart from her relation to Joachim, ought to award to her of all top-line violinists the honour and the responsibility of its first interpretation.

He wrote for approval and support to the Joachims and got both; but neither prevailed against the Nazi government. In the end it was he who prevailed—or to a remarkable extent. Such was the vigour and self-assurance of this man, that he called a meeting of German officials and argued them into granting, as a first point, publication to his firm.

More time passed. The Germans announced and then postponed the date of the first performance in the Reichskulturkammer. However, Strecker had manoeuvred with skill. His right of publication covered disposal of performance outside Germany, and no more was said of a twenty-five-year monopoly. At last the arrangements seemed fixed as follows. Kulenkampf would play on October 19th, 1937, Jelly in London on the 20th in a BBC Concert, and Yehudi Menuhin, to whom Strecker had sent a photostat copy, and who was enthusiastic about the work, would give the first performance on the other side of the Atlantic later in the year. Menuhin wished to play it exactly as Schumann wrote it.

This arrangement was cancelled, and Kulenkampf's performance postponed to November 13th. Menuhin had set his concert for the 3rd, and had to put it off.[12] But the BBC was in a more difficult position. Their planning of music programmes was months ahead of actuality, and alterations were fraught with woe. When a public concert is concerned, and altered for outside reasons, the permutations and combinations of new detail become dauntoning. It was not feasible to find a new date so quickly.

But the Press had got hold of the story, even stating that Sir Adrian Boult, then the BBC Director of Music, and the Assistant Director Kenneth Wright, had left for Berlin immediately.[13] Although this was not the case, the matter had reached national diplomatic levels. Boult advised Jelly to write to the Prime Minister. Now Jelly was no fighter, nor did she like the publicity of self-importance; but she did have a natural pride (or should I say humility?) of possessiveness toward her protégé concerto. So she wrote to Neville Chamberlain, who replied that the Foreign Office was taking up the case with Berlin, and he hoped all would go well, since he personally was looking forward to hearing her in this work.[14]

All did not go well.

The Germans again altered the date, and on October 2nd Strecker wrote to Boult, asking him to postpone Jelly's concert till February *16th* following.[15] The reason for this date, and indeed the reason for so long a postponement, are not clear. At this distance of time Sir Adrian cannot help to make them so, and the minutes of the weekly Music Meetings have not survived the war.[16] No more than Jelly was Boult inclined to this kind of publicity, even in an almost-world première of a never-heard classic. Though the BBC would have liked to give the first British performance as the first in the world outside Germany, he had, when fixing the original date of the Symphony Concert, given Jelly full freedom to play it elsewhere first if she wished.[17] This arrangement still held. But Jelly was neither equal nor willing to organize such a thing; and they both agreed to the February date.

However on October 26th Boult wrote to Jelly saying he had just read in *Signals* that Germany had again changed the date for Kulenkampf, this time to November 26th. It did not affect the BBC, who had retired; but it sent a nasty googly to Menuhin, who was still batting, and had fixed his new date for the 14th.

Meanwhile an excited and grateful Jelly was studying the score.[18] She had been far from convinced of Hindemith's suit-

The Truth About the Schumann Concerto

ability as a reviser, but Tovey assured her that she would find he had done the job well. When her copy arrived in March, she did not like his alterations and was worried also about the proper interpretation of passages he had not touched. At Carnwath in August she, Adila and Palmstierna asked advice of the glass.

According to the replies Schumann did not like the new version either. 'It is not his technique'. Which was only to be expected. Hindemith had not long published his *Treatise on Harmony*, and his heart and mind were in contemporary problems, not traditional ones. Also the concerto was too 'full', and he had made it fuller.

Again according to the replies, there was little that needed doing to the original, and this little could be done by Jelly. It is important to know that Jelly did not touch the glass, that Palmstierna had never heard her practising the work, and Adila only the first movement once.[19] For a quite startling series of swift questions and answers follows in the transcripts on purely musical matters, composition and technical detail. Some passages could be played in a higher register; some of the accompaniment could be thinned out; 'you can take out some of the notes if the harmony does not suffer. You can also use your judgment about bowing and often broaden the tone.'

Jelly asks, for example, about Hindemith's first alteration, which was a register higher. Answer; 'Can you add a few notes and can you play the demi-semi-quavers very strongly and with a firm *legato*? Firm bowing. Not with the runs but the double stops. Do not play in a sharp tone but very broad and smooth.'

And so forth, from the chords at the beginning to be played 'with the low note separately and repeat the low note again' down to details like 'not on a thin kind of *spiccato* but one from the wrist in regular horizontal movement, the bow a little sideways.' 'Keep your outbursts as a complete surprise. Your uncle knew that secret.'

Often there were initial confusions about which passages exactly were intended. Bar numbers meant nothing.

Jelly was not at all at ease about her ability to do the editing;

but she did use her judgment, and the musician in her did not let her down. When she was ready, she went off to Hedenham Lodge, Tovey's Queen Anne house in Suffolk, where they played together, he from the piano score, she from memory of her own violin version. When they had finished, Tovey spun his piano stool round three times, crying 'You see what a good job Hindemith has made of it! You can trust every note of Hindemith.'

Actually Jelly had changed about 200 bars in the whole work, and these only in the violin part. But Tovey's approval of her work rejoiced her so much that she wrote to Anna Robertson 'I am terribly happy and in love with both life and death.'[20]

She was by now convinced that the 'messages' did originate in some sort of spiritual force, though not necessarily in a different geographical habitat.

And so the time drew near for Jelly to play the work, and the news of the 'spirit messages' broke vulgarly on an incredulous public. It broke first in a BBC News Bulletin on September 23, 1937.[21]

Of course reactions differed. There were convinced believers in a spirit world who triumphed. There were sceptics who scoffed at spooks. There were protests against resuscitating before its time a work which was sure to prove dull. And there were the cranks. One lady wrote to Tovey that she was in touch with a Tibetan Lama.[22]

Tovey had written to *The Times* a long letter, which he thought them generous to print in full, defending the disinterment of the concerto now rather than in 1956, when it would be merely a centenary affair with no effect as reparation of an injustice to Schumann's memory. 'Ordinary human intercourse' he observed with insight when part-composing this as a letter to Jelly, 'and the understanding of other people's thoughts by means of reading and writing are as mysterious to me as any other forms of thought-reading.' Then what begins as a hand-written letter of four pages becomes seven sheets more dictated to a typewriter, with a final one of even greater interest added in pen and ink. If only there

The Truth About the Schumann Concerto

were a mediaeval leisure for readers and a Victorian spaciousness for writers today, I would quote it in full.

He accepted neither a 'spiritualistic' nor a 'mechanical' explanation of the messages. He took as analogy a remarkable anticipation of the day when 'music will be directly writeable in terms of phonographic tracks, so that all the thousand and one limitations of musical instruments will be replaced by the more general limitations of the most marvellous phonographic methods.'

In the same way 'it is not impossible that the ultra-microscopic physical movements of grey matter and brain convolutions that accompany thought in living people may someday be traceable as they proceed.' This will not carry us a step forward in connecting mind with matter, but it is as far as mechanism will take us. 'I do not say materialism because materialism became the most abstruse metaphysical tangle as soon as time got mixed up with space.'

Though he does not so define it, Tovey had arrived at the point where many really individual people arrive: that each gloriously unique individual by nature since the beginning of nature (that is to say, all of us) has no significance by himself but is biologically, emotionally, metaphysically and historically part of everyone else in all time and all space.

'I can't wait to find words for my positive belief' he went on 'but I am more and more convinced that the main revelation that awaits us will be something like the discovery that many terms which we use metaphorically have always been so literally true that the stodgiest nineteenth-century materialist need never have misunderstood them—that, in fact, when one person communicates ideas with another by any means whatever, a corresponding amount of personality, or spirit, is transferred; that you and I and Adila have by this time a good deal of Schumann in us; and that that amount of Robert Schumann is *personally* anxious that a piece of his later music should not remain stigmatized as insane.... If we do what is now commonly called 'tapping the subconscious', we can, no doubt, extract from ourselves masses of information identifiable with persons past, or present, which we should otherwise have failed to obtain or not obtained so soon.'

With this explanation, or adumbration, by one who had called himself a scornful sceptic, many open-minded people may agree. The jocular side of the popular press did not; which distressed Jelly.[23] But, as Ernest Newman wrote to her,[24] 'You need not mind if jokers indulge in a little mild humour about the subject; it's a small world, and not everyone sees anything from the same point of view as everyone else.'

Adila was content with a purely spiritual explanation, so long as she was not thereby committed to mediums and ectoplasms: Jelly still disliking emotionalism knew only that what had happened to her had happened. She saw no reason to suppose that the thought or spirit of Robert Schumann had not somehow got into touch with her thought or spirit: which gave her a quiet, warm, pleased sense of belonging to founts of music bigger than herself. But when she tried to get confirmation of past facts, a cloud of midges surrounded her. Colles, for example, was not to be reached on the telephone, and his wife strongly denied that he had ever said he knew nothing about a Schumann *violin concerto.**

Elizabeth Joachim went so far as to write a protest to *The Listener,* saying that many friends of hers and of the Schumann family had always known that the manuscript had been given (*sic*) to the Museum, and that one performance of the work had been given by Adolf Busch, she believed, at Zwickau, which had widened knowledge of its existence. When Jelly, Alexandre and his small daughter Adrienne took the next train to Oxford to ask what she meant by this, she said she was sick of this talk about spirit messages. It had been only in 1934 when speaking to her brother that she had remembered exactly where the manuscript was buried; and she gave Jelly a letter[25] to this effect with permission to use it as she liked. Jelly published it in *The Times*

---

*It must be added, however, that Colles later wrote Jelly a letter full of friendly concern and goodwill, but as he marked it Private and Confidential, I do not quote from it.

The Truth About the Schumann Concerto

with a covering letter which won from Elizabeth Joachim a telegram of thanks.

This flight of the spook-haters had been caused largely by a two-page article in *The Listener*, by Rollo Myers, musicologist and music assistant in the BBC press department, who had telephoned Jelly for information. It gave the facts about the process of location and quoted from Baron Palmstierna's book *Horizons of Immortality*, which was about to be published, very timely but by chance so, on September 23rd. Many of the details about the Schumann concerto affair are given in the part of his book called 'Retrospect'; but in this chapter I have gone by Jelly's own memory and the transcripts. That the three coincide is of course no proof of anything.[26]

Myers spoke of the absolute and unimpeachable integrity of those concerned, and this respectfulness was the rule among the better class of newspapers like *The Times* and the *Daily Telegraph*.

What people really wanted to hear, and what was more important than the method of its location, was the concerto itself; and so came the day of performance, February 16, 1938 in the Queen's Hall with Sir Adrian Boult conducting the BBC Symphony Orchestra. The concert opened with the *Grosse Fugue*, one of Beethoven's last and grandest compositions, and ended after the interval with the *Second Symphony* of Sibelius. Almost all musical Britain was either there or listening-in.

There was a plethora of letters and telegrams for Jelly, one of the most affecting coming from Alfred and Herbert, Schumann's grandson and great-grandson, written in English from Berlin. Rather a solemn little letter, in which both hope to hear the broadcast and which ends 'Our best thanks, dear Miss d'Aranyi, to your violin for singing Robert Schumann's soul.'[27]

Jelly shone out from the black-and-white orchestra in a white and silver lamé dress by Molyneux.[28] As she waited for the opening orchestral section to give her first entry, her habitual expression of contemplative expectation seemed deeper than ever. It was perhaps to her the greatest moment of her musical life so far, a life already rich in great moments. A friend said she looked 'initiate'.

She may have looked so, but for some minutes she felt nothing but the fact that she had not put on the dress before getting ready for the concert, and the shoulder puffs rustled with every movement of her bow arm!

Whether the concerto had been taken as good, bad or indifferent, she received an ovation. And there was an enormous party at the Fachiris' after, with, as one delighted guest wrote, 'a home-made supper far surpassing the usual ones supplied by caterers at parties.' The twelve-year-old daughter of the house helped to see that all guests had everything; and the small figure in white and silver moved among them radiant and triumphant.[29]

The concerto was repeated on the regional wave-length from the big new studio at Maida Vale the following Sunday.[30] Jelly played it in many places later, including Lausanne and Geneva. In Switzerland the critic Moser said of her *'Son bras est plus forte de sa tête:'* but Swiss critics found fault with everyone. This one had even slated Kreisler, and they still slate Stern, to Jelly's indignation. She was to have played it also in Holland in the winter of 1939.

On March 25th she gave it in Edinburgh at a charity concert organized by Rosalind Maitland. Mrs Maitland had heard the first broadcast in a tiny workman's cottage on the shores of Loch Broom, where she was supervising alterations to the Maitlands' highland home at Dundonnell. The gardener brought in his prized wireless set and they listened together. Five weeks before the Edinburgh concert all the expensive seats were sold out, only two rows left at 5s. and a place or two at 3s 6d.[31]

In general the first two movements were preferred to the last, especially the *adagio,* the theme of which Joachim had called 'as warm and heartfelt as anything Schumann wrote,' though he felt that even here the theme meandered and the flow faltered.[32] Ernest Newman agreed with the majority about the first two movements, but with Joachim about the last, always most important because the public gets from this its conclusive impres-

The Truth About the Schumann Concerto

sion. But he hoped the first two would pass into the violin repertory.[33]

This cannot be said to have happened. A few violinists play the concerto, notably Shevrin and Lissi. There is no recording of Jelly's interpretation. At that time the BBC seldom preserved a long programme on processed discs, and tapes were not yet in general use.

This is a pity. But those of us who heard it have not lost all scent in the fumes of more recent sounds. 'The last movement' I have just said to Jelly 'may be a wee bit ordinary for a late work by Schumann; but I can recapture the magic of those octaves after twenty-eight years.'

Jelly's bright eyes smiled, gay and guilty. 'The octaves? In the first movement? As a matter of fact I thought the melody needed strengthening there a bit.'

Use your judgment about bowing and often broaden the tone.

16

The Pilgrimage of Compassion

Celebrity is not all purring in sunshine. An artist in his art gives himself; he may also have to give away part of his personal privacy: especially a performing artist.

If he is poor in people, his celebrity will only aggravate his bitter loneliness, and he can give little. But if he is rich in people, his celebrity will bring him more and more that he can give away. That is why Compton Mackenzie, who often says he should have been called Felix, having been happy as well as lucky, except in health, spends his mornings in such charitable acts as opening cat shows or matters less interesting than Siamese cats.

Jelly too was rich in people, as Adila was. And never in their lives did the one or the other have to give an audition, except to get into the Budapest Academy. Both were generous, impulsively or after thought, because both knew that in all fame there is also luck. And sweetness became a habit.

Celebrities can find themselves in strange junctures. In 1934 Jelly was asked to appear at the Bath Pump Room in a lively sort of evening coyly called 'Happy Night'; during which she performed the Beethoven *Violin Concerto* with the Pump Room Orchestra between what is called 'Light Classical' numbers.[1] She quite enjoyed this.

In 1930 she broadcast in the USA in a programme billed as 'At the Baldwin Half-Hour'. The script takes a lot of believing. At one point a person is instructed to cry impromptu *into applause* 'Why

The Pilgrimage of Compassion

Miss d'Aranyi! You play that Spanish dance just like a Spaniard!'[2]

She had to present the banners at the Leith Hill Festival. But she felt such a fool as she stood with violin in one hand and floral tribute in the other, stuttering, and forgetting what to say or the words to say it in, or any right words, that she didn't sleep a wink on that night's journey to Keswick. To this day she does not know that she had been giving all the same, all the time, without need of being a sleek public speaker.

Celebrity means also meeting other celebrities; and this she greatly enjoyed. After a concert in Oxford Town Hall she went to an Oxford party. It was a lovely June evening, with Jupiter and Mars very close together in a clear sky. She played on the lawn. Einstein was at the party.

It may not be known to everybody that Einstein was no indifferent performer on the violin. He came to the Deneke house the next night, and played second in two Mozart *String Quintets* (*in G minor and in E♭*) with Jelly and Arthur Williams, and with Emma Schotz and Margaret Reid as the two violas. He comported himself with such credit as an ensemble-player, that as Jelly said to him at the end, his Time was relative only twice. On her score he wrote '*Der Haupt und Staats Hexe, Albert Einstein.*'

Jelly stayed often with the Denekes. In 1928 she had had another recital in the Town Hall, and was horrified to find that the same evening Albert Schweitzer was holding a meeting elsewhere in the city for his African mission. She had a good attendance herself, but was upset at having split a potential audience for so fine and dedicated a man in a cause so welcome to herself. She later sent him a cheque.

Like Adila she was always ready to appear for charities. In 1951 the Bishop of Bath and Wells asked her to Bath Abbey in aid of the building fund. He made the appeal himself, and received a cheque from a Roman Catholic, who explained that the Abbey would soon be back in the hands of the Church that built it. This shocked broad-minded Bishop Bradfield no more than had another letter, addressed to Messrs Bath and Wells.

The Sisters d'Aranyi

Between the wars Jelly was continually playing for all sorts of causes from a children's hospital[3] to a society which took care[4] of jobless women over thirty; and in places as different as a Harley Street house with an audience mostly of well-known medical men to Castle Howard, in the Long Gallery (160 feet long and only 23 feet wide with an octagonal chamber halfway along—but the acoustics were unexpectedly good) with an audience of local aristocrats and Gilbert Murray.

As we have seen, the sisters were neither socialists nor slummers, but they were never unaware of other people's hardships and miseries. I do not suppose either approved of the General Strike of 1926, any more than most middle-class folk did. But they did not curse the workers and cry for vengeance. They went to see what they could do. Nobody could do much. Even Lord Haldane[5] did not know what was happening, and thought the Revolution had come. All the Aranyis could do was music. They played. For example the Bach *Double Concerto* in Whitechapel to 'a very rough audience of men and boys'.

This of course solved nothing in a national deadlock with every service paralysed and tanks in reserve for civil war in Hyde Park. Everyone tense with anxiety. Even with dread. Hilda Matheson, just about to begin steering the hardly-born BBC in an exploration of the real point and nature of radio talks, was as concerned as anyone. But seven years later she remembered the effect of this concerto on that audience. It is important later in this chapter.

1926 was the first, and so far the last, real trial of strength between British capital and British labour. A short and drawn battle, leaving the uneasy symbiosis which still obtains. Five or six years later, with less personal bitterness but worse personal suffering, industrial and financial conditions in the whole country began to collapse. The spiritual results were ghastly. People were not now angry. They were baffled and desperate, because nobody knew whom or what to blame, and so could not act. The worst paid were the worst hit. The Means Test, last barrier before actual starvation, could be very humiliating, and cruel,

The Pilgrimage of Compassion

and often unjust. Mines, mills, factories, shipyards closed down. The North of England and South Wales were the most grievous regions.

Jelly herself was in no happy position. In 1931 she was still technically Hungarian: for she held it dishonest for a foreign-born musician to masquerade as a Briton; and it was only at the time of the Silver Jubilee of George V in 1935 that she applied for naturalization: 'out of gratitude'.

But by the winter of 1931 foreign musicians were being excluded from giving concerts in Britain. Even for an International Celebrity Concert the Quartette Instrumentale de Paris[6] was forbidden entry to this country despite appeals on ambassadorial levels: and Tovey was so incensed when a foreign pupil of his was banned from a concert, that he resigned from the Incorporated Society of Musicians.

Jelly never knew if continuous residence would protect her in a country where residence as such hardly exists at law. What did protect her was now not her personal friends, but her profession's need of her. So much so, that when the Ministry of Labour stopped a broadcast by the French violinist Renée Chenet, it was Jelly who was asked to substitute.

By the spring of 1933 it seemed as if nobody could save Britain from the financial fate of post-war Germany. But a number of groups tried to get up some and any kind of help for the unemployed out of such private pockets as could still afford it. Katharine Tennant, for example, a connection of the Asquiths, was trying to organize funds for alternative employment. She asked Jelly if she would give her a recital some time next winter. Jelly said 'Why not now?'[7]

Maybe she remembered the 'rough men and boys' of Whitechapel. Maybe she also remembered, for sheer beauty of sound, the effect of her violin when she had played the Bach *Chaconne* to a few friends in the quiet of Exeter Cathedral.[8] Or maybe she just acted on an inspired impulse. Anyway, Katharine Tennant and she started writing to the Deans of a number of cathedrals up and down the country, asking leave to give public recitals in

The Sisters d'Aranyi

them, beginning with York Minster and the helpful Castle Howard Norfolks not far distant.

When Jelly had played the Brahms *Concerto* in Gloucester Cathedral, she had not been aware of any atmosphere of reverence for a holy place. The Three Choirs Festival had long lost its eighteenth-century sacred origins, and had become a national musical and social event like Handel's *Messiah*. Not that some ecclesiastics did not object. One Bishop refused to preach, and Chapters sometimes refused to let the Festival take place. But it went on all the same.

What Jelly had in mind was something different. With her sense of locality she knew the effect of noble music in a noble building. Both could be put to social use. Compared with the millions needed by the millions, it was nothing. Compared with what she could do, it was everything.

The Deans were eager: she met some in London. She chose works not necessarily sacred, and certainly without the sentimentality of Stainer or Barnby: works which could not only fit a Cathedral but add to it. The *adagio in A minor* from Bach's *Toccata in C* which Siloti had arranged for violin; the *adagio* from Mozart's *Concerto in A major*; the unaccompanied Bach *Chaconne*; the whole of Handel's *Sonata in A*; the *larghetto* of the Beethoven *Concerto*; Purcell's *Air in G*; and the slow movement of the *Mendelssohn Concerto*.

So an hour and a quarter of thoughtful musical masterpieces began to float through the still air from wall to wall of ten masterpieces of architecture.

At each place she was accompanied on the cathedral organ by the cathedral organist, who knew the acoustics better than she could, and who in most cases moderated his multiple giant accordingly. At York this was Sir Edward Bairstow; and in the words of *The Times* Jelly played in a broad[9] style which united her accustomed fire with a special spaciousness inspired by her surroundings. The acoustics here were not, after all, perfect, the first passages of the Handel sounded blurred, and many organ notes got lost in the clerestory. *The Times* would have preferred

The Pilgrimage of Compassion

the grand piano which had been put in the nave but was not touched. However, for beauty of sound as well as depth of expression, the experience, it said, was memorable. For this, as for several appearances, Jelly wore a modest brown and white printed frock she had bought in Brussels.[10] She stood at the choir screen.

This was the start of what the Dean of York in his appeal called 'A Pilgrimage of Compassion'. *The Times* headlined the phrase, and other newspapers took it up.

From York, Jelly went on to Hexham and Durham, staying with friends. At Hexham, J. Dykes Bower accompanied her, and in Durham Cathedral she played the *Chaconne* from the altar steps. A somewhat less banal meaning could now have been given to the words 'an angel with a violin'. Hexham Abbey Church seats 1,000, and crowds[11] were standing. Viscount Grey of Falloden here made the appeal. Jelly had only now realized the full effect she was making. 'I am so moved... I am quite speechless... it has been so wonderful' she said, when some women came up to thank her afterwards in Durham.

It should be remembered that this was in the middle of the summer, and these recitals took place in the evening. In the evening Durham becomes, like Southwell Minster, itself a complex musical composition in shadows and pale gold. They are moving enough without music.

On June 28th she was in Lincoln, with Dr Gordon Slater, in the Cathedral that had once heard the new music of William Byrd. Here her tone developed like organ stops, with a breadth at times rivalling that of the organ.

In Chichester she played from the organ loft beside Dr Harvey Grace, and came down to the Choir for the *Chaconne*. The crowd was so large that many had to listen from the Lady Chapel, and even in the Cloisters.

At Winchester, the acting organist played for her, and at Salisbury George Thalben-Ball, who came from the Temple Church to replace Sir Walter Alcock. The audience in Winchester topped 1,500.

The Sisters d'Aranyi

Thence to Westminster Abbey on July 10th, the first time in history that the Abbey had been loaned for a music recital. Here Adila joined Jelly in Purcell's *Golden Sonata*[12], the *andante* from a Spohr *Duo*, and the Bach *Double Concerto*.

May I remind the reader again of their performance of this last work? No record or rendering I have heard, and no other live performance, has equalled it, certainly not one of the most recent recordings by Kogan and Lizaveta Gillels. To give three or four examples: the quick repeated notes at the opening of the first movement set the intensity of the whole work. Kogan, for whom everybody has justly a very high regard, merely fiddles them: Adila made of them a cry of assertion and re-assertion, so that from then on we were caught up in the vividness of everything in the world: as, I think, Bach wrote it. Jelly made disagreement impossible.

Again, the repeated chords in the last movement: these were a confirmation of vivid solidity after the twofold hope in the loneliness of the *largo*. Kogan and Gillels take them as a romp, indeed the whole movement with them is a rush to catch a train by two skilled, graceful and unequal acrobats. Adila and Jelly, taking this slightly slower, had *fun* with the canon, tossing their delighted reassurance to each other like two celestial jugglers with two different graces beautifully matched. The glory of the work in the Abbey was in no way lessened by their playing from the organ loft against a stained glass window that brimmed with setting sun.

Usually a Dean or Bishop made the appeal. Here it was to have been Mr Stanley Baldwin, but he was kept at a debate in the House, and the Dean made it. There were seats for 3,000—more than for any event since the last Coronation: people arrived an hour early, and hundreds squatted on the floor.[13]

By now Jelly was exhausted and ill. She had spent the previous three days in bed. But this rest, for the time, did its healing work, and the sisters gave of the *Double Concerto* one of the finest performances of their lives. It was of this that Hilda Matheson wrote to Jelly from her country home in Sussex, recalling the

The Pilgrimage of Compassion

General Strike. 'A very different setting and audience, but something of the same response.'

Westminster was to have been the end and acme of the tour, but other Cathedrals offered themselves. Jelly was at Gloucester on July 13th, and at Bristol the day after, where she stood throughout inside the Choir. She stayed the night at King's Weston, the house Vanbrugh built for himself. Purcell must have been near her as she played his *Air* that night.

And so the end of the tour came in Canterbury, a pleasant spiral from its beginning in York. Here she was accompanied by W. T. Harvey. She played the *Chaconne* in the half-dark.[14] By its end the darkness was deeper. So was the silence of the people.

In every place admission and seats had been free, and collections were taken. The recital in Westminster Abbey raised over five hundred pounds, and the whole tour one thousand five hundred and sixty. As a result, the Government added a further thousand. It is pleasant to note that the entire expenses, printing, publicity and organization, rose to little more than forty-five pounds. Less than two per cent!

C. L. Graves in *Punch* wrote some lines of rather augustan verse, praising both sisters and ending:

> Blest pair of Sirens! whose seraphic strains
> Have lately echoed through our noblest fanes,
> Sisters, whose hearts with kindred fervour glow
> To ease our pangs of human want and woe.

And that made another agreeable spiral over jokes about ices and teacakes.

It is not surprising that Jelly received a summons from Windsor Castle to play the whole programme in St George's Chapel with Dr Harris. When she wanted to refuse the offered fee, she was told that the Queen specially wished her to take it, as she was always doing things for charity.

Her work for the unemployed did not end there. She kept on for years in Manchester, Newcastle, again Winchester, St Paul's. And not only for the unemployed.

The Sisters d'Aranyi

More from personal letters than from the press can we recapture the effect she made.

Thus in Westminster Abbey at the worst point of the slump: 'The crowd in the Nave were chiefly working people.... When you played the Mendelssohn something broke over all of us like a wave and transformed the audience. I noticed, when you finished it, that one or two people were very nearly crying, and all were moved. No one stirred for a minute or two; and after an interval they remained serene and tranquil. The expressions on their faces seemed to change somehow and lost that careworn look.'[15]

'In some way the connection between music and listener seemed closer than in many more intimate surroundings' wrote Mary L. McAndrew about Winchester.

This is a test of musicality. A mere virtuoso playing the *Chaconne* in a Cathedral, however nimble and accurate, could have excited as much admiration as in a hall. But nothing more. Indeed the Cathedral might well turn him into an organ-tuner amusing himself after finishing his job. Jelly's humble attitude to music, her intellectual search for meaning, her abandonment of herself to it, made the effect of her playing what can be called only spiritual, as many Deans and others wrote to her. The word 'bless' occurs often. 'This house and our cathedral have been blessed by having you' (Newcastle); 'It blessed the Cathedral and the Cathedral blessed it' (Canterbury). 'The audience were carried away into a different world altogether, rarely thought of and still more rarely visited.' This last of the Mendelssohn *adagio*.

When *Who's Who* asked Jelly for her entry, she wrote firmly at the end of her *curriculum vitae* 'Roman Catholic'. She has not altered this. But she never played in a Catholic cathedral on these ploys, and it meant nothing to her that what *Punch* called[16] these 'fanes' were Protestant. Such denominations were tints to her, and still are. But she felt, every time she played, and not only in cathedrals, that she was being opened to something greater than herself.

This matter is not limited to religious people. 'I wonder if you

The Pilgrimage of Compassion

have any idea of the inspiration people get from your music? Last Monday brought joy into many people's tired hearts.' That was written from Bristol Deanery in June 1943, when the Second War was near touching bottom. Naturally enough, for music is the putting of disorderly sensations into an order. Sensations are coupled with emotions. Emotions to a great degree influence thought. And thought is infinite.

So that apart from mere musical form and the composer's adroitness in solving mathematical problems, we are entitled to find other qualities in music: defiance, guts, gaiety, ruth, pathos, malice, wit, gloom, despair, horror, hate. We can speak justly of the Promethean will of Beethoven, the dreamy wonder of Debussy, the earthy faith of Bach, and so on great or small. We can also justify the words great or small. Even concrete music is Thought (never platitude) by vibration. If ever we reach supersonic music, that will be Thought too.

But music is also public. A symphony in a drawer is in as much a state of suspended animation as a play on a shelf. Most composers are public figures like orators, very much thinking of and into the public's ears. Any composer who ignores this is lost. He has to attract, convince, explain, compel, receive, change, restore, raise, lower, bludgeon, inspire his listeners up to as many verbs as the mind can think of out of an original mental process. The ends of most symphonies, and even of many movements, are calculated with as much showmanship and knowledge of effect, as an act in a circus. Some, if you read the last bars backwards, seem on analysis fully as banal, hackneyed and crude. They do not sound so, because of what has gone before. But for their full effect, even if of a quiet Chehov-like close, the composer depends on place and performer. Both must be available: and both mean people.

In 1933 people were bewildered, tensed, hopeless and helpless. They carried on; but so did their conditions, which seemed to have got out of everybody's control, in the power of superhuman forces none could understand; not even those who seemed responsible for the mess, and who carried on too.

The Sisters d'Aranyi

Anyone who has had anything to do with public relations knows that a big mind speaking truth with clarity is more than a politician. Winston Churchill may not have known that in 1926: in the war years he did. He spoke accordingly. As he rightly said, he did the roaring for the British lion.

It is more than musician too. In the world of music the crisis of 1933 was Jelly's finest hour. If man made great music, Jelly let man hear it, greatly, as it was written. The composers had the music, the people the ears: she had the violin. It was the true heart of Joachim all over again. At that point of time and space it was also the true heart of Jelly d'Aranyi.

PART III

Adila Fachiri

17

Divisions on a Ground

If nature gave Jelly fingers, she gave Adila an arm, formed for the violin. In proportion to the instrument this had perfect length for ease and a growing of skill. Add to this Adila's impetus, which a critic once described as plunging into the music with the boldness of a strong swimmer in the open sea. Add her musical showmanship: Jelly slipped quietly and simply on to the platform, and stood with her violin in one hand, holding her wrist with the other, while Adila made an entrance with a gleam in the eye, knowing she could make any passage she pleased wriggle inside the souls of her hearers. Add to these a nervousness, an ebullience, a surge and a force often called virile (though Adila was anything but a virile person): and you have a very different figure from the receptive Jelly.

At the same time, Adila was no less open to musical meaning, and no less humble toward herself as a musician. She practised from two to three-and-a-half hours every day without fail; often more; and five or six hours if a performance were imminent. On one occasion she practised for a whole six hours in a cabin, returning from Flushing: and on[1] another, the Brahms *Concerto* for the same space of time in a train going to Edinburgh. Especially every day she practised double-stopping, and advised Jelly to do the same.[2] But Jelly saw no point in playing slow things for mere exercise.

Adila's first solo appearance after the 1914-18 War was in

The Sisters d'Aranyi

March 1919 at Bournemouth, where she went, as always, unwilling to be parted for over three days from her husband. She had two dates at Bournemouth: a sonata recital with the Belgian woman composer Juliette Folville, whom she always found a most[3] sympathetic partner; and the other for the Beethoven *Concerto* under Dan Godfrey. Whether or not Juliette Folville had been an actual pupil of César Franck, I have not been able to discover. She certainly played with him or under his direction. This made her a valuable guide in the César Franck *Sonata*, which Adila had been playing through, liked, and decided to play it with only a week to practise. They did not perform it this time at Bournemouth, but Adila did so with George Reeves six days later in the Wigmore Hall (and was furious with *The Times* when Reeves came round[4] next morning dismayed by a bad notice). Juliette Folville was a woman verging on fifty, and their interpretation of the *Sonata* later was an authentic one, especially in the very gradual gathering of pace in the second movement, which was as César Franck himself had insisted.

Adila took some time to re-establish herself. At a concert with Jelly in the Wigmore Hall in May, at which *Sextets* by Brahms[5] and Glière were given, Alexandre (whom I think we may now call Alec) noted in the little diary which for a time he kept jointly, or alternately, with Adila, that Jelly was in wonderful form. A sonata recital with Tovey[6] in June attracted few people; perhaps because the last days of June are not a good date for concerts, or not for a re-beginner. At a rather more important concert she played a John Ireland *Sonata*, but although she notices 'They said I played well', she felt 'nervous and rotten': maybe because Alec could not be present. (After a fallow period Alec had three cases to plead at Geneva.) As late as 1922, when Adila gave in one concert a Mozart, the Beethoven and the Brahms *Concerti*, one critic observed that the great masters of the past had limited themselves to two concerti at one time, and that she had overtaxed her strength.[7]

It was much more the provinces that found her good and gave her confidence. A Paganini *Concerto* at Bournemouth, followed

Divisions on a Ground

by a lyrical holiday with Alec and Jelly at or near Lyme Regis dancing and bathing; big local successes at Oxford and Darlington, and even with a rather sleepy audience at Newcastle; back to Bournemouth again with again Juliette Folville, and for the Brahms *Concerto* under Adrian Boult, again over which she felt nervous, but it went well. At this time she sometimes tended to play the Brahms too roughly, though Birmingham liked her big, bracing style.

These, and many more engagements were well worth while; for they brought in twenty guineas or so, whereas she got only five pounds for a Prom.[8]

Even more than Jelly she was in demand as a paid soloist at private parties, rising through the rich to the royal. The Saxton Nobles, Baroness Knoep, the highly musical Cohens, the Runcimans, Prince Andrew of Greece and naturally her old friends the two royal Princesses. These too were worth while, for she got up to twenty-five guineas for each, even at a time when her playing of the Bach *Double Concerto* with Jelly brought them only ten pounds apiece.

The programmes were suited to the audience[9]; the usual form being a *sonata* by Bach or Sammartini, perhaps a Mozart or Brahms or Beethoven, and then a number of ear-ticklers which depended on the musicality of the gathering. Adila never played down, for most of their hostesses liked good music, and some programmes were worthy of a full-dress public recital. In 1932, for example, she introduced some discerning guests to Tartini's *Sonata in G*, once known as the '*Dido*', which she had rediscovered.[10]

Frequently these were mixed recitals, with Jelly, or a singer, or both. During the Joachim Centenary she and Jelly and Gabrielle Joachim were engaged together for several parties, and when the singer gave Bach's *Erbarme Dich*, Adila played the *obbligato*. During the Schubert Celebrations she and Jelly and Alec took part in the last *quartet in D minor* and the *Quintet in C* (op. 163) with two 'celli at a house in Bryanston Square.

When such parties were in aid of a charity, the fare tended to be lighter, but Adila always tried to be interesting. Thus in 1932 in aid of the Red Triangle Clubs, a very fashionable affair at the Park Lane Hotel with three fashionable opera-singers, Adila and Friedrich Würher played Grieg's *Sonata* (or *Duo*) *in C minor*. They repeated this at Londonderry House. It is not a very great work, and Adila, I think, did not ever play it at a big public concert, but she found it usefully limpid for schools.

Society was eager to hear new foreign performers, especially if their reputation preceded them. The most picturesque in Adila's company were two Hawaiians, wreathed in hibiscus, at the home of Sir Henry Grayson.[11] Here the *lieder*-singer Mark Raphael sang Roger Quilter; Margaret Elwes, daughter of the tenor, made her début; and Adila played six short pieces.

The most fervid in Adila's company[21] was undoubtedly Sasha Cherepnin, young son of the Russian Ballet composer, who had begun his career with, and largely thanks to, her in October 1922. She had met him in Paris, where she played his *Sonata in F* to a music publisher, who bought it on the spot. When Sasha came to London the following month, the Fachiris gave a party to twenty-three people in his honour. Adila and he and the *Sonata* were invited to Lady Deane Poole's because of the success they had had at a Wigmore Hall concert of his works. At the piano young Cherepnin's *fortissimi* sounded like a church organ's, and his music had a tone virile and purposeful, derived from an idiom of reiterated chords. Between these vigorous displays he, Adila and Jelly gave a first British hearing of a *Double Sonata* of Darius Milhaud, which the *Morning Post* called an episode of up-to-date musical gossip. But it was delicate and fanciful and logical at once, ending in a quaint descending unison C major scale: very French.

The most lasting at this period in Adila's company was Nicholas Orlov. A Polish counsellor at the Embassy, Raczinsky, asked Adila to help his compatriot, a wonderful new pianist, who had come to Britain and was shortly leaving again, in February 1924. The Fachiris did find him wonderful, and threw a huge party, for about 100 people, from which he got a number of private

Divisions on a Ground

engagements. He returned in January 1925, full of gratitude and affection for them, dining and playing chamber music, or going to concerts with them. Again in 1926, when he went to Riga, Adila saw him off; and when he came back, he was constantly at Netherton Grove, even while Adila was practising with somebody else. They played Mozart and the *Kreutzer Sonata* at the house of Alec's relatives, and Adila once accompanied him to Eastbourne where he was to play one of the Chaikovsky *Piano Concerti*. They motored down, and the next day to Brighton, and back to London the day after.

In the following January they met at Haslemere, playing with Gaspar Cassadó in Mendelssohn and Beethoven *Trios*. They gave a joint recital at Bangor University, playing Brahms and the ingenious, gracefully contrapuntal Medtner *Sonata in B minor*. This they repeated at the Wigmore Hall in June, with the César Franck and the *Kreutzer*. The hall was full: but the ensemble did not altogether please. Orloff took the opening of the Franck so slowly that Adila could not accept it[13], and the yeast failed to rise. The *Kreutzer Sonata* he could sometimes play as if it were a piano solo with a violin *obbligato* trying rather irrelevantly to get in. No wonder the Medtner work was thought cerebral.

After him came Friedrich Würher, already mentioned once or twice, a Viennese pianist who was in Britain in 1928. He partnered or accompanied Adila in London, the Provinces, and on the Continent. But in him too there was a tendency to overplay both in volume and in *rubato*, though Adila liked playing with him.

Her engagements outside London[14] were now many, if not quite so many as Jelly's. It was as late as 1926, for example, that she was first heard in Bradford, where Jelly had been known and loved for years. Keith Douglas missed her at the station. He was looking for a lady with a violin-case.[15] But Adila had got tired of mislaying her beloved tool (valued in those days at £20,000) and had laid it on a porter's barrow, walking along the platform herself like any other unencumbered arrival. She played in Bradford the elegant, entertaining Mozart *Concerto in D*, and Keith conducted Beethoven's *Second Symphony*.

The Sisters d'Aranyi

However, artists who live a highly social life, as the Fachiris did, find themselves in demand for high social occasions. At the wedding of Cynthia Noble to Myles Gladwin Jebb in 1929, in place of an anthem Adila played the *adagio* from Brahms's *Sonata in D minor* (called by the London press 'Bach's *Air on the G String.*')[16] Society, however, did not order everything, however high the society might be. The memorial service for the Countess of Strathmore in 1938 had been fixed for St Margaret's, Westminster. But when the Dean and Chapter heard that Adila and Jelly were to play violins, they refused outright. Beecham had conducted music there at a society wedding, and people in the congregation had behaved abominably, they said. They were rock-opposed to the request of even the Queen's sister-in-law. So the service was transferred to St Martin-in-the-Fields, where between the Grace and the Address Adila and Jelly played the slow movement from the *Double Concerto*.

If Adila were lagging a bit behind Jelly, when they were together they were incomparable, each to the other and both to everyone else.

From now on they are found for a long time in 'double works' —by which I mean music written for two violins and piano or orchestra. Of these there are not many; but more than might be supposed: and more were written for the sisters.

The following was their full repertoire of existing double works: the two Bach *Concerti*; two or more of the Spohr *Duos*; the Tartini *Double Sonata*; Vivaldi's *Double Concerto in A major*; the Mozart *Concertante in D major* and[17] the same composer's *Concertone in C major* (not often performed, which some found dull, though others likened it to ornaments floating in the air like fragments of rainbows); Pugnani's *Sonata in C*, (a warm soft Southern work with a gallop in the third movement called *Caccia*); Purcell's *Golden Sonata*; Handel's *Sonata in G minor*, which frequently opened their programmes (Adila once played it with two amateur society ladies at a charity concert); and a *Sonata in G minor* by one of the Sammartinis, who did much for symphonic form in the eighteenth century. But the last they played seldom.

Divisions on a Ground

In fact I find only one performance, at the Wigmore Hall in 1931, where it attracted little attention.

There are fewer minor pieces, and very few ear-ticklers: the *Serenade (Adagio and Allegro)* by Sinding; Godard's *Minuit* and *Sérénade*; and an exotic languorous Chilean dance called *Cuecca* specially provided by Norman Fraser. Occasionally as an encore they gave the *Sarabande* or *Allegro* of Leclair.

In their joint playing one critic put neatly the difference between them: 'I should be inclined to praise Miss d'Aranyi especially for her *cantabile,* Madame Fachiri for her breadth of playing.'[18] Once at a delightful Bach concert in the Wigmore Hall in 1933, they sandwiched between the two *Double Concerti* the *Concerto in A minor* played by Jelly and the *Concerto in E major* played by Adila. Adila's playing of the slow movement of this was perhaps her finest achievement as a solo artist, though some preferred the opening movement of the Bach *C major Sonata*. In the last movement she threw logic to the winds. She had flexibility of dynamics, *The Times*[19] wrote, Jelly flexibility of rhythm: but their mutual flexibility in these works was due neither to sloppiness nor waywardness, but to a mutual understanding, of each other and of music. This was like cool flowing water at a time when Bach was often played aridly.

It seems clear, however, that during this period (and I repeat during this period) when Adila was not playing doubles with Jelly, she could be erratic. She could play roughly, with no occasion for roughness, even in an agile display piece. Not having perfect pitch, as Jelly had,[20] she could sometimes play out of tune. She was nervous: her memory played tricks. On occasion in a concerto she might need a whispered bar number[21] from the conductor to regain her footing. But one is startled, remembering her reputation among us, to read that before we heard her, she was as yet unable to play Bach, according to some[22] critics! For she swept us off our feet, or often on to them, and thousands of other people all over the country. Even in London[23] it was said that both sisters had such perfect understanding of Bach that it was impossible to distinguish between them. If there was a difference when they played separate concerti, it was that Jelly was more incisive and brilliant and Adila softer and sweeter.[24]

If Character, as Heraclitus said, is Destiny, it is also musicianship. Jelly had a clear, childlike character; Adila was more complex, tempestuous, and at base self-distrustful. It is often so with people who are belted up to an inner dynamo. They are so eager, so filled with life, that to feel empty is to feel already dead. Adila was one of the fullest.

Like Jelly, she never played for safety. A little brochure with a cover-design by de Laszlo in 1921 collects impressions of her as impulsive, unorthodox, thrilling, colourful, but at the same time 'classical', full of understanding and delicacy.

This dynamo drive, however, can also work in reverse. At the Holywell Music Club in Oxford she fell down some steps and 'hurted' her leg, as she said. This was responsible for her scorn of Schweitzer. She met him after, at the Denekes' where she was staying. She could not get past his bushy eyebrows that hid his eyes from her. Nor could she get past his disregard of her little accident. 'Had I been a little black boy or a monkey, he would have done anything.' And that fixed Schweitzer for her for ever.

Her strong beliefs were part hope, part superstition. 'I never wake up without thinking "Today there will be a miracle"' she used to say to Jelly first thing in the morning. There sometimes was. When the palm of her hand tickled, or when Jelly's did, she announced: 'An engagement!' There often was; and when there were no more engagements, there might be a surprise dividend instead. But all days can bring miracles to the sufficiently perceptive.

Once in Florence, the first time Jelly went there (laden with books recommended by Dr Rendall), Adila hurt a vein in her leg getting into a cab, and had to lie up in their hotel. They were talking for some reason about the Holy Ghost, when to their astonished eyes a pigeon's feather gently floated in through the open window. Duncan Grant, who was more Adila's friend than Jelly's,

Divisions on a Ground

did them a drawing of this incident. They were both taken aback, but Jelly less so, having more sense of humour.

Jelly once hailed an empty hearse thinking it was a taxi. The driver, without stopping, called 'Not yet for you, Lady'. That is a miracle too.

Adila was even vaguer than Jelly at mislaying things, and about dates. Arriving at the Rock Pavilion, Hastings, she found the orchestra already rehearsing, and called out 'Am I very late?' Julius Harrison turned round from the conductor's desk in surprise, and said 'No, you're exactly a month early.' And on one occasion she found she had accepted invitations to dinner at three different houses on the day she had already invited friends to dine at her own.

Her phenomenal energy can be seen in laconic entries of action in her diary: 'Practised 5 hours. Went shopping. Had very successful party about 80 people.' Even with cramp in the thumb at the Queen's Hall, with influenza, with acute depression, she would never give in. She never let others give in. 'She would make a lame horse win a race' says her daughter, Adrienne. During a visit to Paris, or it may have been Geneva, she had this daughter inside her. Titi and her husband had left for England, having ordered a dinner service, which they asked Adila to bring home. As she was incapable of thinking that she was incapable, she spent most of the night, pregnant or not, in packing the service before catching the London train at 8 a.m.

But with all this spiritual muscularity her eyes glowed always warm and kind.

When she went out of Netherton Grove, peace filled the house; a centreless peace like that when a small son returns to boarding school. When she came back, it was filled with whirlwinds and gaiety.

Her eagerness made her an excellent teacher. She had many pupils, at one time[25] twenty-four, the best known afterwards being perhaps Orrea Pernell, the American. As early as January 1921 she brought out Jenny Blank, whose début the *Musical Times* thought should be recorded. Some of them could not pay, but got the same attention, often for two hours at a stretch.

'Play from the *stomach*!' made the diffident jump—and achieve. And her way of saying 'That's it! That's it!' turned into a violinist many a rabbit who might else have stayed in the burrow.[26] Orrea Pernell[27] she launched by taking her, when Jelly was ill, to play in the Bach *Double Concerto* at a Prom: and with another pupil, Diana Cator, she did the same at Norwich. She kept in touch with her pupils, who reported on débuts and professional progress.

Her eagerness made her also a lioness among her peers. A lioness who knew, when she limped, that she was limping; and took measures to cure herself. Study and practice, practice and study, attention to dotted notes and to Joachim's hints on the relation of thumb to middle finger, even reading Mozart's letters before playing one of his concerti: this self-improvement resulted in 1928 in a noticeably surer judgment and a self-control that never spoiled spontaneity. By responding to difficult details she evolved a style of her own. Part of the credit for this must also go to chamber music.

Both in private and on the platform Adila was a leader. A true leader, I mean, with a strong personality which can direct and with a stronger vitality which can inspire. In chamber music she led because the music was more important than she was and she could hear it more clearly than others.

It is not surprising that from all the musicians who night after night played trios and quartets after dinner at Netherton Grove, several ensembles should come out into public. The most frequent member of these was Alec Fachiri.

Although he had chosen the Bar, Alec dedicated every sunday morning to practice, and had great facility in mastering works new to him. He handled his Landolfi 'cello with skill, taste, sympathy and musical understanding. I do not find that he ever played solo in public, or even much to others at home; nor ever in public chamber music without his wife or sister-in-law. He was too nervous. But here was a foundation, and Ethel Hobday built on it. They played at Darlington in November 1919, at Haslemere the

Divisions on a Ground

following February, and elsewhere; and I think it was for this trio that Adila organized three recitals that summer. For the first the hall was very empty. For the second (Beethoven) it was better filled. The third topped expenses by eight pounds. At Sherborne they played Beethoven, and Schubert the next day.

Later on, Alec often joined his wife in piano and violin recitals, so as to open or close with a Schubert or Dvořák *Trio*. His refined style suited well with Adila and Tovey. Once in the Wigmore Hall these played one of Tovey's two adaptations of Haydn *Sonatas for pianoforte with accompaniment of violin and 'cello*.[28] At this recital Tovey's harpsichord was accused of being out of sympathy with the violin family: the viols' would have been better.[29]

This trio gave rise to a less usual ensemble: a string quintet with two 'celli, which the Fachiris raised from the private party playing of Orrea Pernell, Rebecca Clarke and May Mukle, 'cellist of a family long used to chamber music. This played principally for the Schubert Centenary, and a well filled Wigmore Hall heard it in Schubert's *Quintet in C* (op. 163). A little unwieldly, perhaps, but Adila kept it together in her broad command. At this concert she played a delicate little *Conzertstück* which few people had heard.

The same two works were given again in Kensington Town Hall, when George Reeves partnered Adila in the *A minor sonata* (op. 137 no. 2). The *Quintet* was heard in several places in London and outside, with others of Schubert's last works such as the *Quartet in D minor* (no. 14) and the *Piano Trio in B♭* (Adila, Tertis, Katharine Goodson): but the prime reason for the ensemble was the Schubert celebrations, and other works for this combination are hard to find.

Adila like Jelly adored Schubert and took the celebrations very seriously. She organized Würher, herself and the young American singer Harold Dahlquist in three concerts at the Wigmore Hall. George Reeves again accompanied. The instrumental works other than some already mentioned were the *Duo for violin and piano in A, Introduction and Rondo Brillante* which Adila had been

The Sisters d'Aranyi

playing for a couple of years since she revived it, the *Introduction and Variations* on the song '*Trockne Blumen*' (another little-known work first written for flute), the *Sonata for violin and piano in G minor* (op. 137 no. 3): and for piano, the *Wanderer Fantasia*, all the *Impromptus* of op. 142, and '*Grand Duo for Four Hands*' in which Würher was joined by Angus Morrison, but which I cannot identify in the list of works at my disposal.

For sonatas Adila had many partners, from famous soloists like Fanny Davies, Harold Samuel and Myra Hess to less broad but fine artists like John Wills and Bertram Harrison. With Myra Hess in this period she played César Franck and Beethoven *in G* (op. 30 no. 3); but this was at a private house.[30] At one time it began to look as if she and Kathleen Long might set up what Jelly and Myra Hess were setting up. Kathleen Long was younger than Adila, but already known for her sensitivity in Mozart and the French impressionists. At their first joint recital in December 1931 they introduced a *Sonata in E minor* (op. 24) by the Swedish Emil Sjögren who wrote three violin sonatas. Their performance of the *Third Sonata* of Delius gave great charm to this melting work.

The bubbling neatness of Fanny Davies and the healthy sweetness of Adila were a wonderful blend, but they seem to have combined rarely. In December 1926 at the Grotrian Hall they played three Bach *Sonatas*, the one in C minor being known only by its *adagio* and *fugue*. Adila played the unaccompanied one in G minor. She played this so perfectly that Jelly never wished to play it herself, and never did.

In the same year Janáček had had a mild but justified boom in Britain. Adila and Fanny Davies played a *Sonata* of his for the first time in this country at a concert of his chamber music. In November she repeated this with Harold Samuel in a recital at which they also played the little-heard early Beethoven *Sonata in A major* (no. 2). She played the Janáček for some time, at Liverpool and elsewhere. It was felt that her ebullience well suited its passion.

Harold Samuel and she found each other in easy sympathy,

having the same musical alertness and integrity, even if he were more sober and restrained. They were thinking of founding a permanent partnership, which would certainly have rivalled Jelly and Myra Hess. But a small and stupid event wrecked this. After one of their Bach recitals, a young Scottish friend of the Aranyis violently attacked Harold Samuel for daring to play with so great an artist: 'You drag her down!' Samuel may have been aware that some people did not have the ears for the quiet inevitability of his Bach; but being, as I said in a previous chapter, sensitive and modest, he could not defend himself against such rudeness. The remark struck the confidence out of him. He went pale, and never played with Adila again.

The most interesting recital that Adila gave with Maurice Cole was in March 1930, in the first performance of a *Sonata quasi una Fantasia* which the Florentine Castelnuovo-Tedesco composed for her. She had met him ten years before while staying at Bibbiena, where they gave a recital, and when the Fachiris went on to Florence he showed them the sights. The *Sonata* was taken by the London press as slight and confused but agreeable. Maurice Cole was a lively person and when he accompanied Adila and Jelly in the Bach *Double Concerto* he added much to what was called their '*joie de violon*.'[31]

Howard-Jones, Ernest Walker, and Angus Morrison were others—of widely differing styles and applications. The last was a specially able musician. When another pianist had to retire at the last moment from a *Trio* and a Bach *Sonata* at the Paddington Music Club, he read the Beethoven B♭ *Trio* in the morning for the first time, and played with perfect ensemble, though Alec was very anxious.

Of regular 'accompanists'—if that word can be used of an ensemble-player born—Adila's favourite was Ethel Hobday. Her playing, never too intrusive, never too retiring, never too loud, never too reticent, did as much for the smoothness and perfection of Adila's recitals as they did for Jelly's. And as with Jelly, so with Adila she was ideal for concerts in schools. As Jelly's scholastic home was Winchester, so Adila's was Haileybury; al-

The Sisters d'Aranyi

though here Bruce Hylton-Stewart was available at the piano. More than once Steuart Wilson joined them there. There Hylton-Stewart conducted the school orchestra (he did for Haileybury music what Kenneth Stubbs did for Rugby) in the Mendelssohn *Concerto*. But he was not confined to Public School Music. He conducted in the Wigmore Hall, at Oxford, and elsewhere, a string orchestra for Adila and Jelly in all the Bach *Violin Concerti*. The friendship that sprang from these musical meetings lasted all the sisters' lives. It was with joy that he was available when returning from Germany, to play for Adila in Holland. It was good that it should be he to accompany them both at their last appearance in London.

Adila's repertoire was by now very wide, but she was always adding to it things familiar or new to others, or forgotten. In a sense she re-introduced Spohr. In the orgy of 'de-bunking' after the First World War Spohr was not (to use the phrase of after the Second World War) 'Establishment'. He could be called 'Establishment ret^d.' A generation that sniggered at Mendelssohn sneered at Spohr. Adila did not care. She took up the *Scena Concertante*. This is listed among his seventeen *Violin Concerti*, because it is really a concerto though written in operatic form with *arias* and *recitativi* for the opera-minded public of Milan, like a stage *scena*.

Adila first played this at Edinburgh in March 1924, together with the Delius *Concerto* which she had just done at Bournemouth. As Tovey wrote in his programme notes, a concerto in operatic form is bound to be successful (he meant as a musical form) since the classical concerto form itself is a glorification of *aria* form and has in fact no other origin. Spohr, however, could be very sentimental, and the *coloratura* way of writing this work might have come to grief in a modern audience if Adila had not given it with her usual fresh vigour, as a good *prima donna* might have done vocally: and from her hands it was received well when she let London hear it after many years. Lesser artists are advised to be wary of playing it.

The Spohr unaccompanied *Duos for Two Violins* were also

Divisions on a Ground

all but forgotten in Britain. The sisters gave new life to the one in D when they played it at Dublin in 1926. Walter Starkie said that Adila had played this one with Joachim ten days before his death. I do not know where he got this story from; perhaps mishearing Adila herself. The gist may be true but the detail not. Adila was probably not with Joachim ten days before he died, or if she was, he could not have played anything.

This *duo* was written when Spohr was only twenty, before he went into overproduction. It starts *adagio molto*, leads to *allegro*, and ends *in andante con variazioni*. There is a later one which goes from *allegro* to *andante* to *rondo vivace*, and the *rondo* seldom failed to rouse its audience and was sometimes, at least in part, repeated. The sisters played both of these many times, though which on what occasion is not always very easy to find.[32]

In both they created an atmosphere of complete harmony of thought, homely, sometimes lively. This was increased by their harmonizing clothes: Jelly for example in blue when Adila was in maroon: and drew round them screens and palms of a Victorian parlour, as it were, especially when at the Wigmore Hall they played effectively, and quite unaffectedly, sitting down. The *adagio* deepened this. It sounded like a confidence between devoted sisters, gentle, grave, resigned, each in turn speaking her thought aloud while the other returned to soft *pizzicato* thrums, as if to reflective knitting.[33]

Their revival of the Tartini *Double Concerto in F* was a pleasant example of Italian eighteenth-century shapes and graces, if little more. A much more acceptable example was the *Aria and Capriccio* from a *Violin Sonata* in the same key by the Florentine Veracini, Tartini's teacher, which exhilarating work Adila first read, with the Tartini, in 1920. A delight to audiences and to her. I don't think Jelly ever played this. Though the sisters to some extent had the same repertoire, there was no selfishness over pieces. They often said 'Yes, you play that! You play it better than I do.'

Interest in the Jewish composer Ernest Bloch was beginning

The Sisters d'Aranyi

in the 1920s, and Adila found great sympathy in his suite *Baal Schem,* written in 1924. The middle piece, *Nigun,* (usually rendered 'Improvisation') she often played by itself, but as often the whole work under the titles *Three Jewish Pieces* or *Three Religious Laments.* Though critics paid small attention to these, the primeval religious depths in them appealed to her, and through her to audiences who might not otherwise have liked them.

Another new continental work with a religious, if very differently religious, content was the *Concerto Gregoriano* of Respighi. This, though composed seven years previously had had only one previous hearing in Britain when Adila played it at the Eastbourne Festival in 1928. One critic said it seemed to take you up in an aeroplane[34]; and much play was made with references to stained glass windows. The gregorian modes used, especially in the middle movement, might well sound pathless in unnavigational hands. Actually it seems as if Respighi, musical depictor before and after this of the fountains and pines of Rome, had in his mind a crowd moving into a cathedral and coming out again to secular sunlight. Adila's generosity surmounted the double-stopping.[35] She brought the music to exaltation. London critics did not like it, perhaps because it was impossible for Bertram Harrison to bring orchestral colours out of a piano score, and Respighi is best with an orchestra.

Nor were the critics of London kinder to Tovey in the Wigmore Hall in May 1931. But that may have been because for once these two robust horses tended to pull against each other. Dr James Wallace was treated better by critics at Liverpool, for his thoughtfulness and musical logic.

Tovey's unpopularity with the London press gave a mixed welcome to the two earlyish Hindemith *Violin Sonatas* (op. 11). To some ears his arbitrary *rubati* and lack of tonal variety made mere incoherence out of these rather cerebral works. To others both sonatas sounded concise and alert. But in the two somewhat feebly written slow movements he does seem to have reduced Adila's flow of poetry. Dublin, hearing Hindemith for the first

Divisions on a Ground

time, took to the rhythms both in composition and in playing.

In October 1924 the New Kensington Music Club organized a concert of works by locally resident composers. Two out of the six later wrote for Adila.[36]

Arthur Somervell, whose *Conzertstück* she played that evening, gave her his *Violin Concerto* for the first performance with dedication in 1932. This was with the Reid Orchestra in Edinburgh; but Tovey was ill in Suffolk, and his pupil and assistant Mary Grierson took his baton. Somervell at first was distressed that a woman he knew little should direct the first hearing of his only *Violin Concerto*, especially since the BBC cancelled the broadcast of it. But all went so extremely well that he wrote a charming letter to the conductor and a glowing account to her principal.

A London broadcast came later, but as neither Adila nor Jelly kept notices of broadcasts, I have no idea how it was received. Adila played it at several places later, including Torquay (where she happened to be afflicted with shingles) but not very often. In melody and rhythm it was on the romantic side and has not passed into the repertory.

Nor has, unfortunately, the work of the other Kensingtonian. Gustav Holst knew and was stimulated by the work and personalities of both sisters, and long wished to write for them.[37] The result came out in 1929: the *Concerto for Two Violins*, which he dedicated to them. They performed it on April 3rd at a Royal Philharmonic Concert conducted by Oskar Fried. Why it was regarded as intellectual and mathematical I cannot imagine, unless the reason was that this was Holst's label in conservative musical circles. He was certainly a fine contrapuntalist, but the melodies here, never shredded into problems, have the haunting quality of true english folk-song. In the lyrical second movement one such in 5/4 time (Holst found this metre much more malleable than the 7/4 in the *Ode to Death*) is enchanting; and the last movement, beginning from a hushed, dramatic, off-beat theme, is really exciting. Some passages have a Mozartian wit.

The sisters played it under Sir Henry Wood at a Prom in

The Sisters d'Aranyi

September, and under Leslie Heward for a London Regional broadcast in May 1932. It was shortly after composing this work that Holst received the Philharmonic Gold Medal.[38]

In 1930, Vaughan Williams wrote confidentially to Jelly, asking if Adila had told her of his plan to give a London concert to R. O. Morris of Shrewsbury. He knew that like himself she was fond of both the man and his music, but he wanted the idea to be kept secret till all arrangements had been made.

Morris (comparisons were made with Robert Bridges as a craftsman in poetry) cut out eighteenth and nineteenth-century music and went back to Elizabethan polyphony and folk-song. Not copying, but re-creating his own thought in this idiom: not dry nor antiquarian, but musician-like and full of delicacies and fun. The concert took place in the Wigmore Hall. Arthur Bliss conducted an *Orchestral Suite,* a *Concertino in F* for small orchestra, and the *Violin Concerto* which Morris had dedicated to Adila and to which she here gave its first performance. Adrian Boult conducted a *Concerto Piccolo for Two Violins and String Orchestra* in which Jelly joined her.[39] They do not seem to have ever played this again.

The concert had a respectful reception: but Elizabethan and Jacobean music, both in its instruments and its delicate decorations, was made for a few ears at a time in a small space. Modern instruments in more public circumstances can hardly recapture the old or improve on it in the present. As for folk-song, we all know in Scotland what can happen to some exquisite melody, made to be passed quietly round a black house, when it is bawled at thousands by a medallist at a Mod, and what happened to certain tunes in the mouths of the Polish Choir, or even, sometimes, the Orpheus. First hearings of real folk-song and of polyphony need a discernment and adaptation of taste as subtle as first tastings of truffle.

Adila and Jelly made another foray into 'olden style' music when they played with Ethel Hobday at Newcastle in 1934 a *Divertimento in D* (op. 45) by H. Waldo Warner, who had been

Divisions on a Ground

viola player in the London String Quartet since 1907, when it was founded. He wrote much chamber music. This work in its counterpoint was indebted to Bach.[40]

In Ethel Smyth, Adila took as close an interest as Ethel Smyth took in her. In 1928 she appeared in a mixed concert of Smyth works, at which Bertram Harrison and she played the *Sonata in A minor* (op. 7), 'for the third time in forty years' as the composer gruffly numbered the sonata's performances in the programme. (They gave its fourth time at Exeter in 1930). Adila also took the violin part in place of oboe in the *Piano Trio,* one movement of which was then repeated with Helen Gaskell playing the instrument it was written for. Ethel Smyth always liked making things quite clear.

Ethel Smyth also disliked conventions of any sort. Her programme invited the audience to applaud at any point if they felt like it. They did.

Not exactly a new work, but a rare one, and I think a novelty to London, was the *Concert pour Violon et Pianoforte* by Ernest Chausson, César Franck's brilliant pupil. This was given in one of the 'doubles' programmes in February 1933 at the Wigmore Hall. Adila and Würher played the 'solo' parts and the Quartet (Gladys Noon, James Lockyer, Alec Fachiri) was led by Jelly. At this concert Bruce Hylton-Stewart conducted Jelly and a small string orchestra in Kelly's *Serenade.*

Thus far for Adila as an innovator of larger materials. She did the same with smaller ones. Amid the Kreisler cocktails, arrangements of classical *minuets, rondos* and *gavottes,* modern *mazurkas, sarabands* and *berceuses,* Spanish or Hungarian dances, *Ave Maria* and *The Hymn to the Sun,* one finds little unknown bits by friends or contemporaries: a jig by Herbert Hughes called *The Tenpenny Bit, Midsummer Moon*[41] by Rebecca Clarke, a country dance by Frank Bridge, and *Captain Fracassa,* a rumbustious, crazy little work by Castelnuovo-Tedesco when young, which she played 'as one possessed', that is, with fire, tenderness, wit and rhythm. [42, 43]

She even made her own arrangements: an *Arietta* by Pergolesi

The Sisters d'Aranyi

(a gifted young composer who died of consumption at the age of twenty-six); the famous Haydn *Rondo all'Ungherese,* Schubert's song *The Miller and the Stream*; and the folk song *Schwesterlein* as Brahms embroidered it.

With this growing treasure in her pocket Adila went back to Hungary, as we have seen, by way of Italy. It was not her first exit from Britain after the First War. She had been to Paris at the end of May 1920, and found that city 'joyous'.

This time she did not much enjoy Italy.[44] At Arezzo there were violent thunderstorms, and I have perhaps mentioned her dread of thunder and lightning. Her concert at Bibbiena was mostly to Italian noblemen and their wives, and admirals and others, with varying musical interests. Alec and she loved Venice and were sad to leave it, though they could not find a good hotel. They were sadder still in Vienna, where the hotels were full and they had to bribe their way out of Austria: and saddest of all in Budapest, in spite of an emotional welcome from Taksony. There was an insolent servant in Adila's old home, who ran her father, and when rebuked pretended to commit suicide ('I wish she would have dyed' Adila stabbed into her diary). They found Budapest 'terribly changed' after the Béla Kuhn failed revolution and with Admiral Horthy named 'Regent' by the nobles of Hungary. Adila had as little sense of politics as Jelly, indeed she saw no connection between politics (or timetables, or policemen like her father), which were altogether irrelevant except as a means, and music, which was relevant to everything. But both she and Alec were disappointed in the Hungarians. Not a present or two for their wedding nor preparations with Dienzl for a concert, nor dinner with Béla Bartók, nor fun found on St Margaret's Isle without mosquitoes, nor a wedding anniversary supper in the country with Alec alone and a bottle of fine Tokay, nor playing the Mozart *A major Concerto,* with its barbaric, Turkish freak in the middle, as a winged artist in the Academy that had fledged her, wiped out the dismay of this visit. Coming home was fully as bad. Neither she nor Alec ever thought of reserving rooms in

Divisions on a Ground

advance, and had to sit up all night in the Hall of a Vienna hotel, with the result that when they got home to London they hated that too.

Yet they went on going abroad. The South of France, where they spent Christmas in 1920 and 1921, not only introduced them to prominent Europeans like Prince Danilo of Montenegro and the Duchess of Aosta, but to musicians like Georges Lauweryns, to whom Adila played and made him enthusiastic about her, and Halphen, a *sonata* of whose she played at sight. Lauweryns[45] came and presented her at Monte Carlo. These connections led to engagements.

Adila's musical trips abroad, which were more numerous than Jelly's, were not always successful. In March 1920 she was on her way to Germany, but in the boat to Ostend had a kind of nervous breakdown or crisis, so that she had to return in the same vessel when it turned round for Dover, and she stayed nine days in bed under doctor's orders. In May 1922, however, she spent some days in Paris by herself, having a wonderful time and playing at a private party. Then Jelly arrived for the Milhaud *Double Sonata* at the Salle des Agriculteurs. It pleased Adila to find Francesco Mendelssohn after fifteen years grown into a nice young man and a promising musician.

In June of that year her father came to London for a holiday of a couple of months and took Adila and Alec back to Hungary with him. They had trouble on the journey. Adila left her handbag behind at Victoria Station, so that they had to wait for a later boat till the bag caught them up, after which there was a bother over Alec's visa, and they all had to spend the night in what Adila called the Windsor Castle Hotel and did not enjoy it at all. With their usual lack of provision they had to search Salzburg for a hotel and finally arrived with relief at a little house in the woods at Velden in Carinthia, which they had rented in advance for two months. Here they played music and tennis, and Adila practised Schumann for the Archduke when he came to tea after having had them over to lunch at Liechtenstein. Later all the Liechtensteins came to the Fachiris'. It rained most of the time.

The Sisters d'Aranyi

Taksony left for Budapest on November 1st, and the Fachiris a fortnight later for home, after another Liechtenstein party at which they gave comic presents and music.

For those who enjoy it, and have dignity and liking, and have or can make themselves have the money, this kind of life can be fun. To the Fachiris it was. But I think the main object of the holiday was to settle Adila's nerves. This object was only partly achieved. On the journey to Munich Adila had what Alec describes as 'her shivers' in the train. But Munich helped. There they had orgies of private chamber music in a friend's house and went to a supper given by the Bavarian Princess and King Ferdinand of Bulgaria. The royal presence was less important to Adila than was her playing with Bruno Walter, who was one of the most subtle accompanists in Europe.

At Munich they attended five Wagner operas, a joy I cannot share with them, especially after hearing Anna Russell on the subject. Even more they enjoyed Dresden and Berlin, where Adila met again her relative Paul Joachim and had an evening with the Mendelssohns, playing a Schubert *Quintet* for which Alec was loaned a 'cello that had been Piatti's. So, at last, they returned to London and found that Alec, who had taken a legal position with the League of Nations, had earned £365 for his work at the Hague. This must have gone some way toward paying for an expensive holiday.

It would be wrong to say that Adila's continental reputation was made as a result of these high-level diversions: doubly wrong to suppose they were undertaken with that object. Neither Adila nor Jelly was ever a careerist. But these certainly helped, for on the high social level one met (if the area were right) people who counted in one's own profession, and whom one wanted to meet anyway. Through the Mendelssohns Adila gave a sonata recital with Carol Szreti in Berlin shortly after Francesco von Mendelssohn had had his début. This might not have happened but for such family friendship.

She gave two more recitals, in Vienna at the Mittlerer

Divisions on a Ground

Konzerthaus-Saal, and at the Hague, which was presumably due to Vienna repute. After this year Adila was continually crossing the Channel for concerts.

One year she played with the Berlin Philharmonic the Mozart *Concerto in A*, and another the Beethoven *Concerto*. She appeared with Elizabeth Schumann at an evening of the 'Concordia' at Vienna, and gave a solo recital in that city. She played the Beethoven at Schevening, and had recitals with Würher at Cologne and Munich. She took one of her preferred British accompanists, Julie Lasdun, to Italy, to the Accademia di S. Cecilia in Rome, to the Opera House in Malta. At the British Institute in Florence Castelnuovo-Tedesco again accompanied her. She found Italian audiences less warm than British or Teuton ones, but had a big success, with dates for following seasons.

After the Santa Cecilia concert she was summoned by Mussolini to Palazzo Venezia. Although non-political, Adila firmly disapproved of the fascist régime and had no wish to go. But excuses of lack of time were not accepted; and after her interview she had the honesty to admit she had found Il Duce personally charming—as several dictators are reputed to have been in private life. He said he was disappointed that she had not brought her violin, because he also played and had wished to hear her. He received dozens of violins as presents, which he did not know what to do with: 'one man needs only one violin.' 'So whenever I hear of a poor musician who has none, I send him one.' He said also that had he been Governor of England, he would not have allowed Nash's Regent Street to be destroyed.

In her life she had three audiences with the Pope, the last, in her later years, a personal one. She had to be helped to rise from her knees, but found the audience deeply moving.

Adila was constantly asked back to these European music centres. At Munich and Berlin she played the *Concerto Gregoriano*, and at Frankfurt, and at Vienna where she played also the Beethoven *Concerto*. With Würher she gave the Castelnuovo-Tedesco *Sonata* at Vienna. With Jelly and Ethel Hobday she toured Spain and played in Brussels. She gave two concerts in

The Sisters d'Aranyi

four days, at Uppsala, and another at Cracow. In 1935 Jelly and she toured Portugal together. Suggia was again helpful: but on the voyage home (again no advance planning) there were no berths available and they had to have three mattresses spread on the floor of the children's day nursery, surrounded by rocking-horses, tiny chairs and Humpty-Dumpties hanging from the walls.

From all these trips Adila came home to a steady increase in demand.

Even the somnolent gramophone monopolies listened with half an ear from their opium dreams of dance music. She made her first recordings in 1924. Trifles, of course: business men so often immortalized good performances only if they were sure of quick returns. She rehearsed four light pieces with Ivor Newton, 'to play for the gramophone' as she put it, or 'on the gramophone.' As a result a gramophone and some records were installed at Netherton Grove. But when Adila went to hear herself, she thought very little of it. Naturally enough. Electric recording did not start until 1925, and Adila sounded as Caruso and Patti did: noise from a woollen bag heard through a cheese-grater.

However the record sold well enough for her to be invited to make another the following month; and again next year. This time she played 'in the gramophone'.

She was the first serious British musician to appear on British television[46], when it was in its experimental, Baird, stage in 1932. Special make-up was needed, and Adila to help the staff did her own, fascinated at smearing her face biscuit yellow and filling out her lips in black.

But life is not all joy and success: nor was the indomitable Adila to be unacquainted with grief. She suffered with her relatives in Budapest. She mourned her Aunt Tatiana.[47] She was desperate when her mother died. And on her fell the brunt of the death of her father in 1930.

Jelly was in New York and Titi and her husband were in Boston. Nobody knew that Taksony was ill, though Titi had her suspicions. They had met seldom since the women-folk left Hungary sixteen years before, but all had written often. In fact letters from Jelly and Titi arrived two days after Taksony died, and an affectionate one from Adila, happily, five days before.

Adila was ill with an abscess and in bed when the news of her Aunt Tatiana's death arrived. Again this time she was ill and in bed.[48] But she and Alec left London at once and arrived in time for the funeral. It was the custom for mourners to kiss the coffin; and when Adila's turn came, she did not notice that it had a glass top, so she never saw her dead father's face. She was glad of that.

Taksony was only seventy, but before he died he had changed, becoming gentler and milder. He had been looking forward to a three or four month visit to London in June, for which he had ordered a new evening suit. Particularly he wanted to see his little grand-daughter, for whom he had bought a stock of picture-postcards to send two or three each week.

On the night of Monday, March 4, he did not feel well. His doctor found nothing serious, but the next day suspected that his patient would not live. Taksony had no fear of death after all, when he arrived there, but was sad that his children could not be with him. 'They say' Adila wrote to her sisters, 'his veins were bursting round his heart, and gradually he bled to death inwardly.' He died serenely the next day.[49]

Budapest gave him a military funeral, with a thousand police, 150 mounted police and the police band. Owing to the Hungarian thaw the cemetery was flooded, and most of the *cortège* remained outside. He had been saving, to leave something to his children. His savings amounted to £500.

18

The House in Netherton Grove

The Fachiris moved into their real home on the First of April, 1919 and lived there for the rest of their married life. Jelly took up permanent abode with them in 1927.

The principal bedroom seemed to Alec the most beautiful of the rooms; but to Adila all was lovely. It was a big house with plenty of rooms for guests and several public ones, their favourite being a kind of library called the Green Room.

Within a fortnight they gave a house-warming with thirty-five people, who included Tovey and Vladimir Rosing, the Russian singer who had settled in England in 1915 and was famous in opera and the realistic character songs of Mussorgsky. A kind of higher-voiced Chaliapin.

Adila and Alec inaugurated their new life by playing to their guests the Brahms *Double Concerto for Violin and 'Cello* with Tovey as orchestra. From then on, the list of people who played there reads like a list of nearly all the public concerts we would have clamoured to get into.

The space was not big enough for crowds, however, and they built-on in the garden a big new dining-room. This connected with mirror-panelled double doors to the studio, so that over 100 people could be seated in ten rows of ten. Over the studio were the bedrooms. The colour scheme of the studio was of its period: black walls, a blue ceiling, and a gold strip picture-rail.

Post-prandial music here was never premeditated. It was more

The House in Netherton Grove

like a *ceilidh*. A *ceilidh* in a castle. Cernikov, the conductor Claude Powell, Louis Fleury with his flute, Tovey, Hubermann, George Reeves, Rebecca Clarke with viola, May Mukle and 'cello, Philip Heseltine ('Peter Warlock'), the Baron d'Erlanger who rehearsed Adila in his *Poème,* Lobkowitz, Rumschitzky, Reynaldo Hahn, Maurice Besley, Adrian Boult and Arthur Bliss, Béla Bartók, Brosa without his Quartet and the entire Busch one, these are only a few and in the first two years.[1]

Many also were the non-musicians with diverse and sometimes conflicting interests, whom Adila hostessed into enjoyment. She could do this even at sticky social luncheons such as all hostesses have to give from time to time; and these did not worry her. Before one of them she was walking back from the shops with Anna Robertson when a fire engine passed. Adila insisted on following it, and watched the fire so long that her guests at home arrived before she did. Arms full of flowers, she swept into the room crying 'Darlings, do forgive me! Please arrange these flowers while I change for lunch.'[2] The ice dissolved in her flood.

It was the kind of house that people did not want to leave. The last of the 150 guests at the re-housewarming in 1922 left at two in the morning; and this was no exception. The gatherings were anything but solemn. If Beethoven were to be played, he was played respectfully and well; but afterwards he was in shirt sleeves, especially if anyone had been giving a public concert and needed to let off steam. So you might see Harold Samuel dressed up as Queen Victoria singing comic songs at the piano. Or Würher acting a latecomer to a concert, or accompanying wildly as Jelly danced *à la Argentina.* Or Orlov playing for musical chairs. Or Myra Hess accompanying herself as a senile opera star.[3]

After her last recital of the series in which she and Jelly played all the Beethoven *Violin Sonatas,* Myra Hess sat down and played the 'Black-Keys' *Etude* of Chopin by rolling an orange in her right hand up and down the notes (without a wrong one).[3] Quite a number of serious musicians like fooling about musically.

Even the learned Tovey caught the infection. He could dramatize. A. H. Fox-Strangways describes a dinner party at which with

The Sisters d'Aranyi

the serving of the dessert, music was heard. Tovey leapt from his chair and paced about crying 'Adila! Have I gone mad? I thought I heard *music!*' The decanter stopped circulating and the music was heard no more, and Tovey sat down; 'but still palpitating visibly.'[4]

It is no special pleading to say that the food was among the best in London. Society papers said it. Especially when Adila prepared it herself; for she loved cooking. Having sacked the servants one Friday, and the new ones not to arrive till the Monday, she spent the weekend spring-cleaning and cooking, while Jelly in her room with an unmade bed practised and noticed no difference.[3] Another time Adila gave a dinner for sixteen people when the cook was taken ill. She cooked everything.

'Do come, Charles! *On mange bien chez Fachiri*'[5] was Jelly's coaxing invitation to her hostess's son when staying with her old friends the Fishers at Canterbury. This became a family saying in the archiepiscopal palace; '*On mange bien chez . . .*' The wines may not have been on quite the same level; for I am sorry to record that neither Adila nor Alec understood or even greatly liked drinking. Indeed they were often amused by what seemed to them the pure *mystique* of a restaurant waiter sniffing a cork.[6]

Sometimes one ate not only well but surprisingly. One grand evening of music, supper and dance, to which came Princess Helena Victoria and half the Diplomatic Corps, every kind of classic supper dish stood on the buffet. But the guests neglected the soup and the salmon when in came a huge silver bowl filled to the top with hot sausages.[7]

Orlov was the pianist on that occasion: for Adila engaged either a famous musician to entertain her guests or else an unknown talented one. She liked to pass on to others the lift she had had so easily.

She lived in the grand manner, with five servants. Even her exaggerations were grand. When she had to wear glasses for reading, she wore them with jade-green frames.[8] She had the good breeding that can break the rule of good breeding and remain well-bred. Even with outrageous remarks.

The House in Netherton Grove

The day the Maharajah of Kutch[6] came to a banquet, Adila hired four footmen, and did extravagant shopping with Jelly and the Austrian cook. Their anticipation of the oriental sweet tooth was justified when the Maharajah (in a pink turban and spectacles) devoured throughout the meal not only the little dish of pink and white sweets in front of him, but the little dishes in front of everyone else, which were one by one tactfully passed up to him. Although the chief guest, he was sitting at some distance from his hostess, who scandalized everyone by suddenly roaring up the table 'How many vives haf you got?'

Some of her sayings had a grim humour. For the Silver Jubilee procession they had good seats in the Mall. But Adila suffered from almost chronic internal trouble. One of the passing horses lifted its tail, and Adila moaned 'O how I vish I vere that horrrse!'

Even her own nervousnesses before concerts she could get wantonly out of proportion. 'She doesn't have to practise and feel nervous' she remarked enviously as her Liverpool taxi passed a prowling prostitute. 'How lucky that voman is!'

And so at Netherton Grove few leisure hours passed without laughter. Fun written down and printed can sound silly; so I won't try to define the evening when Adila received her mother and sister as dinner guests,[9] dressed in her husband's clothes. But Fachiri laughter rings to this day in one man's ears.

When Volterra, 'that great but desperately nervous pianist' as Jelly called him,* first came to London, he had no suitable protection from the rain, so he went into a shop to buy a raincoat. Seeing that he was a foreigner, the assistant gave him one in the continental style, with flaps along the shoulders; but Volterra did not know. Completing the outfit of the perfect English gentleman, he bought a tweed cap to look like Sherlock Holmes. That evening he dined at Netherton Grove, and was puzzled, as he opened his raincoat and fumbled in his dinner-jacket pocket to pay his taxi, by hearing loud laughter from the front door, where Adila, Alec and Jelly were

---

*He was so paralysed with nerves before his first recital in the Aeolian Hall, that Adila had to push him physically on to the platform.[10] But he was a wonderful pianist in the judgment of the Aranyis.

The Sisters d'Aranyi

in convulsions. Alec later insisted on lending him a top hat to go back to his hotel.[11]

He has told me this story quite without rancour. Fachiri laughter was so full of spontaneous human warmth that it could offend only people with a deliberate lack of humour: and such among their friends were few. The whole house seemed air-conditioned with this spiritual warmth. Tom Spring-Rice spoke for hundreds when he wrote to Jelly: 'You are right, there's not a house in London where I always find so warm, so affectionate a welcome as 10, Netherton Grove.'

Warmth, generosity, was the source of all Adila's actions. When she spring-cleaned, she did so with a will: and that meant, with her, gusto. Having slabbed paint on the studio walls, she went out into the garden and slapped it on to the railings.[12]

Her response to nearly everything was as immediate as that. Many a guest who admired (say) a piece of old china was embarrassed at having it pressed on them as a gift.[8] When once she liked anyone, that person could do no wrong. Hence she was often taken advantage of, especially she and Jelly together after Alec's death, as was noticed and said to a friend of theirs by their hire-service driver, when he came to fetch away the *Beethovengesellschaft*.[8]

'Hurricane House' a pupil of Adila's called it. 'That happy and chaotic League of Nations' says Anna Robertson, 'one Greek, two Hungarians, Swiss governess, Austrian, German, Irish maids for ever changing.'[13]

It is now Anna Robertson's turn to take the centre of the stage.

She first met the Aranyis, when she was very young, at Carmichael House near Tinto Hill, where her friends the Rankens lived. Later they moved to Kersewell (Mrs Ranken wrote it Cursewell during the torment of moving) near Carstairs Junction. At both houses the Fachiris and also Jelly spent many holidays and periods of rest after Scottish concerts: for Mrs Ranken, before she married her crack-shot Major, had been a Marion Bruce whom Adila had known as a student in Berlin.

Anna Robertson started as Adila's and Jelly's admirer and be-

The House in Netherton Grove

came their administrator. She also became the loved and loving friend especially of Jelly. Her qualifications for the post of administrator were three: merriment, devotion, and as complete an inability to spell or type as Jelly's and Adila's. Also she was unyieldingly loyal and dependable, two qualities needed in one who was to be to a pair of celebrities 'friend, right hand, scribe, pianist and on occasion chauffeuse.' Her duties (the right description would be 'two-way favours') did not stop there. She paid accounts—and ten years later bills for house alterations were still being presented. She grappled with income tax forms. She acted on last-minute appeals from Adila, or from Jelly in Brussels, imploring Darling Anna to go to the silver writing table in the corner of Jelly's bedroom at Netherton Grove and find two cheques in the 'top right-hand draw', because Jelly has asked her bank to invest £600 for her and will be overdrawn if these are not presented. This must be an early letter, because for the rest of her life Jelly called her 'Snookie'. (Pronounced as with a Sh, this was the name of a mischievous Hungarian imp in one of the stories Adila used to tell.)

It was she who found (how often!) things mislaid or left behind, corresponded with agents and music societies, reconciled conflicting dates, sometimes shopped for meals or for a whole party,[14] chose trains and somehow got either or both of them to the right place by the right time.

She was a unique boon to the two—indeed the three—unpractical musicians at Netherton Grove; and when she went out of it, they decided they could have no one to replace her. For in the early 1930s she developed tuberculosis and spent years in and out of Scottish hospitals. Jelly felt like a little dog lost without her. She hated London with 'no grumpy darling little Snook' (both sisters used *kish,* the Hungarian for 'little' as a sign of affection) bumping into her at every step. Jelly, worst of correspondents except to Adila and her father, kept writing letters of love and admiration for Anna Robertson's courage and humour and patience; letters which did much to save her from the spiritual despair which sometimes accompanies the graver stages of that malady.

The Sisters d'Aranyi

In one such letter Jelly gave her news of a certain Robert Gell, whom she met after a recital at Norwich. She liked him very much. 'Devotion' she wrote 'like his for you is a moving thing.'

Everyone liked Anna Robertson, and missed her. She had charm and good looks as well as humour and reliability. Jelly and Alec were both struck by her good looks when they met her, unexpectedly and after a long time, at Glyndebourne.[15]

At last in 1937 she was cured, and took a small cottage at Colman's Hatch in Sussex, whence she wrote wittily to Jelly about the morals of the village, one neighbour having gone to prison, another having killed himself, and others engaging in bloody fights.[16] While she was there, the Aranyis saw quite a lot of her, but she was not well enough to take up her 'duties' again.

Then she returned to Scotland, to Dirleton; and Jelly could see her only when she went north for concerts. It was a little consolation to both that a blackbird in the garden there sang the first two bars of the *Rondo* in the Beethoven *Concerto*.[17]

When the Second World War broke out, Anna Robertson returned to hospital life, but as Red Cross nurse not patient, having passed the necessary exams. Jelly's admiration grew for her courage in the kind of work she did, which included often sittings at the bedside of the dying. But in some people wars can supply the otherwise lacking physical reserves that the mental purposes demand. When the war was over, Anna Robertson married Robert Gell and went to live in a cottage at Roslin, where she still is, which was to be of deep importance to Jelly though she saw it only once. But more of this later.

Her absence caused a recrudescence of chaos in Hurricane House, ever-continuous telephones being now unanswered by ever-continuously practising violins. But the parties went on, engagements were made, and even kept, Adila filed away programmes and Jelly made hers into little bundles.

The truth was that in the heart of the hurricane was tranquillity. 'I never heard a cross or jealous word between Adila and Jelly', Mrs Gell says; Alec and Adila loved one another, and Alec

The House in Netherton Grove

and Jelly were devoted. When, early on, her '*Sai*' got a bad notice in *The Times*, it was Adila who was furious. 'Damn that man!'[18] He's a fool and doesn't understand music.' They never complimented each other, but praised each other discerningly. Nothing blocked their mutual love or their evaluations.

Adila mothered Jelly. They both were apprehensive of accidents that cripple. When Jelly and Titi went to America, Adila's final instructions arrived at ss *Olympic* in Southampton docks with a huge mass of flowers. Jelly was to be particularly careful with train doors and lifts—and do not please look out of windows. Adila promised to take similar precautions herself.

She did not always. She liked to lean out of railway windows, when steam trains could blow burning cinders into your eye. She was once doing so on the way to Malaga, where the track passed through fields of coloured and sweet-smelling flowers. 'I wish we could stop here!' Jelly sighed. And the train stopped, with a jerk. Adila could see up the curve that the locomotive had derailed itself.

At Christmas time Adila waylaid any parcels that arrived, and hid them till Christmas Eve, which was their time for presents: and Adrienne did the same for her aunt when her mother died. Jelly had that childlikeness which makes people want to cosset a person and prevent evil from hurting them. It was part of her magic.

In the tranquillity of her personal life Adila filled her spare time like any other intelligent woman; for she was not all swirl and bustle. She liked reading; Jane Austen in particular, and later Anthony Trollope when the Trollope boom brought him new readers. She enjoyed Burton's *Arabian Nights*, being neither prurient nor prude. She read few popular novels. Scott she had detested but she suddenly fell for him. Travel, biography, decent books on religion, even Bertrand Russell, whom she always much admired.[19] These were her likes.

Few hobbies she had but many diversions: tennis, swimming, gardening in later life, bridge, poker, films and the game called scrabble. Though she liked subtle food, she could also enjoy bread and cheese. If she revelled in society, she also looked forward to quiet weekends in friends' country houses or days by the sea in a hotel. She always took her violin, and practised.

The Fachiris went seldom to the theatre. Sometimes they were taken in a party, and could find the play rather trashy. But Adila was struck by entertainments as diverse as *Juno and the Paycock*, Grock, and Sacha Guitry in *Mon Père Avait Raison*. She could not like Stravinsky, not even *Mavra* at the Russian Ballet in Paris.[20]

When she and Alec had something to celebrate, they went out to a favourite restaurant, like Les Gobelins, the Savoy or the Carlton, the Ivy or Simpson's: and when they felt merely like going out, they made for the Imperial or the Good Intent nearby.

Their private life, in short, was that of any happily married couple; for there are such things as happily married couples; and as with many such, after ten years a daughter was born.

Alec was delighted, being fond of children: so much so, that when they gave children's parties, as they had done before their daughter's birth, Alec came back early from the Temple to devote himself to the small guest of the afternoon.

And as with most parents, the daughter caused them both worry and joy. She fell, and both were anxious. She had her first tooth, and both were glad. She had spots, and even Jelly in America had to be kept informed by telegram when the diagnosis was made, even though it was a common ailment. Adrienne had a baby flirtation with a Spanish painter at table, and because by now she could talk, she asked questions. This was a friend of Cassadó. He did a drawing of mother and daughter. On her first birthday they gave, as parents do, a party. With a conjuror.

Adila was never a besotted mother. In fact she could laugh at even her motherhood. When the baby was less than a month old, the nurse handed her to Adila to hold for a moment while she did something else. Adila in a gorgeous dressing-gown took her, and little Adrienne set up a howl. Adila handed her back. 'I'm not her type' she said ruefully.[21]

And Jelly was much more than aunt. When Adrienne was

The House in Netherton Grove

small, if Adila were ill in bed as she frequently was, Jelly would not leave the house, because she was needed to clown for her little niece.[22] But soon Adrienne showed an aptitude for the violin as unmistakable as her aunt's or mother's. Jelly was again in demand. By the time Adrienne was eleven, when she had finished her homework, Jelly had always to go and practise with her in the Green Room.[23]

They had a dog called Caesar, a fox terrier, to complete the domestic picture. I imagine him rough-haired, like King Edward VII's Caesar. The Swiss governess, another Anna, used to tease him by calling '*Souris! Souris! Souris!*' When Casals came one evening, he was complaining that he had not slept a wink at the Piccadilly Hotel because of a mouse in the room. He spoke in French. Caesar arose and hunted.

In fact it was all normal.

But normal households also have illnesses: and here was a dark shadow. Neither Adila nor Alec was ever for long fully well. Common influenzas could keep Adila in bed from six to nineteen days. Often she gave concerts when she should have been in a sickroom.[24] But she had a fierce disregard for bodily weaknesses. This she had always had. When twelve years old, she was passing a house in Budapest where builders were at work, and a piece of quicklime lodged in an eye, which was delicate ever after and gave trouble when she was in Berlin with Joachim. A doctor there advised glasses. Adila was furious. 'There's nothing the matter with my eye!' she roared.

Alec's health was a more grave matter. He too had a contempt for weakness, but his lungs were not controllable by contempt. As early as 1920, during an attack of whooping cough (painful to adults) he started to expectorate blood. Although he assured Adila that this was from the throat only, she dreaded worse explanations. An X-ray in 1926 revealed nothing; but he was continually finding himself unable to go to work from heavy colds and congestions and fevers that would not abate. His work gave him small chance to better his condition, which needed rest and fresh air. For from 1919 he had more and more cases to handle, long

The Sisters d'Aranyi

hours of study and strain in far from healthy surroundings. Later his life was a rush between London and The Hague.

(Incidentally it is something of a shock to discover at this point that Alexandre Fachiri was naturalized only in 1919. Up till then he had been a citizen of the U.S.A.)

In 1938 it was largely through his international efforts that at last 'India of the Princes' remained in the Commonwealth to be. These efforts drained his reserves. He was very ill for weeks. Six doctors could not get his temperature down. In the end it was a homoeopath who discovered that influenza germs had settled permanently in a lung that must have been weak from childhood. This was then confirmed by a specialist, who found scars on the tissue. No medical person seems to have known what should be done.

That was in the middle of February. On March 27, 1939, he died, of double pneumonia and complications.

Adila took his death as well as any woman can who is in love with her husband. Jelly wrote her admiration to Anna Gell, that Adila was ashamed of being broken. And 'Adrienne' she continued 'loves her Daddy more than ever.' But life at Netherton Grove was finished. Adila could not bear the place. It is wise advice to a bereaved wife or husband that they should either fill their home with friends and flowers, or get out at once to a new place as different as possible. This latter Adila and Jelly tried to do.

First they went to the Rankens in Edinburgh for such comfort as an oldest woman friend could give. When they returned to London, they looked for somewhere to live. The two best women violinists living were humiliated and frustrated in this process.

They looked first for furnished rooms[25]. They found dingy, depressing ones only. Then they accepted Ralph Hawtrey's offer to live with him as paying guests. But this took time to arrange, and they borrowed a flat for five days. Two days before the day for the move to Elm Park Gardens, they went round to decide what they would need. They thought best to have two rooms, two extra beds, and a maid and charwoman of their own.

Hawtrey's two maids promptly gave notice, though it had been

The House in Netherton Grove

for a trial of only three months. A compromise of three weeks made them feel, as they left the house, downhearted and lost and not wanted. That was at eight in the evening. They had intended to buy something for their supper, but the shops were shut. At last the faithful Baron Palmstierna came to their rescue. He had asked them to dinner that evening, but Adila wished to be alone with Jelly. Now they went round in the hope he might still be in. He was, and took them out to a comforting dinner, said they must obviously find a flat of their own, and asked in the restaurant if anyone knew of any. In this way they moved to Chesil Court in Manor Street, where Adila cooked breakfast and supper, lunch was available downstairs, and they had to do all the housework themselves. Which was the best thing for both of them. Adila bore up, and Jelly, no longer 'morbid' as she said, 'believed again'. And so for three months or so they began to build their new life together.

Then war broke out.

19

Last Years

If Titi has appeared seldom in these pages, it is because she appeared seldom in public. Very occasionally she was well enough to accompany one of her sisters at a private concert or party. But she often came with her mother or husband to Adila's parties where she was as gay and witty as anyone, and could make people laugh and cry at the same time with her descriptions of things seen or done. Her own parties were gay too, gayer and better, some said, than those at Netherton Grove.[1] But the flood of public music which fountained into Adila and Jelly only spilled over into her.

The nervous trouble that afflicted most of her life flared up more often and more fiercely as she grew older, and from time to time she found herself happier and safer with the company of nurses in nursing homes, latterly at Northampton. At other times she came back to social life only to return again to her bodily convents, and there was little that could be done for her.[2]

She spent her time and some of her psychoses painting pictures, an art she took up when she was about forty-five after two years of study. These are far from negligible artistically. In all that I have seen there is a strange and well rendered atmosphere of apprehension.

She had a sister-in-law who took the veil; and this stimulated her to depict the *Marriage of a Nun to Christ*. The girl's eyes are mystically exalted; her hands, deliberately long, form a triangle which jabs harshly toward the softly dreaming face. Two smiling girls support her. The head of one is poised to grasp the novice's hair, and the arm, fat and foreshortened like a baroque nymph's, is curiously disturbing.

The Temptation of Eve is mature and haunting. Against a background of rectangles like angles of wall, the face is in hard profile with a reflective, aware, and very feminine eye. The hand holds an apple of so dark a crimson that it seems a ball of blood. The treatment is free and assured, and an Italian painter has found in it something on a level with Chagall. If Titi was not well known as a pianist, she might well be better known as a painter.

The Second World War oppressed both Adila and Jelly. Humanly its predecessor had been a tragedy; musically this one was at first a disaster. All public concerts[3] were automatically cancelled with the imposition of the Blackout; and it was a long while before the inhabitants of London and other towns groped their way back into theatres and concert halls. To the sisters it seemed as if the end of their usefulness had come: and so, unfortunately, in a sense it had.

Neither of them was either more or less nervous of bombs than anyone else. Adila indeed returned to her childhood's motto 'Where danger is greatest, help is nearest.'[4] Jelly admired this, even if she were not wholly convinced. But a furnished flat was no place for two middle-aged ladies with at least three musical instruments of considerable value. It was this, and not cowardice, that made them leave London in November 1939.

They first stayed for a short time in Hertfordshire, then went to their friends the Donald Somervells at Ewelme Old Rectory in Oxfordshire.[5] Here they spent a large part of the war, came to love the place, and later built on a bungalow site a small cottage which they called The Garden House. It had a grey-tiled roof and rose-pink walls. Adila developed her arts of gardening.

Adrienne was sent to boarding school, to everyone's grief. But the middle part of the war she spent in the Master's Lodging at All Souls, Oxford, where she finished her education under such people as David Cecil. By 1943, however, the flood that fountained

The Sisters d'Aranyi

showed every sign of being about to cascade into Adrienne, and she went to the Royal College of Music, for general musical education and violin lessons with Albert Sammons.

At Ewelme Adila and Jelly met another evacuee, the pianist James Sherrin, who had been for two years accompanist to Brahms's friend Raymond Zur Machen. In chamber music they found him exceptional and took him to St Andrews for a joint concert. He had no money, never grumbled or complained, and played for love. Jelly, writing this to Anna Robertson, repeats the word Love in capitals. He was just the right kindly affectionate person to encourage and comfort them when they felt unwanted; and they made plans to help him, financially also, by a concert in aid of Anna Robertson's Red Cross in Edinburgh. This would at least bring him three guineas.

Outwardly Adila was the same impulsive, downright, generous woman she had always been. But she was far from being happy or at ease. If she had a fear, she still had to master it, and that meant sometimes mastering other people. Thus she had a neurosis about flying. She had to go to Scapa Flow to play to the Navy. The tiny military plane which took her from Inverness was the first and I think only experience she ever had of flying, which she found even worse than her fear of it. She thundered at the pilot 'Don't smoke! It's dangerous!' And when safely landed but still on edge, she marched into the Navy-occupied hotel where she was to spend the night, demanding 'Who is the manager here?'

But inwardly the heart was out of her. The Somervells were as kind and good friends as could be, but the house was eleven miles from a railway station. Travelling, as she had to do to CEMA and other concerts, was in her state of health painful as well as uncomfortable, as it was to Jelly.

At first they played mostly together: in the Temple Church, in the Sheldonian Theatre at Oxford with a small orchestra. Adila tried to form a string quartet when they went for a holiday to Scotland in 1942. But the heart was out of Scotland too for her, since Tovey's death in 1939: Tovey, to whom she had written when his hands were too crippled to play any more 'I could

Last Years

never, never thank you enough for all your help and teachings—not only in music, but in other things.'⁶

As she went on in life, at times she thought she learned less and less. This might mean progress or might mean decay. At that time it felt like decay. She gave lessons; she played in the provinces; she went to school after school. But with one exception she played nothing new.

In March 1942 she gave the first performance of a *Suite for Violin and Small Orchestra* (op. 101) at Windermere, where its composer Armstrong Gibbs lived, and she gave its first broadcast under Sir Adrian Boult in September from Manchester.

In June 1943 after a London absence of about seven years, she reappeared in the Wigmore Hall, but again with nothing new. This was at a Bach concert with the Jacques String Orchestra. She played both *Violin Concerti*, the unaccompanied *Chaconne*, and with Bertram Harrison the *C minor Sonata*. It gave pleasure and consolation to people, as wartime music did when it got going again; but without the old glory.

In November of 1943 Adila and Jelly returned to London, to another furnished flat, in Basil Mansions. The war was turning from exhaustion and apathy and destructive stalemate to hope and endeavour with Stalingrad and the long withheld Second Front. But London was different. Friends were away or busy with war work. Rationing was dire. A cook like Adila cannot begin without an onion nor end without butter: butter was served out in inches, and if anyone came by an onion, they put it on the mantelpiece for its beauty. Although Adila gave two other London concerts that year, continued her provincial trips and even played twice in Rome after the war, so far as I can make out another seven years had to pass before she played in London again.⁷

However in 1951 three things of importance happened in her life. She had her sixty-fifth birthday: she gave an important concert in the Wigmore Hall: and Adrienne got engaged to be married to a young Italian she had met on holiday. Adrienne was by now a violinist with a fine technique, lovely bowing and a deep intuition for music.

The Sisters d'Aranyi

It was once said of T. S. Eliot, at an older age than Adrienne now had, that he had all the qualities of a great poet except the wish to be one. The same could have been said of Adrienne as violinist. 'Adrienne's playing is very beautiful' Jelly wrote to Anna Gell[8] in the middle of a letter about other things, as if she had just heard her practising and broken off to listen. And Jelly never passed opinions on violin playing from favour or prejudice.

Maybe Adrienne felt weighed down by the family name and the Joachim blood. She found practising not beauty but labour: and although in her hands in later years her great-great-uncle's violin was served almost as it had always been served since he first had it, the life of a professional performer was not her choice. That of a young wife in Florence, making new friends and welcoming old ones on visits, was more to her liking: and so for a while she passes from this chronicle.

The concert in the Wigmore Hall was important for three reasons. First, in the Bach *Concerto in E* Adila was accompanied by a small string orchestra without a conductor. This went swimmingly. It was not the first time she had done such a thing. In 1943 she and Jelly had played with an unconducted double string-quartet in Hampton Court. They had no necessity to lead with gestures, the unanimity was so perfect: whereas Max Rostal, trying a similar experiment, found violent gestures necessary. When Jelly told me this, she compared it with the difference between Queen Victoria and the Empress Eugénie sitting down after plaudits at the Opera. The Empress had to look round for her chair, the Queen sat down like a professional.

Secondly, Adila had at last prepared a novelty: the entire sequence of Brahms-Joachim *Hungarian Dances* in the arrangement for violin and piano. All twenty-one of them: and programme notes by Adila herself. With the help of Béla Bartók. From which last it appears that some of the tunes could be ascribed to Panna Czinka, the musical mistress met in chapter 3. Adila's mind at this moment must have made a fine spiral over her Budapest childhood.

These dances were by now regarded as homely and old-fash-

Last Years

ioned and romantic, compared with the true Hungarian rhythms of Kodaly and Bartók, which had been rejected as non-national and highbrow twenty-five years before.[9] But her playing of their waywardnesses as on the spur of the moment had something of gipsy playing in it, and came as a revelation to the London public which had forgotten her.

The third, and most cogent, reason for calling this concert important is that Adila was right back to her old form, and from then on had a new lease of musical life.

As if to show that she was no old-fashioned string in an old-fashioned style in a quaint little old-fashioned vogue, when she next performed the dances with Sherrin in London (March 1952) she added a *Tartar Suite* by Mostras and Lobachev, Soviet collectors and arrangers of Tartar songs and dances, of whom the former was an authority on Turkmenian music.

Adila found a family resemblance between this music and that of the true Hungarian gipsies; so close that she suggested as an explanation of their unknown origins perhaps the Altai Mountains: and defended in her programme notes this Tartar-gipsyish music for its 'rhythm and its nostalgic memories' with as much firmness as she defended some Wieniawsky virtuoso pieces she was playing. Virtuoso pieces are fun to play, and the fun the public had from them when Adila played was rightly ascribed by the press to the perfect skill of a rediscovered virtuoso of top rank.

Her word 'nostalgic' reveals a new mood in Adila. When she repeated the *Tartar Suite* in London in 1955, she also played for the first time in public the little work Béla Bartók had written for her after the success of the Budapest Academy concert. It was Bartók who named it *In Remembrance of November 23rd*; under which title she gave the world its first hearing after fifty years. The youthful, Straussian little work sounded romantic and parlour-like[10] to a generation to whom Bartók, who had died in 1945, then stood among the four or five most advanced composers of the time.[11] But Adila's charming and wistful way of playing it justified its belated introduction, and she had many requests to repeat it, as she did the following year.

The Sisters d'Aranyi

I would not like to give the impression that she returned to fame as a manipulator of jolly rhythms or collector of nosegays. Her interpretation of the Brahms *Sonata in G* with Sherrin was not only as musicianly as ever, it had also a new authenticity. She had studied this with Joachim. Toward the end of the last movement Joachim was particular about complying with the composer's request over the *poco rit.*;[12] and Sherrin confirmed that Raymond Zur Machen was the same. They resisted the temptation to end *ritardando*. Adila followed them, and in the place where the violin takes over the accompaniment *pizzicato*, she contrived as Joachim had done to make it sound like a harp.

These are small details, but indicative. In her lonely nostalgia for the past, Adila was improving not only her technique, but on her youth.

In the Bach *Chaconne* too, if perhaps she never possessed Jelly's consummate ease, there was freshness, breadth and grandeur more than ever. Her bowing was even better. By now the older she grew, the more she could learn. She went from strength to strength.[13]

During this time she went to stay with Adrienne in Florence and was glad to find her happy and to give a concert or two there; and Adrienne came on a return visit later.

Adila was now getting on to seventy and evidently thinking much about the past. Her programme notes read like spiritual footnotes as much as musical news. In June 1955 she gave a talk on Béla Bartók at the International 'Cello Centre; a simple friendly talk about him as man and composer, from which I have taken one or two details in other chapters. But she gave no more important concerts.

True in 1956 she played three *Sonatas* at the Wigmore Hall with Rainer von Zastrow (Schumann *in D minor*, Beethoven *in C minor*, and one by Respighi also *in C minor*). But her rare appearances gave the press an opportunity to make obvious innuendoes. 'Much of the music'[14] the *Daily Telegraph* wrote 'demanded a power of tone and a vigour of attitude which she was unable to sustain. But there were moments of Schumann's op.

which recalled the high-spirited yet distinguished style which made Mme Fachiri's name.' Almost exactly the same words were used by the critic of *The Times*. Almost as in a conspiracy.

There were no Proms, no Philharmonics, no Hallés; not even chamber music. Many of her old conductor friends had retired or died. But her absence from the concert platform was not due to that.

The career of a public performer is like running in a dream: however fast you run after slower runners you never overtake them. Public performers must never disappear. If they do, they must not reappear. How many actresses who have left the stage to marry, find when they wish to return that because their old continuum has stopped they are not allowed to start anew? With Adila there was no ageing in musical spirit nor slackening of technique. Quite the reverse, according to friends who could judge. Adrienne says that to the very end when her mother played the Mozart *A major Concerto*, the sound was 'like what comes out of a dolphin's mouth in a fountain if you take your finger off the spout.' Clear, purposive, free, refreshing. And at least as late as November 1959 Adila felt her powers actually growing. 'I now will learn the Bach *Sonata* (solo) *no. 3 in A minor*' she wrote to Adrienne. 'Somehow it will go as I wanted it to go but never dared to tackle. Music needs a life's experience to do as one feels and wants.'

The circumstances of her last recital were characteristic of both sisters. They had locked up their house, and found in the interval at the Wigmore Hall that nobody had brought a key. Jelly took a taxi and got a young officer from the nearest police station to break in by the bathroom window. They were expecting guests, and had already prepared snacks, so that Jelly was able to entertain young Charlie (or Harry) to beer and sandwiches. When he left, he forgot to take his pocket torch; and Jelly had to call out in the silence of the evening street 'Charlie! Charlie!' (or Harry! Harry!) 'you've forgotten your torch,' to the great interest of tickled neighbours.

However in 1957 both sisters fell ill, and for both there was now considerably more joy in the past than in the present. Their mutual love was imperishable; but both were lonely without Adrienne. So while Jelly was convalescing the following March with snow covering the ground outside, they came to what Jelly called 'the terrific (and now it seems a terrible) decision.'[15] They would sell the Garden House if they could, and emigrate to Florence. At least there loneliness would be filled.

Adila went over and chose the new house, at Bellosguardo. She returned with a sinusitis that kept her in bed for a fortnight. And when the time came for the flitting, she was hardly well enough to get up, let alone see to everything in a rush.

Jelly followed later, thinking she would go for eighteen months. Even that was a wrench. England was specially kind to her that year in 'glorious country, loving friends, good concerts' she wrote to Adrienne.[16] So it was harder for her than for Adila, though she knew it would be good to be with her sister and niece and nephew-in-law.

Her mind went back not to romantic memories but to wry ones: a dream, in fact, of Anna Robertson's about the Last Judgment, which had become a parable for Jelly.

The dreamer was sitting with others on an endless horizontal pole poised between clouds above and below. Everyone had to jump into space, and if they had faith, they went up; if no faith, down. The dreamer felt she had not faith enough even to jump; so stayed still until she was the only one left. The pole then grew hotter and hotter.

So felt Jelly at Ewelme.

She tried to persuade herself that the house at Bellosguardo was quite near houses where the Brownings and other great ones of the past had lived, and that surely they must have left a happy atmosphere.

And as it proved, life at Bellosguardo had many compensations for both of them. The sisters made music in houses and villas. Adila gardened, learning yet more widely in the two acres. And in gardening she was as methodical as when studying a new concerto: she even kept count of the number of roses on each bush.

Last Years

They intended to go back to England soon on a visit, and to give a few concerts whose fees would help expenses. But their proposed hostess had a demand for arrears of income tax and had to live as quiet as a church mouse for half a year.

Adila did go back on visits. She regretted them. Her image of Britain now differed from the reality. Even in a *de luxe* hotel with wonderful food, she hated the cocktail bar, where the inmates all looked wicked and dissipated. She found the English, despite their daily baths, dirty compared with the Italians. London saddened her, with its now impossible traffic, its people all dressed the same with three horrible hair styles: 'like marionettes'. The sensations and advertisements of the newspapers nauseated her. And the kind of people she met were not the kind she had met. The old order to which she belonged had vanished.[17]

But while there she kept on practising, and giving some lessons, and her friends gladdened her. Especially Rohan.

Rohan de Saram was a very young 'cellist from Ceylon, for whom Adila had a deep maternal love. He lived with the Denekes at Oxford. This time Adila found him more adorable than ever, and when he played he looked so like Alec that Adila burst into tears. He wanted to buy Alec's 'cello; but Adila was loth to take money for it and gave it to him on loan instead.

Such moments did not make up for the general ugliness of life in England to Adila's eyes. She felt they were lucky to be able to live in Florence. In Florence she could still be herself. She could still whirl and exaggerate. She had a cat, which got on everybody's nerves. When it died, she had a baby's coffin made and lined with pink and lavender, and buried it in the garden with a cross over the grave. There are times for some people when they have to exaggerate their own sincerities.

In Tuscany too there could be friends. On August 12, 1959 Adila and Jelly went to Siena for the day, where Casals was giving a final 'master lesson' to a group of musicians. They met in Count Chigi's 'glorious drawing-room'. Casals who was then eighty-three ('but had more life in his playing than even a sixteen-year-old boy' Adila said) dismissed everybody when he saw them, and hugged them and kissed them, and could not believe they had really come. They sat on a sofa talking of old times and friends, and all three of them were the better of this. Casals wanted to send a message to Adrienne, who was in England on a visit; so Jelly tore a piece of a cheque out of her cheque-book, and kept this message in her fiddle-case till Adrienne returned.[18]

Jelly went once to Britain with Adrienne. They gave concerts in Durham and Bath and Oxford. At Oxford Adrienne played the César Franck *Sonata* and some of the *Hungarian Dances*. At that time she was also playing the Brahms *Sonata in A*, Tartini's *in E minor*, and the Beethoven *'Spring' Sonata*. She was Hope to her mother. 'I prefer' Adila wrote to Jelly—one serious violinist writing to another, 'Adri's playing to Stern's.'[19] Isaac Stern had just given a concert in Florence and Adila deeply admired him. But she insisted that Adrienne get used to playing solo. If it was her unreliable memory which made her nervous, then according to Adila who knew all about perfidious memories, with regular practice of at least four hours a day, this lack of confidence would go, as it had with her. 'You *have everything*' she wrote to her daughter, 'and only get muddled by lack of practice.'[20]

Adrienne had a success in these concerts. That did not help her.

In 1960 Adila and Jelly were asked to play the Bach *Double Concerto* with Dr Hylton-Stewart in St. James's, Piccadilly, for World Refugee Year. The church was packed, and the collection reached £174. But what touched them most was the endless queue of friends who came to see them afterwards. About which Jelly was guarded in writing to Adrienne in Florence. 'It was all very moving and we played our best—well, that's that.'

They did their best: and may I here copy out what *The Times* said of that best in 1925, thirty-five years before?[21]

'The whole effect is finely satisfying, the solo parts stand out the more clearly for this difference in style' (classical restraint, romantic warmth) 'while the pull, first one way then the other, seems to give the whole interpretation great vitality and interest.'

I do not agree that Adila was 'classical' and Jelly 'romantic'

Last Years

Both could be either: like Beethoven. And if *The Times* thought their consort best with Jelly in the lead, because 'hers is the more decisive temperament, while Madame Fachiri is more sensitive to suggestions,' many people, including myself, thought the exact opposite. When Adila led, Jelly came in with a will; but Jelly was every bit as sensitive to suggestions as Adila; and Adila controlled.

However 'pull' is an accurate word. It was true in 1925. It was probably true of their first performance of the concerto in Vienna in 1908. As true also of this last time in the Britain they had loved, and which had loved them; when they played it so gloriously together.

In October 1962 the BBC broadcast a recording made by Adila and Tovey for the National Gramophone Society in 1927 of Beethoven's last *Violin Sonata* (op. 96 in G). Sir Edward Boyle, in private life an accomplished musicologist and old family friend, thought this better than Adila had feared, even if Tovey's playing sounded by 1960 standards 'old-fashioned and explosive.'[22] This was the only time Tovey's voice was recorded; for he had strong convictions that to omit the repeats destroyed the structure. At the end of the exposition his voice is heard on the disc telling Adila to go back to the beginning.

That was Adila's last acknowledgement from Britain during her lifetime.

In December she went into a nursing home for a minor operation on an abscess. Both sisters were happy that in Italy it is permitted, indeed welcomed, for the second bed in a private ward to be occupied by a relative. After four days they went home, but Adila's heart grew worse, and they went to a clinic for treatment. In addition to other chronic troubles Adila had always had high blood pressure. A blood vessel burst and she died in her sister's arms on December 15, 1962. '*You* can do without me' she said to Adrienne, but she was worried about Jelly[23], remembering how she had helped and mothered Jelly from the very days in Budapest when she had dressed her dolls.

Inside her handbag, some days later going through her things, they found a small white woollen rabbit.

Epilogue at Bellosguardo

Jelly died here when the first two parts of this book were more or less in their present state. She approved of what had been so far written. My intention had always been to close with an epilogue, written perhaps in the present tense, a backward look at her life, a kind of actuality programme. This is not now possible.

But although the number of pages has swollen inadvisably, there are still other angles, lights and lines to be added if the picture is to be anything like complete.

We left her with the Cathedrals Tour in 1933, which ruined her health and was in one sense the destruction of her. Like most public performers she had fortitude to appear when bed would have been better for colds and fevers, and even to make long journeys in draughty trains. Rarely did she miss an engagement from sickness: a BBC date because she was suffering from 'absecces' (word she never could spell) in the nose: another time when she was substituted by Orrea Pernell.

As a rule these afflictions did not affect her playing, and once with a very heavy cold she thought she had never played the Bach *Chaconne* better.[1] But when her general condition was low and her body quite exhausted, she realized she was not playing well and decided not to touch the violin for a couple of days.[2]

The number of times she sprained an ankle was abnormal for one life. As we have seen, book-years ago, anxiety and a bad circulation caused a vexatious irritation in her bowing arm, and even rashes. This bad circulation, combining with graver troubles, incapacitated her after the Cathedrals Tour. She was staying in the West of England, and fell while moving along a corridor of a country house at night. She broke a bone in the little finger of the left hand.

At the time she was mourning the loss of Tom Spring-Rice; but her spirit conquered both grief and the injury. At her next appearance a friend thought she played the *Kreutzer Sonata* 'with an inspiration of sadness almost overwhelming.'[3] But very soon after this she again fell, slipping on a polished floor, injured the base of her spine, and suffered slight concussion, so that a future visit to Aberystwyth had to be postponed.[4]

These accidents, and perhaps some sense that she was destined to lose in one way or another almost all the friends she was most fond of, further inflamed her proneness to rheumatism, already affected by the nights in violinists' frocks in cold and damp cathedrals. Arthritis set in, all up the right arm, and spread to her legs; and from then on she was never wholly free from pain.[5] Arthritis or worse.

Work and pain were an unpleasant combination, she decided; but made light of her troubles to her friends, who were content with 'lumbago' or 'sciatica' as explanations.

But in December 1934 a more alarming affliction came to torture body and mind.

Although Jelly suffered no more than most people from sore throats, she had in 1928 gone to bed with a septic one after returning viâ Vienna from her Budapest holiday with the Fachiris. She got up for concerts at the Queen's Hall and Derby, where she wore a gossamer scarf round her throat[6]—and hated doing so for fear people might think she went in for such kittenish things.

Now in 1934 after another train journey, to Aberdeen, she started another septic throat. For Christmas she went to a country house in the south of Scotland, where the infection spread to the mastoid gland. A local doctor gave the wrong treatment and a specialist from Edinburgh did a minor operation on the ear-drum. This misfortune, which cost her £100 and the loss of a tour to

Epilogue at Bellosguardo

the Canary Islands, made her seriously ill and understandably anxious.[7] She was afraid of losing her absolute pitch, possibly being left deaf; and from a Beethoven-like terror of what malicious mouths might say, insisted on calling her ailment 'septic throat'. She lost nothing of her hearing or pitch; but her general condition grew worse. Her bowing was affected, more slightly than she feared it might be (for Sidney Newman among others found no falling-off in her later years),[8] and perhaps she did fade a little in her unique 'magic'. So low was her state of nerves that she, who hardly knew fear, was agonized by Baron Palmstierna's car-driving on perilous corners during a summer holiday in North Devon. And sometimes her fingers were so stiff that they could hardly guide a pen.[9]

What got her out of this was her own spirit. Not only in the religious sense, though that too made memorable her playing at a private memorial tribute to Tom Spring-Rice in December 1934. I do not mean that Jelly thought about God or Death while playing: she thought about music. But a friend places her well on this occasion by saying 'Whether it is death or any other form of sorrow, there *is* another view and you can tell us of it, and I know no other artist who can or does.'[10]

Jelly knew she had played well. 'The dying flames of my popularity' she wrote to Anna Robertson after the 'impish' Brahms *Concerto* at Gloucester criticized on p. 134 'have been blown to a volcano vomiting flames.' But all the same, she seems to have kept to her old repertoire for a very long time, adding only a new light piece or two, the *Dudak* from *Schwanda the Bagpiper* at Sidmouth and a *Rondo* by the Piedmontese Leone Sinigaglia (who was delighted she had done it) at Liverpool. She broadcast frequently on Empire wavelengths.

In March and April 1935 she was in Holland, playing the Mendelssohn *Concerto*. The following February at one Edinburgh concert she played Joachim's, the Bach *in A minor* and the Brahms. To this she had gone expecting two orchestral rehearsals, but there was only one, and that was rushed, because the wind section had to leave for a broadcasting date. But she was glad to hear how Tovey, in spite of staff difficulties and frustrations, had improved his orchestra.[11] She played nothing new at the Lewes, Coventry or Canterbury Festivals, nor at the many recitals she gave in London or outside.

In 1937, however, she made a musical discovery. For years she had not played the Bach *'Sonata for Violin with figured Bass'* but while on holiday with friends in Scotland, she decided to restudy it, and worked the speed of the *allegro* to what Adila called *'brillante'*. The next afternoon Adila and Alec were at the 'glass game' and to Jelly's consternation it spelt out 'Bach says play it slow'. Trying it slow the following day she could make no sense of it, and her hostess Maisie Kelly could not find her copy of the *Bachgesellschaft*. Next time the glass advised her to look in the volume of this work which contained a work by Vivaldi 'if we remember aright'.

Jelly did not then know that any work by Vivaldi had been published with Bach; but at a rehearsal in the RCM for another Gloucester Festival, she asked Sir Hugh Allen if she could see the *Gesellschaft*. Sure enough, two works earlier than one by Vivaldi came the Bach *Sonata* she was looking for. The 'description' said that Bach had indicated the repeated E notes to be doubled *in unisono* (open and stopped alternately), but that this was not printed owing to its impracticability at the speed *allegro*.

She now considered the work itself. There was no figured bass. There was no indication of speed whatever. It was a mere convention that the first movement should be played fast. She spent much time till she mastered it as Bach evidently intended; but the effect, she said, was 'unearthly'.

Strangely, I find no evidence in programmes or press cuttings that Jelly ever performed this work in public. But she never told me that she did not; and the musical public must have been interested in this new sounding of an old work.

Nor do I know what Jelly meant by the 'dying flames of my popularity'. And now I cannot ask her. The evidence is all to the contrary. At the Leith Hill Festival in 1936 the scene was 'unprecedented'. She had played Bach's *Concerto in A minor,* and

Epilogue at Bellosguardo

three of the *Hungarian Dances,* which were received 'with the wildest enthusiasm'. She then mounted the conductor's rostrum, faced the choirs, and played Bazzini's *Suite de Concert* from beginning to end, 'a simply marvellous display of execution and harmonics' which was received with such 'almost frantic delight' that she could not leave without adding a Spanish dance by Manuel de Falla.[12]

Many of her appearances up to, and during, the last war were for charity. In particular she braved worse arthritis by her second cathedral series. After one she sent the Dean a cheque, but he destroyed it, saying her own expenses were high enough for her. She also had many professional dates all over the country and on the radio, going to Brussels in March 1937 and to Holland again the following February. Early in the war she played with Myra Hess and Cassadó in the National Gallery.[13]

During the Second War a fund for the men in minesweepers was helped by her with yet more recitals in sacred buildings, Portsmouth Cathedral and St Columba's Church, Pont Street, among them. In Hereford Cathedral in 1941 her red-robed, gold-belted figure gleamed before a moss-green frontal and five gilded arches with the altar cross shining on her head.

The courage of the people of London in the first, worst 'blitz' won her admiration so immediately that she got up many recitals in aid of the YMCA Mobile Canteens. This social giving of music resulted in another summons to Windsor Castle, where she was accompanied by the organist Dr W. H. Harris. It also resulted in a late recognition of her services to music with the CBE in 1946. She kept the programme of that recital: all familiar noble reflective or peaceful works, Purcell's *Air,* Bach *'on the G string',* the Handel *Sonata in A,* slow movements from the Mendelssohn and Brahms *Concerti,* and *The Lark Ascending.* It may have been that she was playing for charities, but she kept hardly any programmes, and no press cuttings, and never spoke to me of what she had done or not done in those years.

One can trace her only through letters, her own or other people's. Like most of us she was often weary with the slow

The Sisters d'Aranyi

and at times uncertain course of the war. But it may well be that she felt she was not wanted as an active musician when she was not yet fifty years old. 'Very little work' she observes in a letter to Anna Robertson at the end of 1940 'mostly a good deal for the YMCA'. And again in 1943, 'not many engagements for me. Going to Dublin on Dec. 10—if I can get a passage—to play Beethoven.' Then she adds 'That will be fun.'

Not irony, but pleasure.

It was a strange fading-out of a very fine artist still in her prime. I admit I cannot account for it by facts: there are none. And Time in some people's memories tends to magnify rumours more than recollections. Easy to say that as Adila was lost because her husband died, so Jelly was lost because her sister was. There may have been a deeper wound than that. If wound there was, it was perhaps dealt by Myra Hess, who lectured Jelly for a whole hour, as she had done apparently to Adila previously, and as good as told her that she was crippled and could no longer play. 'I am a corpse—musically' wrote[14] Jelly to Anna Robertson with a grimness as near to bitterness as ever she came.

The causes of this, however, nobody seems to know. Accumulations of small vexations, perhaps, that fuse into distress and turns friends to enemies overnight: social things that have nothing to do with musical ones. When I asked Jelly why that wonderful partnership with Myra Hess came to an end, did they quarrel, or what was it, she said firmly 'The war', and nothing more.

It could hardly have been political, though I seem to remember a left-winger about this time saying the Aranyis were 'fascist'. It was a generic word used by many left-wingers of anyone who was not on their wing in the same battle. It could sting, and stick. But as we have seen, it could not stick to Adila or Jelly, though it might have stung, if they heard of it. Adila made outrageous remarks about anyone or anything, but fascist she was not. As with many Hungarians of her upbringing sometimes these could be antisemitic; but Adila had several Jewish friends, and made new ones, even commending a married couple for their cleverness and

Epilogue at Bellosguardo

goodness and charm to Adrienne when they were going to visit Florence. As for Jelly, she was too simple in her enthusiasms to be political at all, and too tolerant, and like Adila too upset by violence to be an -ist of any kind, least of all a racial or oligarchic one.

True, Jelly moved in the blue rather than the red. She played at an Astor wedding in the autumn of 1945. She often stayed at Hever Castle, and was rapturous about 'our beloved Prime Minister' when writing from there to Anna Robertson in 1939: 'I can't tell you how wonderful he is—so truly, so divinely simple. No fuss, no hurry, no red cases, just a fellow guest wanting more and more music.' Her admiration was partly because he liked music, but partly because Neville Chamberlain could tell a story against himself, about some Eton boys who went to see his return from Munich and preferred, as a thrill, seeing a man having a fit whose false teeth had to be taken out.

The younger and gay Jelly adds in an aside 'P.S. In the future keep my autographs—P.M. asked for one.'[15]

If the spirals in our lives can cause pride or pleasure or gratitude or self-searching, it must have been a confused Jelly who with the Fachiris left Ewelme because of spring cleaning in April 1940[15] and went to stay with the Hawtreys in Elm Park Gardens.[16] In the early years of that second world war, mistrusting what the future held, she had the same room as in the First World War, when the gifts of the future seemed boundless.[17]

Neither did the end of the war bring her much. I find traces of few appearances, and very few on concert platforms.[18] In June 1946 she played in Bristol Cathedral for charity (and was gently chided for charging a lodging only and not full expenses). In 1954 she played three times in Bath (Pump Room, Symphony Orchestra, Abbey Church). Here James Sherrin played with her.[19] Even Ethel Hobday had gone. She died at her Kentish home in 1947.

Bath was always a favourite place with the Aranyis. Lady Noble was sure to be in the audience, if indeed she had not inspired the concert, as she had done with so many for them. And her great-grandfather had been the engineer Brunel to whom Mendels-

The Sisters d'Aranyi

sohn had written in 1844 asking him to be kind to the boy Joachim. To feel change is not always to conquer time.

And then, for a while, Jelly like Adila came back. In June she played with her friend Iso Elinson at a private house in Oxford, and on a bitter September evening gave the Bach *Concerto in E* in Winchester Guildhall. Then silence for another three years, till again with Sherrin she played *The Lark Ascending* in St Mary's Church, Ewelme, where Robert Birley made the appeal. From there she was invited to give the Vivaldi *A minor* and Mozart *G major Concerti* at the Hexham Festival. But Adila and she lived at Ewelme, and at Hexham Jelly had friends.

After Adila left for Florence, Jelly had six concerts in October, one being at the University College of Wales, Aberystwyth.[20] This was like a farewell to Arthur Williams. And another wistful spiral was that at one of her last recitals in Britain she should include not only Kelly's *Jig* but also a fantasy of his called *'Gallipoli'*, which unless it was some special arrangement for violin of the *Elegy* I take to have been the first performance of a hitherto unrecorded work.[21]

Emigration, this time, was no easy thing for her. In the letter in which she announced the 'terrible decision', she enclosed a snapshot of Anna Gell taken in 1937, and commented in her gentle way 'I love it and it makes me feel most nostalgic.' Nor can she have been at first very happy when the break was made. The house at Bellosguardo looked ugly to her, neither an old villa nor, though new, a very modern house. But she found the view over to Montemorello and the northern hills 'heavenly', and the garden filled with flowers was set in one of the parts of the Italian countryside where there are still a few song-birds. She had a book on birds, and loved to watch and identify them.

Being quite without self-pity, it would never have occurred to her to scrutinize what she had made of years past or would do with years to come. Nevertheless with her love of places and events and her active memory she could not but be to some extent nostalgic.

One November morning, depressed after influenza, she tried

Epilogue at Bellosguardo

to concentrate on 'something lovely.' She found two havens of thought. One was the cottage at Roslin, where Anna Gell lived, about which she wrote for news, of the rabbits, of the specially made sink, and any changes, so that she could imagine it as it really was at that moment.

The other was Archbishop Fisher's 'Pilgrimage of Goodwill'.

Sensitive to places, I have said more than once before. She spoke to me of many, especially of Holkham Hall, where she found tears in her eyes as she handled a manuscript of Leonardo da Vinci and a thickly bound letter of Columbus to Queen Isabella saying he believed he had found China. It excited her at Ilkley to 'be so near *Wuthering Heights*.'[22] The condition of Coleridge's tomb so worried her that she wanted to give a concert for its restoration.[23] She particularly loved Scotland and the Scots.

But sensibility can make one also hate or despise places and events. In her youth she was glad to have seen the Derby, because then she need not go to it again. She had a girlish disillusion over an Albert Hall fancy dress ball: 'Everyone thinking of their own dress, and all individuals lost among 4000 brilliant costumes.' She despised small talk and gossip, and after one such unpleasant lunch party went to bed at 6 p.m. 'which was lovely'; and Adila came up to her room in the evening. 'That was perfect'.[24]

She was born flirtatious and remained so all her life. A chuckle may be allowed at a note she made when she was twenty-seven. 'I never talk about school to those under twenty, never about death to those above fifty, and when I get one between thirty and forty I talk about books (if well read) and make them recite love poems and by the end of the dance they are terrified of me— and then I know j'ai gagné ma cause.[24]

During the First World War she was asked to play the *Chaconne* to a priest. She did not then like playing just for one person; but he was going to the Front and she found him a fine character. That, however, did not stop her from trying-on a little 'Tentation de St Antoine', harmless—and substanceless. St Antony won.[24]

Though self-regard vanished once she had begun to play, she

was always aware of her appearance on the platform, so that it is useful to get glimpses of how she prepared herself. In a Welsh public hall she stood out in white and silver from a bright bank of flowers and greenery, with her face in shadow and her hair flushed in the glow of a red lamp which lit also the tip of her bow.[25] Sometimes she wore a full, old-fashioned gown, almost a crinoline, gracious and billowing, which according to one critic was as much responsible for her eight or nine encores as was her fine playing.[26] Sometimes she looked 'like a picture by Alfred Stevens' in a full-skirted pink dress with a pink ribbon in her hair.[27] In a church she wore black and white. For she shared Adila's love of good clothes both on the platform and in ordinary life.

Adila's love of good food too. But unlike her sister Jelly got herself a meal only once. She had refused to go to a cinema with Adila and Alec because an injured arm was still painful: but in their absence she felt hungry and boiled herself an egg. Very proud she was, of knowing how. And aware she was of the more than physical value which luxury food can have for those who are ill or don't usually get it: when Arthur Williams was having a bad bout she sent him turtle soup and chicken breasts, which while he enjoyed them, made his lion-cub of a dog stare at him in amazement, 'thinking it was Xmas.'[28]

She was aware too of what even dull food can mean to those who can't afford any. Anna Robertson once took a rather slummy short cut from her flat in Chelsea to Netherton Grove. She was astonished to see Jelly coming out of a fish-and-chips shop. Jelly had been going for a walk and had noticed two urchins with their noses pressed against the window of this but with no money, and had taken them in for a meal.[29]

She was almost as vague as Adila in leaving things behind on visits or losing them at home, a brooch, a cross, shoes. She was vague about many small material things, not knowing when Bank 'Holydays' were, and seldom conscious of distances between where she would be and where she would like to be: Keswick from Edinburgh, for example, when she planned a flying visit.

Epilogue at Bellosguardo

And time and time again her letters are written in trains on notepaper of a house just left. Her handwriting was so difficult for anyone not used to it, that Dr Rendall once asked her to mention her fee on a postcard since only he would be able to read it.[30]

She greeted her own foibles with the same laughter as she did those of other people. Fans could be funny. One correspondent was so stirred by Jelly's playing that she went out into her garden and sang *Madam Butterfly* in the rain.[31] Another reproved her for giving too melancholy short pieces, when she was only a public entertainer and should 'do as the public wants, as Kreisler does.'[31] Arthur Williams told of a Welsh taxi-driver who had heard 'Kreesler and Kubelik' but thought they were not in the same street as Jelly, by whose playing he had been so carried away that he drove straight home after it, forgetting he had a passenger.[32]

'Smashing' was the opinion of more than one school she played to; and her school recitals made many admirers for life. This she was shown in her later years. Returning to Florence in the train from Pisa she was asked in a couchette by a middle-aged man if she were not a famous violinist, and they had a gay journey together. After her death he wrote: 'like every Eton boy of the 1920's I was deeply in love with her.'

The first time she had been recognized in a train, by a Winchester boy in 1920, made her feel she belonged, and was no more an enemy alien. But fame can be like a child's toy too quickly chosen: when you get it at last home it may not be quite what you thought you saw in the shop. And many famous people have longed to be sure they were wanted for themselves, not for their gifts. As we have seen, this happened to Jelly. Then even her playing gave her no pleasure. She felt she had played the *Adagio and Fugue* better two years before. 'Will it always be like this?' she wrote like a cry in her diary. At another recital she felt as 'if she had played in German.'

When things went better, she renewed her resolve to improve her playing, for though she was sometimes satisfied with the way she had played, she was never self-satisfied because of it. To the end of her life her mind was open, and as late as 1952 when Titi suggested no *crescendo* in the second subject of the *Kreutzer Sonata* Jelly found she was right.

Sometimes hearing a fine fellow-artist's work spurred her into improving her own. Toscanini's in particular the first time she heard it. But she was frank about it and them. 'D'Alvarez bellowed and Hubermann miaowed' was her disrespectful young comment when the latter played Mozart.

'It's safety first in violin playing today' she said to me, 'especially in bowing. In the Brahms and the Schubert Trios for instance, there are passages of repeated notes which Joachim and the older violinists like Hubay and Ysaye took as a "flying *staccato*"—the notes detached but in a single movement of the bow. Today even celebrated violinists take them *spiccato*. Easier, but much less thrilling. The older way was perilous and for that is avoided. Nobody dares throw their bow about. They play on the string for fine safe clarity.'

The new and lazier way began with Heifetz, 'who would never take a risk like that,' Tovey said to her joy, after she had played three *concerti* at a single London concert. She thought Heifetz sacrificed feeling and charm to technique, and was glad she didn't at all disappear next to him.[33] Great was her admiration for David Oistrakh, 'one of our giants. But he too plays for safety.' For Isaac Stern she had almost worship, as Adila had, especially after they retired to Florence and he came there. His Brahms *Concerto* according to Jelly was 'beyond words, although he was dead tired having flown from the USA' too late for a rehearsal and having to run through with the conductor in his hotel room. 'He played like a God.'[34] The next day he came round to see them and played on all the Aranyi violins.

Adila had first heard Kogan's recording of the Brahms *D minor Sonata* in 1961, and wrote in one of her daily letters to Jelly who was in Britain, 'At times wonderful, but we could tell him a lot.'[35] But Jelly, when Kogan came to Florence, found him better than Oistrakh. In his first notes she recognized a new master. She went round to the Artists' Room and was delighted that he knew

Epilogue at Bellosguardo

her by name and fame. The Kogans came to supper at Bellosguardo, he speaking German, his wife only a little French. Jelly was convinced that nobody would play as he had without some religious faith. She asked if he were religious. He answered 'Not a little, but much.'

He returned in 1965. This time in the Artists' Room he said he had a little gift for her, but as he was leaving on the early train next morning, would she come round now to his hotel to fetch it? She went expecting some small souvenir of Moscow, perhaps a coloured view. The Kogans were standing in the hotel hall beside a large parcel, which contained an electric silver samovar, bulky homage he had been trailing round Europe for weeks.

Another 'wonderful humble simple great man' was Richter, whom she met at an after-concert dinner given by the Volterras at 1 a.m. When Jelly praised his playing, he said sadly what a long programme it had been, and how badly he had played in Ravel. Talking of New York, again sadly he said he had given seven recitals in the Carnegie Hall and at six of them had played badly. He told her he never played the *Emperor Concerto* nor the *G major*, because he loved listening to these; and when he played a work himself he could never listen to it.

Paganini is reported to have said, surprisingly for him, '*Bisogna forte sentire per far sentire*.[36]' Jelly not only felt fully enough to make others feel, she lived fully. I use the word as Vaughan Williams wrote of Gustav Holst, 'If to have "lived" it is necessary to have eloped with a *prima donna*, to have played mean tricks on one's friends, to be dirty or drunken,—if life means no more than that, then indeed the word has little meaning for a man like Holst.'[37]

I have described Jelly's 'open-ness' or receptivity to music. She was also open or receptive to life, which flowed through and out of her in all its better forms as music did. Her heart was receptive too, and one is surprised that she never married. If Kelly had lived, something might have come of that. Perhaps if Tom Spring-Rice had. 'Loyal, charming, gentle Tom' as Admiral Kelly called him,[38] who once gave a recital in a private house with Jelly and

The Sisters d'Aranyi

the Fachiris, where he had to use a piano... 'must have been kept in an Inferno for bad pianists' was Guy Liddell's description.[39] 'But he played so beautifully and was so nice about it.' After his death his music collection was offered in 1934 by his uncle, who succeeded him, as a Memorial Library in the Royal Irish Academy of Music. Jelly and Ethel Hobday played Bach and Brahms in aid of this at the Saxton-Nobles' house in Knightsbridge.

But either Jelly loved the wrong person, or the wrong person loved Jelly. Jan Masaryk, son of the founder of modern Czechovakia, himself a statesman and diplomat, wrote her many letters and notes, both when Envoyé Extraordinaire at the Ministry in London and after he returned home. Affectionate, respectful, a little indulgent, beginning 'Dear Friend' or 'Dear Child' or 'Dear Little Lady' (he was eight years older than she); enclosing flowers, pansies for their sweet scent, or a couple of wildflowers.[40]

A long letter from Prague in December 1931 gives a clue to his attitude. 'I wish I could do more than being an understanding friend or uncle or some damned thing.' But his 'funny idealistic work' trying to untangle 'this horrid array of short-sightedness' left him no time for any other occupations. He was wholly dedicated to a liveable Europe. And if one were to take as a norm the series of frustrated telephone calls, dates with Jelly cancelled, and apologies for changed necessity, they would have seen each other only at concerts.

He and his family continued to correspond with her, especially his young, musical and emotional niece. What happened I do not know, but the last word from Berta—on a postcard—is 'I am not sure if I am allowed to write to you at all. At least I shall always be allowed to think of you.'[41]

Jelly was appalled to read of his death in the London evening newspapers of March 10, 1948. Patriot to the point of being almost non-party, Masaryk had decided that the Communist revolution was, for all its shortcomings, the best thing for his country, and became Foreign Minister in the Communist government. Early in the morning his pyjama-clad body was found by a woman

Epilogue at Bellosguardo

cleaner under his window in the ex-Royal Palace. Only a fortnight before, the same thing had occurred with an ex-Minister of Justice, who left a suicide note. The official statement said that Jan Masaryk too had been suffering from insomnia and depression, but he left no note. He left the draft of an invigorating speech which he was to have made on friendship with Russia, and had shown no signs of depression the evening before. Political parties accused each other of causing his death, but the truth has not yet been made clear. His humour, humaneness, wholehearted absorption in his country had made him loved by his people both during wartime broadcasts and later. They wept in trams and at street corners.

Two other famous men felt for Jelly what she could not fully return. In her little diary of 1922 she remarks 'Tovey's declaration is one of my greatest memories', but she was too much in fond awe of him for richer feelings to grow, though they continued to play music together with excitement and laughter. In the same entry she mentions 'George, who frightened me with his letters, so sentimental written in bad French and in spite of this great beauty I could never fall in love with him.'

This was George Herbert Leigh-Mallory, the mountain-climber who from an early age and through his entire life prepared himself for an eventual conquest of Mount Everest. Only one of his letters in bad French remains, a teasing one from Charterhouse in 1912, when Jelly was nineteen.[42] Other letters do, from 1917 on. Jelly was godmother to his child and a loyal friend of his wife. In one letter only did Mallory write more perhaps than in more thoughtful moments he might have intended, and that was sent by Jelly to his wife, who said 'You and I both know George so well not to trust him absolutely. I would as soon not believe in God as not believe in George.' Her belief was justified.[43]

But in 1924 when Mallory by lecturing and 'slaving' had raised funds[44] and departed in T.S.S. *California* for his final attempt on Everest, he wrote long letters to her, describing life on board, himself sucking a peppermint sweet, drowsy ideas and honestly confused thoughts.[45] In Tibet he remarked in whimsical dismay that Jelly's smiling face keeps coming and going before his eyes. And even in his last letter he longs to see her head coming throught the slit in his tent.[46] It is late at night. Outside are '300 little black donkeys about as high as my hip,' which recalls to him the extraordinary significance of the donkey in Fra Angelico's *Flight into Egypt*, 'bearing in perfect uncomplaining meekness the troubles of the Holy Family.' He says he will come back after Everest, the tactics of the attack on which are his show; he speculates on Jelly's reaction to him when he does; and he ends 'Do keep a warm place in your heart for donkeys, surtout for this one.' She always did.

There was no slackness nor ill in him, physically or morally. His strong will and lifelong concentration got him and a companion when last seen, going strong to well inside the last thousand feet of the summit for a final try before the expedition must end in failure. What happened nobody knows. They never came back. Sir Francis Younghusband was never sure that they did not reach the summit and postponed collapse till they faced downward. But no signs of any kind seem to have been found by the later British Everest expedition. To fail at the very last moment, on the other hand, seemed out of character with Mallory.[47]

Such were the men Jelly remembered at Bellosguardo: big minds, generous, amusing, modest, honourable and dedicated. Fops and meanies, pomposity and self-esteem she could not abide. Indeed in many of her friends she admired the very qualities she did not know she had herself. 'What an attractive person you've painted' she said after reading the first two parts of this book, 'but I don't recognize it as me.' For as she grew older, her self mattered less and less to her.

This last quality outstands before I bring these chronicles and memoirs to an end. Time after time different people called her, in her presence or absence, 'a saint'. It was nothing mystical. It was not a manner of speech. It derived from an incorruptible modesty.

She would stop, for example, to encourage street musicians

Epilogue at Bellosguardo

(who deeply moved her), saying to Anna Robertson with tears in her eyes 'But Snookie! I might have been in their place.' Which made her friend feel very humble.[48]

Any kind of misfortune had to be dealt with at once, and quietly. A sum of money to a woman heard of, injured in an air-raid; an abrupt journey to a University town where the husband of an acquaintance had just been murdered by a student, and Jelly stayed the whole day with the widow, whom she knew only slightly: dozens of instances. She had no philosophy for such piteous crises, except one of patient openness to proportion, which she never thought of formulating. 'This will have to mingle gradually with all the beauty and goodness in life, which also exists.'[49] Ruth Draper, who in private life had a similar sweet impulsive spirit, herself thanked Jelly for her wisdom and counsel, when her close Italian poet friend was killed by Blackshirts.

If she could not reach her friends, she wrote to them: and 'with pen and bowstring you strike in such a way' Arthur Williams told her 'that a small handful of words (or notes) fills a page (or a hall) with pleasure.' Pleasure of an assuaging kind, as Anna Robertson found throughout her long illness; for to be so open to the facts of good and evil in life, to the music and the pain, meant a quietude under her own griefs and high spirits alike. It was the quietude of an untroubled child, as many of her idioms of speech and behaviour were those of a child.

She did not even have to write, she could be written to. After her death a lady wrote that she had lost her naval husband in the First World War and her son had been killed shortly after. When Jelly heard that she had been writing to her son every Sunday, she asked whether it would help if she wrote to Jelly instead, even with nothing to say: and this had continued every Sunday for years.

Several times she took her violin to hospitals. She was made a Governor of the Middlesex Hospital in acknowledgement. She did like now playing to one person alone, and did so, softly in bedrooms, to the very sick, to the dying. This made her ashamed of her bouncing health and the gay outer world she brought into

The Sisters d'Aranyi

their wretched hours. Even if latterly she had no bouncing health, she left behind her in the sick room much of her own world, where music and tranquillity meet.[50] Even tulips and roses sent from a florist's could have this effect if the dying person had known her: and when Maisie Kelly was distracted by the death of her four-year-old son, the result of Jelly's playing was magical.[51]

After Adila's death some people thought that Jelly seemed hardly to care much about this world. Adila had replaced her mother, and on both Jelly had depended in the same way. In a sense this was true, in another not. Jelly was always open to this world; and spent hours playing and caring for Adrienne's child, who seemed as strangely connected with Adila as Adrienne's birth itself had seemed connected with Madame d'Aranyi, after so many years of marriage. Life, other people, this world, continued to radiate in Jelly to the end.

At the same time she seemed to have seen through death, except as loss and sorrow to the living, and to belong as much to the future world she was firmly convinced of, as to the Present, rich, beautiful and exciting though this could be.

She had by no means given up playing. She practised every afternoon. She gave concerts in friends' houses and villas and played unseen in the American Church (her place of worship) or at such ceremonies as the Mass of the Artists in SS Apostoli, where she kept to the full her power of turning the architectural meaning of eight centuries, through classical composers, into music for today. Often in place of Adila, Adrienne played with her: notably in the Spohr *Duo*.

The culmination of Jelly's playing in Italy was also her last concert. She gave it with Adrienne on the evening of October 5, 1965. She was inspired, as always, by the place. This was the Castello del Trebbio, a solid mediaeval castle on a high rounded hill in the Mugello, some twenty miles north of Florence, which its owner, an Englishwoman of breeding and sensibility, has made as comfortable as a country cottage despite its spaciousness. Here in the dining-room they played the Handel *Double Sonata*, the Bach *in C major*, and the Vivaldi *in D*.

Epilogue at Bellosguardo

An unalterable engagement prevented us from being there; but she rang up my wife next day in full exuberance. 'Maresa *darling;* I'm sorry I couldn't come to your show' (the opening of a sculpture exhibition Jelly had looked forward to) '... Yes, last night was unique—such a *wonderful* place, and so still, and my violin behaved beautifully.'

She seldom used inaccurate words about important things, and never about her performances. Everybody agreed about the behaviour of her violin. So at the very end she had a quiet reassurance that even if professional platforms had neglected her, and whatever she may have thought about herself, her gifts had not abandoned her nor the music failed to flow through.

Her death on March 30, 1966 was swift. She contracted a kind of water on the lung, which put too much strain on her already weakening heart; and she collapsed before most people knew she was ill. She was happy and peaceful, not even resigned, indeed in a tranquil way eager for the next adventure. For she was as open to death as to music and life.

The day before, a friend in Oxford had received a letter from her. The last words are:

'The Spring's here, new life appears, and love is everlasting.'

Hand-list of Music and Composers

ANTALLFY-ZSIROSS. *Berceuse*, 128.
BACH, J. S.   49, 105, 119, 123, 133, 135, 150, 169, 172, 175, 213, **223**, 270, 280, 306. *Adagio and Fugue* 49, 141, 277. '*Air on the G String*' 44, 70, 271. *Chaconne for solo vln from Partita in D mi (no. 5)* 107, 117, 129, **141–2**, 179, 207, 208 seq, 212, 257, **260**, **267**, 275, 306. *Concerti for vln* 175, 230: *Concerto for vln in A mi* 223, 257, 269, 270: *Concerto for vln in E* 119, 141, **159–60**, 223, 257, **258**, 274, 304, 306: *Concerto for vln in G mi* 120. *Concerto with figured bass* 133. *Double Concerto for 2 vlns*: *in C mi* **63**, 70, 222: *Double Concerto for 2 vlns*: *in D mi* **49–50**, 58, 59, 82, **83**, 105, 141, 143, 155, **156**, 168, 206, **210**, 219, 222, 223, 226, 229, **264–5**. *Erbarme Dich* 219. *Jesu, Joy of Man's Desiring* 176. *Sonatas for vln & clavier* 219, 228, 229: *Sonata for vln & clavier no. 1 in B mi* 303: *Sonata for vln & clavier no. 2 in A* 172, **177**: *Sonata for vln & clavier no. 3 in E* 303: *Sonata for vln & clavier (two movements) in C mi* 228, 257. *Sonata for vln with figured bass* **270**, 298. *Sonata or Suite for solo violin: no. 1 in G* 228: *Sonata or Suite for solo violin: no. 2 in A mi* 101, 105: *Sonata or Suite for solo violin: no. 3 in C* 223. *Double Sonata for 2 vlns & clavier: in C* 74, 284: *Double Sonata for 2 vlns & clavier: in G* 107. *Sonata or Suite for solo 'cello* 84, **161**. *Toccata in C* 208 seq.
BANTOCK, SIR GRANVILLE. *Songs*, 154, 306.
BARTOK, BÉLA.   23, 26–30, 40, 44, 130, **135–40**, 151, 236, 243, **258–9**, 260, 295, 307. *Allegro Barbaro* 138, **140**, *Canon*, 27, 29. *Concerto for vln (posthumous)*, 27, 139 & n. *Duo*, 27, 29. *In Remembrance of November 23rd*, 27, 259, **310**. *Kossuth symphony*, 30, 135. *Piano works*, 138, 140. *Sonata for vln & pf: no. 1 in C sharp mi* 130, 136, 138, 140, 145: *Sonata for vln & pf: in C* **138–9**, **140**, 178. *String Quartet no. 2*, 178. *Suite for Orchestra no. 1*, 135.

287

BAX, SIR ARNOLD. 67
BAZZINI, ANTONIO. *Ronde des Lutins*, 43, 69. *Suite de Concert*, 271.
BEETHOVEN, LUDWIG VAN. 102, 106, 135, 142, 150, 173, 213, 219, 243, 272, 307. *Concerto for vln in D op* 61, 32, **43**, 47, 55, 59, 83, **123**, 127, 153—4, 164, 165, **169**, 204, 208 seq., 218, 239, **248**, 269. *Concerto for pf no. 4 in G*, 279: *Concerto for pf no. 5 in E flat*, 279. *Grosse Fugue*, 201. *Piano Trio*, 102, 221, 227. *Piano Trio: in C mi*, 107, 182: *Piano Trio: in B flat op* 97, 229. *Romance in G*, 73, 142. *Ruins of Athens*, 47. *Sonatas for vln & pf*, 166, 174, 182, **184-5**, 243: *Sonata for vln & pf: no. 2 in A op.* 12 *no* 2, 185, 228: *Sonata for vln & pf: no. 5 in F op.* 24 *Spring*, 52, 128, 264: *Sonata for vln & pf: no. 7 in C mi op.* 30 *no.* 2, 124, 138, 260, 303: *Sonata for vln & pf: no. 8 in G op.* 30 *no.* 3, 185, 228, 303: *Sonata for vln & pf: no. 9 in A op.* 47 '*Kreutzer*', 61, 73, 128, 138, **140**, 221, **268**, 278: *Sonata for vln & pf: no. 10 in G* (*op.* 96), 124, 265, 303. *Sonata for pf in F sharp* (*op.* 78), 64. *String Quartets*, 33. *String Quartet: in B flat no.* 13 (*op.* 130), 298. *Symphony no. 2 in D* (*op.* 36), 221.
BÉRIOT, CHARLES AUGUSTE DE. *Scènes de Ballet*, 41.
BIHARI. *Rakoczy March*, 39.
BLISS, ARTHUR. 234, 243.
BLOCH, ERNEST. *Baal Schem*, 231-2.
BRAHMS, JOHANNES. **32-5**, **37**, 41, 49, 67, 68, 85, 102, 106, **119**, 122, 123, 150, 167, 168, 187, 189, 219, 256, 280, **295**. *Academic Overture*, 168. *Concerto for vln in D* (*op.* 77), 123, **134**, **155**, 217, 218, 219, 278, 302. *Concerto for pf*, 49. *Double Concerto for vln & 'cello*, 188, 242. *Sonatas for vln & pf*, 56, 118, 174, 218: *Sonata for vln & pf: in G* (*op.* 78), 73, 84, 101, **260**: *Sonata for vln & pf: in A* (*op.* 100), 159, 264: *Sonata for vln & pf: in D mi* (*op.* 108), **32**, 63, 81, 174, 222, 278, 304, 306. *Piano Quintet in F mi* (*op.* 34), 106. *Piano Trio*, 87, 278: *Piano Trio: in C* (*op.* 87), 159, 303. *String Quintet with second viola in G* (*op* 111), 108, 298. *String Sextet*, 218. *Schwesterlein*, 236.
BRAHMS-JOACHIM. *Hungarian Dances*, **37**, 57, 61, 73, 75, 107, 122, 147, **258**, 264, 271.
BRIDGE, FRANK. 67, 120, 122, 235. *Piano Pieces*, 174. *Sea Suite*, 153.
BRUCH, MAX. 150, 167. *Concerto for vln no. 1 in G mi* (*op.* 26), 50, 167, 180: *Concerto for vln no. 2 in D mi* (*op.* 44), 57, 76.
BUSONI, FERRUCCIO. 181.

Index of Music and Composers

BYRD, WILLIAM. 209.
CARTIER, JEAN BAPTISTE. *La Chasse*, 107.
CASTELNUOVO-TEDESCO, MARIO. **229**, 239. *Capitan Fracassa*, 235, **309**. *Sonata quasi una Fantasia for vln & pf*, 229, 239. *Ritmi*, 309.
CHAIKOVSKY, PETER ILYICH. *Concerto for vln in D (op.* 35), 57, 70, **143**, 145. *Concerto for pf*, 221. *Piano Trio in A mi (op.* 50), 102.
CHAUSSON, ERNEST. *Concerto for vln, pf & strings*, 235.
CHOPIN, FRÉDÉRIC. 33. *Black Keys Etude*, 243. *Fantaisie in F mi*, 47. *Funeral March*, 89. *Nocturne in A*, 70.
CLARKE, REBECCA. 105, 227, 243. *Midsummer Moon*, 235, 309.
CORELLI, ARCANGELO. 31. *Variations on La Follia*, 74–5, 128.
COUPERIN, FRANÇOIS. *La Précieuse*, 107.
CRAXTON, HAROLD. *Alman*, 145. See also under Galuppi.
CZINKA, PANNA. 39. *Hungarian Dances*, 258.
DEBUSSY, CLAUDE. 67, 177, 213. *En Bateau*, 107. *Sonata for vln & pf*, 107.
DELIBES, CLÉMENT, *Coppélia*, 154.
DELIUS, FREDERICK. 67. *Concerto for vln*, 230. *Sonata for vln & pf no.* 3, 228.
DIENZL, FRANZ. 236. *Spinning Song*, 70.
DOHNANYI, ERNST. *Sonata for vln & pf*, 128.
DVORÁK, ANTONIN. 67. *Concerto for vln in A mi*, 44. *Piano Quintet in E flat*, 105. *Piano Trio*, 227. *Romantischstücke*, 109. *Terzetto for 2 vlns & vla*, 298.
ELGAR, SIR EDWARD. 34, **117–9**, 153. *Cockaigne Overture*, 153. *Concerto for vln*, 119. *Sonata for vln & pf in E mi*, 116–7, 118, 145.
ERLANGER, BARON FRÉDÉRIC D'. 243. *Poème*, 243.
ERNST, HEINRICH WILHELM. *Grand Variations on a Theme of Rossini's Otello*, 31.
FACHIRI, ADILA. *Arrangements*, 235–6.
FALLA, MANUEL DE. 140. *Spanish Suite*, 179, 271.
FAURÉ, GABRIEL. *Sonata for vln & pf*, 56, 116.
FIGUERIDO. *Desuetlar del Niño*, 158 182,.
FRANCK, CÉSAR. **218**, 235. *Sonata for vln & pf*, **124**, 145, 159, **174**, 177, 182, **218**, 221, 228, 264, 304. *Variations Symphoniques*, 177.
FRASER, NORMAN. *Chilean Dance (Cueca)*, 223.
GALUPPI, BALDASSARE. *Pieces*, 179.
GATTY, NICHOLAS. 179. *Bagatelle*, 179.
GIBBS, ARMSTRONG. *Suite*, 257.

289

T

GLIÈRE, R. M.   *String Sextet (op. 1)*, 218.
GODARD, BENJAMIN.   *Adagio Pathétique*, 44, 57. *Duettino for 2 vlns and pf:* 'Minuit', 70, 223: *Sérénade*, 223.
GOOSSENS, EUGÈNE.   *Sonata for vln & pf in E mi (op. 45)*, 142.
GRAINGER, PERCY.   67.
GRIEG EDVARD.   48, 168, 306. *Berceuse* 74. *Sonata (or Duo) for vln & pf in C mi* 220.
HALPHEN.   *Sonata for vln & pf*, 237.
HANDEL, G. F.   150. *Messiah*, 208. *Sonata for vln & pf in A*, 208 seq. *Double Sonata for 2 vlns & pf in G mi*, 69, 222, 284.
HARTY, SIR HAMILTON, 134, 143, 169. *Concerto for vln*, 166.
HAYDN, FRANZ JOSEPH.   17, 33.   *Rondo all' Ungherese*, 236. *Sonatas for pf with vln & 'cello*, 227. *String Quartet no 2 in F (op. 77)*, 105: *String Quartet no. 41 in D mi*, 298.
HINDEMITH, PAUL.   *Two Sonatas for vln & pf (op. 11)*, 232.
HOLST, GUSTAV.   67, **233-4, 279**, 308. *Concerto for Two vlns*, 233. *Fugal Concerto for Oboe*, 144. *Ode to Death*, 233.
HUBAY, JENO.   41, 43, 46, 58, 131, **138**, 147, 182, **278**. *Hungarian Rhapsody*, 43. *Scenes in a Country Inn*, 182. *The Yellow Cockchafer*, 182. *Zéphyre*, 44.
HUGHES, HERBERT.   *Jig, Tenpenny Bit*, 235.
HUMPERDINCK, ENGELBERT.   48.
IMRÉ, MAGYAR.   39.
IRELAND, JOHN.   *Sonata for vln & pf*, 218: *Sonata for vln & pf in A mi no. 2*, 171.
JANÁČEK, LEOŠ.   228. *Glagolithic Mass*, 302. *Sonata for vln & pf*, 228.
JOACHIM, JOSEPH.   16, 26, **31-7**, 40-5, **47-54**, 55-7, 58-64, 66-8, 75, 79, 81, 84, 94, 122-3, 129, 140, 147, 161, **167-9, 181, 188-90, 192-5**, 202, 214, 219, 226, 231, 251, **260**, 278, 295, 296. *Hungarian Concerto*, 62, **167** & n., 168-9, 269, 302. *Hungarian Variations*, 55, 168. *Overture to a Comedy by Gozzi*, 168. *Maria*, 167. *Romance: in C*, 56, 63: *Romance: from Hungarian Concerto*, 61-3.
KELLY, F. S.   61, 66, **73**, 83, 84, 89, 101, **109-11, 120-2**, 126, 186, 279. *Aghadra & other Songs*, 120. *Cycle of Lyrics*, 73, 120. *Elegy for Strings & Harp*, 109, **121**, 274. *Gallipoli Fantasy*, 274, 311. *Jig*, 122, 145, 274. *Monographs*, 120, 121. *Prelude for Organ*, 120. *Serenade for Flute and Strings*, 110, 116, 120-2, 235, 298. *Sonata for vln & pf*, 110, 121, 186. *String Trio*, 106, 110, 122. *Youth Pageant*, 122.
KODÁLY, ZOLTÁN.   259, 307.

Index of Music and Composers

KREISLER, FRITZ.   31, 107, 128, 155, **156**, 182, 202, 307.
LALO, V. A. E.   *Symphonie Espagnole*, 127.
LECLAIR, JEAN MARIE.   *Allegro*, 223. *Sarabande*, 223.
LEKEU, GUILLAUME.   *Sonata for vln & pf*, 107.
LEROUX, XAVIER.   *Le Nil*, 142.
LISZT, FRANZ.   14, 18, 30, 34, 40, 47, 67, 68, 72 n, 147.
LOCATELLI, PIETRO.   *Suite*, 116 & n.
MALIPIERO, FRANCESCO.   *Canto della Lontanezza*, 129.
MARSICK, M. P. J.   *Scherzando*, **145**, 157.
MENDELSSOHN-BARTHOLDY, FÉLIX.   31,**33**,51,150,162,230,273. *Concerto for vln in E mi*, **131–2**, 133, **157**, 161, 182, 208 seq, **212**, 230, 269, 271, 302. *Hebrides Overture*, 168. *Piano Trio in C mi (op. 66)*, 221. *Sonata for 'cello & pf*, 102. *Variations Sérieuses*, 84.
MEDTNER, NICOLAI R.   *Sonata for vln & pf in B mi*, 221, 298.
MILHAUD, DARIUS.   *Double Sonata for 2 vlns & pf*, 220, 237.
MORRIS, R. O.   *Concertino in F for small orchestra, Concerto for vln in G mi, Orchestral Suite, Piccolo Concerto for 2 vlns & string orchestra*, 234.
MOSTRAS AND LOBACHEV.   *Tartar Suite*, 259.
MOZART, WOLFGANG AMADEUS.   15, 33, 106, 129, 156, 176, 219, 221, **226**, 228, 278, 307. *Concertante for 2 vlns & pf in D*, 222, 306, **307**. *Concerti for vln & pf*, 123, 127, 131, 170, 218: *Concerto for vln & pf, in B flat (K 207)*, 179: *Concerto for vln & pf, in D (K 211)*, 144, 311: *Concerto for vln & pf, in G (K 216)*, 82, 169, 274: *Concerto for vln & pf, in D (K 218)*, 179: *Concerto for vln & pf, in A (K 219)*, 55, 161, 208 seq, 236, 239, **261**. *Adelaide Concerto for vln*, 191. *Concertone for 2 vlns in C*, 222. *Haffner Serenade*, 74, 140. *Rondo in G*, 305. *Sonatas for vln & pf*, 145, 174, 185: *Sonata for vln & pf, in G (K 301)*, 303, 308: *Sonata for vln & pf, in F*, 304: *Sonata for vln & pf, no. 3 in D (K 7)*, 120, 303: *Sonata for vln & pf, in E flat*, 73: *Sonata for vln & pf, no. 15 in B flat (K 31)*, 124, 174. *String Quintet in E flat (K 174)*, 205: *String Quintet in C (K 515)*, 302: *String Quintet in G mi (K 516)*, 108, 205.
MYASKOVSKY, N. Y.   *Symphony no. 5*, 163, 302.
NARDINI, PIETRO.   *Concerto for vln in E mi*, 116, 129, 142.
NICHOLSON, SIDNEY H.   *1914*, 121.
PAGANINI, NICCOLO.   31, **32**, 42, 91, **279**. *La Campanella*, 72 & n. *Capricci* 35; 74, 107, 116, 174, 179. *Concerto for vln*, 218. *Moses Variations on a single string*, 43, **70**. *Le Streghe*, 129.

The Sisters d'Aranyi

PALMGREN, SELIM. *Pieces*, 298.
PARRY, SIR HUBERT. 67 n., 101, 308.
PERGOLESI, GIOVANNI BATTISTA. *Arietta*, 235.
PIANELLI. *Villanella*, 305.
PORPORA, NICCOLO. *Minuet*, 107.
PUCCINI, GIACOMO. *Madam Butterfly*, 277.
PUGNANI, GAETANO. *Double Sonata for 2 vlns & pf in C*, 222.
PURCELL, HENRY. 211, **306**. *Airs*, 128, 271: *Air, in D mi*, 128: *Air, in G*, 208 seq. *Double Sonata for 2 vlns no. 9 in F (The Golden)*, 107, 210, 222, **306**.
QUILTER, ROGER. *Songs*, 220, 306.
RACHMANINOF, SERGYEI V. *Preludes*, 174.
RAVEL, MAURICE. **83, 145 seq**, 156, 279, 307. *Gaspard de la Nuit, Berceuse*, 304. *Hommage à Gabriel Fauré*, 147. *Introduction & Allegro for Harp &c*, 146. *L'Enfant & les Sortilèges*, 146. *Ma Mère l'Oye*, 302. *Sonata for vln & pf in G*, 149, **175–6, 177**, 180. *Sonate en Duo for vln & 'cello*, 145. *Songs*, 145, 300. *String Quartet*, 145, 298. *Tzigane*, **146–9, 158**, 164, 177, 181–2, **183**, 300, 304, 311. *La Valse*, 147.
REED, W. H. *Elégie*, 160.
RENDALL, EDWARD. 107. *English Dances*, 120.
RESPIGHI, OTTORINO. *Concerto Gregoriano*, 232, 239. *Sonata for vln & pf in C mi*, 260.
RIMSKY-KORSAKOV, NICHOLAS A. *Hymn to the Sun*, 235.
RONTGEN, JULIUS. *Concerto for vln*, 168—9. *University Symphony*, 168.
SAINT-SAENS, CHARLES CAMILLE. *Concerto for vln no. 3 in B mi*, 69, 107. *Habanera*, 57. *Rondo Capriccioso*, 49, 56, 57.
SAMMARTINI, GIUSEPPE or GIOVANNI BATTISTA. *Sonata for vln & pf*, 219. *Double Sonata for 2 vlns in G mi*, 222.
SARASATE, PABLO. 123, 129, **161**. *Spanish Dances* or *Suite*, 44, 49, 56, 57, 107. *Zapateada*, 49.
SCHÖNBERG, ARNOLD. *Five Orchestral Pieces*, 68. *String Sextet*, 115.
SCHUBERT, FRANZ. 33, 102, 106, 142, **181**, 219, 227. *Ave Maria*, 235, *Conzertstück*, 227. *Duo for vln & pf*, 109, 227: *Duo for vln & pf in A*. 303. *Grand Duo for 4 hands*, 228. *Introduction & Rondo Brillant*, 227. *Introduction & Variations on Trockne Blumen*, 228. *Impromptus (op. 142)*, 228. *The Miller & the Stream*, 236. *Piano Trio*, 102, 107, 227, 278: *Piano Trio no 1 in B flat (op. 79)*, 84, 92, **181**, 227, 303.

Index of Music and Composers

Sonata for vln & pf, 102, 161, 175: Sonata for vln & pf, in A mi, 227: Sonata for vln & pf, op. 137 no 2 in G mi, 228. String Quartet no. 13 in A mi, 298: String Quartet no. 14 in D mi, 219, 227. String Quintet with second 'cello in C, 227, 238. Wanderer Fantasy, 228.

SCHUMANN, ROBERT. **31**, 33, 35, 49, 122, 188 seq, 237. Clara S., 67, 102, 189, 192. Eugénie S., 192–3. Concerto for vln in D mi, 161, 188 seq, 305. Fantasia, 188. Garden Melody, 107. Piano Trio in F (op. 80), 303, in A mi 311. Sonata for vln & pf in D mi, 83, 260, 261, 306: Träumerei, 43, 44.

SCOTT, CYRIL. 67.

SIBELIUS, JEAN. 150. Symphony no. 2 in D, 201.

SINDING, CHRISTIAN. Serenade for 2 vlns & pf (Adagio, Allegro), 69, 70, 223.

SINIGAGLIA, LEONE. Rondo, 269.

SJÖGREN, EMIL. Sonata for vln & pf in E mi (op. 24), 228.

SKRYABIN, ALEXANDER N. 67. Prometheus, 67, 296.

SMYTH, DAME ETHEL. 67. Concerto for vln & horn, **166**, 302. Piano Trio, 235. Sonata for vln & pf in A mi (op. 7), 235.

SOMERVELL, SIR ARTHUR. 166. Concerto for vln, 233. Conzertstück, 83, 233. Sonata for vln & pf, 166. What You Will, 166, 311.

SPOHR, LOUIS. 32, **33**, 230, 306. Concerto for vln, 47. Duos for 2 vlns, 138, 210, 222, **230**, 284, **308**: Duo for 2 vlns, in D, 230-1, 308: Duo for 2 vlns, no 2 in B mi, 308: Duo for 2 vlns, in A mi, 107, 308: Duo for 2 vlns, in G mi, 57, 61, 308. Scena Concertante for vln & orchestra, 230.

STRAUSS, RICHARD. Sonata for vln & pf in E flat (op. 18), 131.

STRAVINSKY, IGOR. **124-5**, 138, 151, 250, 307. Firebird, 144, 307. L'Histoire du Soldat, 124-5. Mavra, 250: Pieces for String Quartet, and for Clarinet, 125. Pributki, 125. Pulcinella and Sacre du Printemps, 68.

SZYMANOWSKY, KAROL. 151. Concerto for vln no. 1 (op. 35), 151. La Fontaine d'Aréthuse and Tarantelle, 132.

TARTINI, GIUSEPPE. 306. Concerto for vln, in D mi, 69, 70: Concerto for vln, in E mi, 264. Sonata for vln & pf in G mi (The Devil's Trill), 42, 44, 49, **156**, 179. Sonata for vln & pf in G (Dido), 219. Double Sonata for 2 vlns, 222.

TOVEY, SIR DONALD. 34, **48-9**, **53-4**, 61-3, 65, **66-68**, 73, 82, 121, 125, 126, 167-8, 171, 189, 192 n, 198, 207, 227, 230, 232, 242, **256-7**, **265**, 270, 278, 296, 305. Cadenzas, 169.

VAUGHAN WILLIAMS, RALPH. 67, 78, 82, 119, **149–50**, 157, 179, 234. *Concerto Accademico for vln*, 149-51, 311. *Job*, 167. *The Lark Ascending*, 134, **157–8**, 271, 274.

VERACINI, FRANCESCO MARIA. *Aria & Capriccio from Sonata for vln in F*, 231.

VIEUXTEMPS, HENRI. *Ballade et Polonaise*, 63.

VIOTTI, GIOVANNI BATTISTA. *Concerto for vln*, 106.

VITALI, ANTONIO. *Ciaccona*, 158.

VIVALDI, ANTONIO. **132**, 149, 169, 270. *Concerto for vln in A mi*, 132, 274. *Double Concerto for 2 vlns in A (op. 3 no. 5)*, 222. *Double Sonata for 2 vlns in D*, 284.

WEBER, CARL MARIA. 33.

WEINBERGER, JAROMIR. *Schwanda the Bagpiper (Dudak)*, 269.

WEINGARTNER, FELIX. *Sonata for vln & pf in D*, 133.

WIENIAWSKY, HENRI. 259. *Légende*, 42. *Valse Caprice*, 70.

WOLF, HUGO. *Songs*, 306.

WORMSER, ANDRÉ. *The Prodigal Son*, 154.

WOOD, SIR HENRY. *Fantasy on Sea Songs*, 154.

ZANYTSKY. *Polonaise*, 70.

ANON. *Syncopated Study*, 47. *Ta-Ra-Ra-BOOM-De-Ay*, 47. *Scherzando* (other than by Marsick), 145. *Trio*, 307.

Additional Notes and References

Chapter 1. Childhood in Budapest
This chapter is almost entirely compiled of notes taken during weekly talks with Jelly d'Aranyi for several years.

Chapter 2. Music Prospect
In general, as in Chapter 1.
1. Typescript of a talk given by Adila Fachiri on Béla Bartók to the International 'Cello Centre, June 23, 1955. The postcards exist.
2. August 18, 1963.
3. *The Life and Music of Béla Bartók* (London, 1953), p. 14.
4. *The Letters of Robert Schumann*, selected and edited by Dr Karl Storck (London, 1907), p. 284. Written from Düsseldorf, February 6, 1854.
5. Jeffrey Pulver: 'Brahms and the Influence of Joachim', *Musical Times*, February 1, 1925, p. 23. When writing for violin or string quartet, Brahms often had Joachim in mind, according to an article in the *Spectator*, August 24, 1907, p. 255.
6. Florence L. May, *Life of Brahms* (London, 1905) Vol. I p. 69.
7. Much of this detail is taken from *Musicians on Music*, ed. F. Bonavia (London, 1956).
8. Mary Grierson, *Donald Francis Tovey* (London, 1952) p. 94.

Chapter 3. Violins and Fiddles
1. Florence May, *op. cit.* Vol. I, p. 222.
2. Ignazio Balla, *Budapest* (1931) pp. 131–2.
3. *Ibid*, pp. 134–5.
4. January 1931, (Vol. XII) pp. 36, 40.
5. Sir Henry J. Wood, *My Life in Music* (London, 1938), edition of 1946, p. 234.
6. August 11, 1900.
7. January 19, 1906.
8. Talk by Adila Fachiri as Chapter 2 note 1.

Chapter 4. To the Death of Joachim
1. October, Vol. XXXI, p. 336. Quoted by the editor in a review: *Harold Bauer: His Book*. Adila's letter was written from London SW 10.
2. J. Ma. Corredor, *Conversations with Casals*. Eng. transl. by André Mangeot (London, 1956) p. 97.

3. Letter from Adila to *The Times*, July 18, 1940, after Tovey's death.
4. J. Ma. Corredor *op. cit.* p. 97–8.
5. Letter from Adila in *Music and Letters* Vol. XXXI, 1960 No. 3 pp. 282–4. A long letter written from Ewelme.

Chapter 5. Viâ Elsewhere to England
1. *Nieuedauraut*, The Hague, February 12, 1908.
2. Article on Joachim in *Spectator* August 24, 1907.
3. Margaret Deneke, *Ernest Walker* (1951) p. 76.
4. *Ottoline, the Early Memoirs of Lady Ottoline Morrell*, ed. R. Gaythorne-Hardy (London, 1963) p. 277.
5. *Ibid*, p. 168–9.

Chapter 6. Music in Britain and Abroad
1. Percy Scholes, *The Mirror of Music* (London, 1947) p. 207.
2. J. Ma. Corredor *op. cit.* p. 94.
3. Percy M. Young, *Elgar O. M.* (London, 1955).
4. *Dictionary of Modern Music and Musicians* (London, 1924), article on Wood by Englefield-Hull, its general editor.
5. *Ibid*, Article on Skryabin by Boris de Schloezer. This concert took place on February 13, 1913.
6. A. L. Bacharach (ed.), *British Music of Our Time* (London, 1946) (paperback) p. 116.
7. Most of the facts about Tovey in this chapter are taken from Miss Grierson's *Donald Francis Tovey* (London, 1952) pp. 86, 100, 121.
8. Details of these continental tours are from local press cuttings.
9. Unless otherwise indicated, all unpublished letters quoted are in the possession of Sig^a. Camilloni.

Chapter 7. An Advantage of High Society
1. Virginia Woolf, *Roger Fry, a Biography* (London, 1940) p. 50.
2. Mary Grierson, *op. cit.* p. 111.
3. Letter from Guy Liddell to J. d'A. July 28, n.y.
4. Obituary of Sir Alexander Maitland Q.C. *Scotsman* September 27, 1965.
5. Letter from an old friend to A. F. February 24, 1959. This writer was the 'cellist who had a cold as related on p. 103.
6. Letter from F. S. Kelly to J. d'A. January 14, 1914.
7. Letter from Leonard Borwick to J. d'A. November 21, 1913.
8. Undated programmes. One, in Mrs Dalliba's house, 9 Langford

Additional Notes and References

Place, Abbey Road, was under the auspices of the Music in Wartime Committee.
9. This may have been in 1934. (programme).
10. Letter from Steuart Wilson to J. d'A. 1912.
11. Unidentified press cutting. May be apochryphal.
12. J. d'A. Entry in diary, January 2, 1920 (actually written in a diary of 1919).
13. Letter from J. d'A. to her mother, undated.
14. J. d'A. Entries in diary, February 22, August 26, 1920.
15. R. McNair Wilson, *The Empress Josephine* (London, 1932/1952).
16. Letter from A. F. to J. d'A. in England June 12, 1961.
17. Letter from J. d'A. to her mother, undated, perhaps 1915. 'Malheureusement j'aurais' (by the train arriving at Paddington at 10.40) 'à venir en l-er, car nous irons plusieurs ensemble.'
18. *The Autobiography of Margot Asquith* (London, 1920), p. 82.
19. J. d'A. Entry in diary June 24, 1920.
20. Letter from Mrs Asquith to J. d'A. September 10, 1918.
21. J. d'A. Entries in diary 1920.

Chapter 8. Enemy Aliens
1. *Who's Who*, 1914.
2. *The Gramophone*, Review of this recording. June (1928?).
3. Letter from Roger Fry at Durbins to J. d'A. August 25, 1917. Also Virginia Woolf *op. cit.* p. 225.
4. Letters from Bertrand Russell to J. d'A. January 25, July 29, 1915.
5. According to J. Ma. Corredor *op. cit.* p. 59. This, however, is news to Jelly.
6. In 1914. Hesketh Pearson, *The Last Actor Managers* (London, 1950) pp. 13–14.
7. Letter from Mrs Gell to the author.
8. The quotations in the rest of this chapter are from MS letters and poems sent to Jelly. This one, 1914.
9. From Balliol. 1914 or –15.
10. From 'Cherwell', where he had gone into wartime lodgings, autumn term, 1914.

Chapter 9. Wartime Music
1. Letter from Fanny Davies to J. d'A. January 29, 1915.
2. From a few aphorisms written in at the end of the diary for 1922, which stops in April.

The Sisters d'Aranyi

3. Obituary in *The Times*, March 28, 1939.
4. Letters from Alexandre Fachiri to J. d'A. August 9, 1919 and February 26, (1928?).
5. Concert programme. The singers were Edith McCullogh and J. Campbell-McInnes.
6. I.   Bach, *Sonata for Vln. with accompaniment of figured bass*. (J)
      Mozart, *Sonata for vln, & Pf. in G* (K. 301) (J & LB)
      Palmgren, Various pieces (LB)
      Medtner, *Sonata for Pf. & Vln.* (A. & LB)
  II. Beethoven, *4tet no 13 in B♭* (op. 130)
      Violin solo (J); but she doesn't remember what.
      Haydn, *4tet no 41 in D mi.*
  III. Brahms, *5tet for 2 Vlns, 2 vlas, & 'Cello in G.*
      Dvořák, *Terzetto for 2 vlns and vla.*
      Mozart, *5tet for 2 Vlns, 2 Vlas, & 'cello in C.* (2nd viola, André Mangeot)
  IV. Ravel, *4tet*
      Violin solo (A), again Jelly does not remember.
      Schubert, *4tet in A minor.*
7. Unfruitful to attempt a list, as many of the surviving programmes are fragments, and there is at least one letter of thanks from a cause for which there is no programme.
8. Anonymous article in a supplement to *The Wykehamist* No. 966, November 7, 1950. Rendall used to call Jelly "Goddess", according to this writer.
9. Letter from F. S. Kelly to J. d'A. December 15, 1915, at Cape Hellas, Hood Battalion, RND Mediterranean Expeditionary Force.
10. Letter of May 4, 1916 from 29 Queen Anne Street, Cavendish Square.
11. Letter of August 9, 1916, from Hood Battalion, BEF France.

Chapter 10. Drawing Flames
1. p. 892.
2. Entry February 10, 1919 in a small joint diary kept by Adila and her husband.
3. Entry March 18, 1919 in J. d'A.'s diary.
4. The *Serenade* consisted of *Prelude, Idyll, Minuet, Air & Variations* and *Jig*.
5. D.M.F. in an unidentified Birmingham newspaper.
6. Percy Young, *Elgar O.M.* (London, 1935) pp. 192, 198.

Additional Notes and References

7. October 27, 1919.
8. Entry February 29, 1920 in J. d'A.'s diary.
9. *Dictionary of Modern Music and Musicians*, and *Who Was Who*.
10. Percy Scholes, *op. cit.* p. 285.
11. Entry May 2, 1920 in J. d'A.'s diary.
12. Programme in the author's possession.
13. Letter from F. S. Kelly in France to Sir G. Henschel, who had asked if he had been composing. Copy in J. d'A.'s handwriting.
14. Letter from Lord Monteagle to J. d'A. March 17, 1927.
15. J. H. E. in unidentified Yorkshire newspaper 1933.
16. Several entries in J. d'A.'s diary.
17. April 30(?), 1920.
18. Entry in J. d'A.'s diary, June 28, 1920.
19. Article by J. d'A. in *Music and Letters*, 1927 no 2 April. pp. 191–7, on Beethoven's *Violin Sonatas*.
20. Account of performance of *Histoire du Soldat* and of the new violin taken from J. d'A.'s diary.
21. *Daily Mail*, October 1st.
22. Details from J. d'A.'s diary.
23. *The Wykehamist*, November 20, 1920.
24. as 22.

Chapter 11.   Béla Bartók
1. *Musical Opinion*, December 1931.
2. *Morning Post*, November 25, 1921.
3. *Musical Times*, 'London Concerts' January 1, 1922 p. 44.
4. *Boston Daily Mail*, November 3, 1931.
5. A further account of Jelly in this Concerto is to be found in Samuel Langford, *Musical Criticisms* (ed. Neville Cardus) (London, 1929) pp. 83–84.
6. *Birmingham (Post?)* September 8, 1934.
7. Philip Heseltine 'Béla Bartók' in *Musical Times* March 1, 1922 p. 164.
8. Pierre Citron, *Bartók* (Paris, 1963) p. 89.
9. Quoted by H. H. Stuckenschmidt in *Neue Musik*.
10. Letters translated by Count Teleki (one) and the rest by Mrs Marya Hörnes November 9, December 7, 26, 1921, February 2, 1922.
11. Letter to J. d'A. November 9, 1921.
12. *Musical Times*, February 1, 1930.
13. May 8, 1922.

The Sisters d'Aranyi

14. Adila Fachiri, talk already quoted.
15. Pierre Citron *op. cit.* p. 48.
16. In *Musical Times*, January 1, 1924.
17. December 5, 1923.
18. Percy Scholes, *op. cit.* p. 732.
19. Letter from Nigel Law to J. d'A., December 1, 1922.

Chapter 12.   Ravel: Vaughan Williams: Szymanowsky
1. Personal reminiscence by Mrs Jean Cleland, who was standing offstage.
2. Having been to Llandudno for the first time in September 1924, she was asked back for two concerts the following Good Friday and the Saturday after.
3. Letter from J. d'A. to Anna Robertson February 22, 1935(?).
4. Unidentified local newspaper referring to a performance at Sidmouth.
5. Norman Demuth, *Ravel* (London, 1947) p. 37.
6. *Music and Letters,* 'When Ravel Composed to Order' 1941, No. 1 p. 58.
7. Bolero, *The Life of Maurice Ravel* (N.Y., 1940) p. 194.
8. Article by André Coeuray in *Dictionary of Modern Music and Musicians*.
9. Programme note referring to concert at Groton School, Massachusetts.
10. As stated in *The Times,* according to Rollo H. Myers. *Ravel, Life and Work* (London, 1960) p. 67.
11. p. 68.
12. Ravel and Gil-Marchex played a transcription of *Ma Mère l'Oye*, the soprano Marcelle Gérard sang *Schérérazade* to Ravel's accompaniment, and among other songs, for the first time in Britain *Ronsard à Son Ame*, which Ravel had dedicated to her, with Gil-Marchex at the piano, who then played *Gaspard de la Nuit* and *Berceuse. Tzigane* ended the programme (*Daily Telegraph,* April 28, 1924).
13. *Neptune,* March 31, 1928.
14. Letter from Scott Goddard to J. d'A. June 29, 1927.
15. Ursula Vaughan Williams: *R.V.W.: a Biography* (London, 1964) p. 156.
16. *The Music of Vaughan Williams* (London, 1954) p. 97.
17. *Vaughan Williams* (London, 1963) p. 412.

Additional Notes and References

Chapter 13. Variations on Various Themes

1. Sir William Beveridge, *Power & Influence* (London, 1953) p. 173-4.
2. *The Sketch*, February 21(?), 1926.
3. Letter from J. d'A. to Anna Robertson, July 4, 193(?). She describes the occasion as a 'horrible Ball affair at Dorchester House for Archie's Club.'
4. *Eastern Daily Press*, October 1, (1924).
5. *Daily Telegraph*, October 8, 1924. The *Daily Express* of about the same date called her gift for getting inside the music 'uncanny.'
6. *Oswestry Border Counties Advertiser*, November 18, 1931, of a concert directed by F. O. Morris in Shrewsbury Town Hall. Neville Cardus, *Ten Composers* (London, 1945).
7. *Musical Opinion*, March 1926.
8. April 1, 1925.
9. September 3(?), 1931.
10. Undated letter from A. F. to J. d'A.
11. Entry in J. d'A.'s diary October 31, 1920. She was human enough to record that the Hall was fuller than the previous Sunday, when Szigeti had been playing.
12. *Manchester Guardian*, October 21, 1925. Jelly used the word 'ear-ticklers' in an article on 'Some Thoughts on Violin Playing' *Farrago* (Oxford, 1930) pp. 107-11. She said their only *raison d'être* was to act as 'medium between public and players—players in their less exalted mood, when the something divine that is bound to cling to them while playing the great works falls away from them and they stand in nothing but their "personality".'
13. Hubert Foss, *Ralph Vaughan Williams, a Study.* (London, 1950) p. 115.
14. Sir Ralph in personal conversation. Also letter from J. d'A. to Anna Robertson, June 20, 1940.
15. May 1926.
16. H.G. in *Musical Times*, November 1, 1927 of a performance in the Wigmore Hall, October 3, 1927.
17. Letter from Rosamund Fisher to Adrienne after J. d'A.'s death, April 2, 1966.
18. *News Chronicle*, October 9, 1930.
19. *Bromley District News*, December 12, 1930.
20. Letter from J. d'A. to Anna Robertson, November 21, 1934(?).
21. Undated letter from Augustus John to J. d'A.

22. Vol. II. In July 1920 he wrote thanking her for sitting all morning in a most tiring position.
23. Entry in J. d'A.'s diary, July 13, 1920.
24. *Daily Mail*, undated.
25. Letter from Mrs Gell to J.M. June 18, 1966.
26. *Birmingham Mail*, January 18, 19(?).
27. 2,002 in the afternoon, 1,106 in the evening. *Irish Times*, January 12, 1926.
28. F(rancis) T(oye) in *Morning Post*, March 7, 1927. Most of the review is a scornful attack on Myaskovsky's Symphony already mentioned.
29. *Daily Telegraph*, March 7, 1927. This critic liked the Myaskovsky.
30. Letter from Ethel Smyth to J. d'A. December 29, 1926. In this she says 'If you have time, please look at the passage after 37 in slow movement, which you said wasn't violin *mässig*. You'll see that all the same it will sound jolly—like the squeezing of an agonized sponge. And any double stopping that doesn't come out smoothly I will change for something that does!—Smoothness being essential.'
31. Also the 1st performance in England of Janaček's *Glagolithic Mass*.
32. *Daily Express*, October 24, 1930.
33. Virginia Woolf, *Roger Fry*, p. 107.
34. Letter to J. d'A. from 'Mary', July 15, 1931. I have forgotten who this ungushing friend was, and failed to note it.
35. Letter of July 14, 1931.
36. Grierson *op. cit.* p. 150.
37. *Musical Opinion*, December 1930.
38. Joachim, Brahms, Mendelssohn.
39. Unidentified press cutting; of performance at Sheffield.
40. October 16, 1928.

Chapter 14. Myra Hess and America
1. Letter from J. d'A. to Anna Robertson, March 30, 1935(?).
2. Howard Ferguson says: as a small boy he did accompany music-hall turns, helpless with laughter when one with a deep speaking voice opened as a male soprano.
3. *Birmingham Post*, November 22, 1928.
4. Letter from J. d'A. to Anna Robertson, February 22, 1935.

Additional Notes and References

5. In Knightsbridge, home of Mrs Saxton Noble: Thursdays March 15 and 22, 1917(?). Works played:
   I. Brahms, *Trio in C*
   Beethoven, *Sonata for pf & vln in C minor* (no. 7)
   Schubert, *Trio in B♭*
   II. Schumann, *Trio in F*
   Bach, *Sonata for pf & vln in E*
   Unannounced composer, *Trio*
6. April 30(?), 1920.
7. Name suppressed.
8. Brahms *in D minor*, Mozart *in G*, Beethoven *in A minor*.
9. *Daily Sketch*, October 5, 1925.
10. *Derby Express*, date illegible.
11. Because it is spelt *Piskos*.
12. The Old Rectory, Badingham, near Woodbridge, Suffolk.
13. Letter from Myra Hess to J. d'A. October 13, 1935.
14. *Derby Advertiser*, September 11, 1925.
15. *Sonatas* by Mozart *in D*, Beethoven *in G* (op. 96), Brahms *in A*, and the Schubert *Duo in A*.
16. *Sunday Pictorial*, October 23, 1927.
17. October 21 or 26, 1927(?).
18. *Daily Telegraph*, October 20, 1927.
19. J. B. in *Glasgow News*, January 29, 1926, who said that Elizabeth Schumann was heralded by authoritative trumpet notes on the part of Ernest Newman, her star paled beside the stars known as Jelly d'Aranyi and Myra Hess.
20. *Musical Mirror*, November 1925.
21. *The Observer*, February 27, 1927. Lelia Morgan, Francis Russell.
22. November 5, 1927. They played a Bach *Sonata in B minor*, Schumann *in A minor*, Mozart *in F*, Beethoven *in G*.
23. November 6, 1927.
24. November 6, 1927. But see note 22.
25. *Musical America*, January 14th.
26. Letter from V.W. to J. d'A.
27. Unidentified.
28. *Musical America*, January 14th.
29. *Catholic Herald*, June 15, 1928.
30. June 10, 1928.
31. June 11, 1928.

32. J. d'A. article on Schubert (MS).
33. Both of December 16, 1928. They played Brahms *in D minor*, Mozart *in G* (K. 301), Beethoven *in A minor* (op. 23) and the César Franck.
34. Unidentified press cutting.
35. The Bach *E major Concerto* and *Tzigane*.
36. The same works as at their London farewell concert.
37. Percy Scholes, *op. cit.* p. 215.
38. The writer in the *Sunday Times* was H. F. (Hubert Foss?). The pleas were made often.
39. H. F. in the *Sunday Times*.
40. From the typeface I fancy this unidentified cutting is from *The Times*.

Chapter 15. The Truth About the Schumann Concerto
1. Letter from Guy Liddell to J. d'A. September 23, 1933.
2. Letter from Donald Tovey to J. d'A. 'April-May-June 1933.' 'Why does planchette make Schumann use French or Italian keynames?' he asks.
3. Pulls of an article kindly lent me by the BBC, undated, possibly 1938, by D. Millar Craig, who had known and played with Joachim as a young man.
4. November.
5. Details of these sessions are given in Palmstierna's *Horizons of Immortality* (1937) pp. 352 *et seq.*
6. Telegram from Baron Palmstierna to the Fachiris, received September 14, 1933.
7. Programme notes, Courtauld-Sargent Concert, November 13/14, 1933.
8. Letter from Baron Palmstierna to Pamela McKenna in Berlin, November 2, 1934.
9. Unidentified US newspaper, September 24, 1937.
10. Letter from J. d'A. to Anna Robertson in Switzerland, redirected under swiss postmark, 25 III 37–11.
11. Article by Edwin Evans in *Time and Tide,* February 26, 1938.
12. David Megidoff, *Yehudi Menuhin* (London, 1956) pp. 183–5.
13. Wireless or Radio Correspondents of *Nottingham Journal* undated and of *Sheffield Independent,* September 30, 1937.
14. Letter from Neville Chamberlain to J. d'A. September 25, 1937.
15. Copy of letter from Strecker to Sir Adrian Boult, October 2, 1937.

Additional Notes and References

16. Letters to the author from Sir Adrian Boult, February 2, 1966 and from the Librarian, Broadcasting House, March 31, 1966.
17. Letter from Sir Adrian Boult to J. d'A. February 19, 1937.
18. Letter from J. d'A. to Anna Robertson as in note 10.
19. Palmstierna op. cit. from transcripts. Jelly confirms.
20. Letter from J. d'A. to Anna Robertson September 7, 1937.
21. Letter to the author from the BBC Librarian as in note 16.
22. Letter from Donald Tovey to J. d'A. September 28, 1937. 'Lhamas sic must expect silly people to be sloppy and inaccurate in transmitting their messages, but it is worse than inaccurate to imply that the broadcast of Schumann's violin concerto will loosen a wonderful flood of Thought Power to flood the earth.'
23. Letter from Anna Robertson to Jelly October 1, 1937.
24. February 18, 1938.
25. Dated September 29, 1937.
26. Letter from Baron Palmstierna to J. d'A. August 31, 1937.
27. February 14, 1938.
28. Letter from 'Wilma' to J. d'A. February 17, 1938.
29. Letters from P. J. Murray Smith to J. d'A. February 17th and from 'Robinia' to Adila Fachiri February 16, 1938.
30. Letter from Nelly Tucker to J. d'A. undated.
31. Letter from Rosalind Maitland undated. Letter to the author from Professor Sidney Newman.
32. Donald Tovey, Edinburgh programme notes.
33. Letter from Ernest Newman to J. d'A. February 18, 1938.

Chapter 16. The Pilgrimage of Compassion
1. Jelly also played the Bach-Siloti *Adagio*, a *Villanella* by Pianelli, and a Mozart *Rondo in G*, accompanied by Wilfred Wade.
2. In the d'Aranyi papers. The 'Host' was Alois Havrilla.
3. Great Ormonde Street. The concert was organized by the Peter Pan League; possibly the house was the Barrington-Wards'.
4. Letter from Helen Waddell to J. d'A. April 20, 1936, asking her to play for this society at an At Home in Lady Astor's house. 'The Over Thirty Association.'
5. In a personal interview with the author, when the latter was collecting news and views for a *tertium quid* news-sheet called *The British Independent*.
6. *Woking News*, December 11, 1931. The Quartette was replaced by Adila, Jelly, Ethel Hobday and Gladys Ripley, who sang Brahms,

The Sisters d'Aranyi

Wolf, Bantock, Grieg, Leoni and Quilter. Besides Bach, Tartini and Spohr the Aranyis played Mozart's *Concertante in D*.
7. *Yorkshire Post*, June 19, 1933.
8. Letter from an Exeter friend, June 19, 1933.
9. June 23, 1933.
10. Letter from J. d'A. to Anna Robertson (1933).
11. Attendance and other details here taken from press cuttings in a folder among the Aranyi papers.
12. Described as being for 2 violins and orchestra. It is in fact one of the sonatas in four parts (this one in F) but the two lower parts are usually taken by a keyboard instrument, sometimes with a 'cello playing the bass line. The sisters found in Purcell something of the purity in joy and in grief that they found in Bach. Purcell was getting better known: on November 4, 1938 *The Times* suggested they play more of him. A most proper suggestion, on which however they did not act.
13. *The Tatler*, July 19, 1933.
14. Postcard from E. M. D., Canterbury to J. d'A. July 18, 1933.
15. Letter from 'Sylvia K.' to J. d'A. July 10, 1933. This may be Mrs Kennedy, wife of Kennedy of *The Times*.
16. July 26, 1933.

Chapter 17. Divisions on a Ground
1. Entry in A. F.'s diary January 17, 1926.
2. Adrienne Camilloni in talk with the author.
3. Entry in A. F.'s diary 1919.
4. Ditto, March 19, 1919.
5. With Williams and Tomlinson as extras.
6. June 26, 1919. Brahms *D minor*, Mozart *B♭ major*, (I don't know which) Schumann *in D minor*. A. F.'s diary.
7. B. V. in *Musical Times*, December 1, 1922. The same critic thought her Bach *Chaconne* in a following concert 'rather tired' and preferred her in the less exacting *Concerto in E*.
8. Extracts from A. F.'s diary.
9. Details of these private concerts taken from programmes etc., in two large albums in the Aranyi papers.
10. At the Hon. Agatha Beaumont's, 121 Mount Street, May 4, 1932.
11. *The Sketch*, June 12, 1929.
12. From entries in A. F.'s diary, autumn 1922.
13. F. B. in *Musical Times*, August 1, 1929. Almost all the critics agreed about their incompatibility.

Additional Notes and References

14. For example, Cloyne, Munich, Haslemere, Edinburgh.
15. *Bradford Daily Telegraph,* November 26, 1926. After the concert Keith wrote in her programme:

> Beethoven at times can be dreary—
> To hear him for long makes me weary:
> Not often my heart
> Gets a thrill from Mozart,
> But he's different when played by Fachiri.

It being *de mode* among the younger musicians in that decade to decry Beethoven.
16. Fortunately unidentified.
17. Strictly speaking, *concertante* is an adjective describing passages where two or more soloists do not behave differently from the *ripieno*. It dates from older music, and I do not think it should be applied as a noun to this work.
18. F. T. in unidentified cutting dated in ink April (or) May 27, 1931,
19. *The Times,* January 28, 1921.
20. Adila once wished to hear how Kreisler had taken a certain passage of Beethoven. Anna Robertson borrowed a record and a portable gramophone, which she put on at 78 instead of 80 r.p.m. This of course lowered the pitch, but Adila did not notice. When Jelly came in, however, she was aghast with fear that either her hearing or mind was going. Jelly first discovered she had absolute pitch as a child in bed when she rubbed her fingers round a medicine bottle and knew the note. But Adila had very selective hearing. Once in Geneva in the company of Bartók, Kodaly, Milhaud and Ravel she heard for the first time the *Firebird,* and remarked on the use of saxophones. The others laughed, but Stravinsky later was astonished that only she should have heard it. (Letters from Mrs Gell.)
21. Professor Sidney Newman, in talk with the author. He stopped the orchestra to whisper the bar number, but few in the audience noticed.
22. B. V. in *Musical Times,* November 1926.
23. *The Times,* September 22, 1927.
24. *The Times,* September 3, 1931.
25. Letter from A. F. to Anna Robertson undated (1934?).
26. Letter from Mrs Gell to the author, March 26, 1966.
27. Adrienne Camilloni says O. P. was Adila's first pupil.
28. Grierson *op. cit.* p. 331.

The Sisters d'Aranyi

29. *Musical Opinion,* June 1931.
30. Grove House, Regent's Park.
31. The phrase was used of both Adila and Jelly by a writer in *Musical Opinion,* Newcastle, February, 1931.
32. Some of the confusion caused by programme printers and journalists which the chronicler has to sort, can be seen from the following. In a Derby programme one finds the *Duo in D minor* as one of three in op. 3; at Newcastle it is op. 39, and in the Wigmore Hall and *The Times* op. 67; (a work containing *Duos in A minor, D major* and *G minor*). This contained a *Rondo,* as did a Duo called D major by critics of recitals in the Wigmore Hall (another one), Woking and Madrid, but in Madrid the middle movement is called *largetto*. According to a critic of yet another Wigmore Hall recital the movements of one unaccompanied Duo were *Allegro-Largo-Allegro,* but in Oxford the middle movement is called *Adagio* by the press. When the earlier work was given at Blackpool as op. 3, the divisions were added correctly; but when the same opus was printed in yet another Wigmore Hall programme two critics called it op. 67. Further, on examination, the *Duo in G minor* seems to be written in D minor, with one flat in the key signature and the B♭'s added where needed. One has to know a lot before one learns a little.
33. Actually, according to Adrienne, Adila and Jelly played most often *Duo no 2 in B minor*.
34. *Brighton Herald,* November 10, 1928.
35. *Era,* March 5, 1930.
36. *Daily Telegraph,* October 29, 1924. The other musicians were Norman O'Neill, Frederic Austin, Sir Hubert Parry and Katharine Eggar.
37. 'These rehearsals were a joy. It was exciting to sit down to a meal at which four different languages were spoken at once. And it was exciting to be called "darling!" so frequently by both his hostesses. He was not used to it and at first had a bit of a shock. But he soon found he liked it. Gushing fervour he could never have put up with for one moment. But this abounding vitality, although it might be exhausting at times, was certainly very pleasing.' Imogen Holst, *Gustav Holst* (London, 1938) p. 143.
38. Ursula Vaughan Williams, *op. cit.* p. 180.
39. *Daily Telegraph,* November 15, 1930, *Sunday Times,* November 16, 1930.

Additional Notes and References

40. Programme note, Old Assembly Rooms Newcastle, January 18, 1934.
41. The correct title may be Midsummer *Noon*.
42. *Morning Post*, January 26, 1921.
43. Adila introduced, besides this piece, another by the same composer called *Ritmi*. The Captain is a character in the Commedia dell'Arte.
44. Details from A. F.'s diary.
45. *Petit Monégasque*, January 1, 1921.
46. Letter from Mrs Gell to the author, March 26, 1966.
47. Entry by Alec Fachiri in diary, October 3, 1919.
48. As note 46.
49. Letter from A. F. to her sisters Titi and Sai, March 11, 1929.
50. Actually 5,000 pengös.

Chapter 18. The House in Netherton Grove

1. These and other details in this chapter are taken from A. F.'s diary.
2. Letter from Mrs Gell to the author, March 26, 1966.
3. As above.
4. Article on 'Donald Francis Tovey' *Music and Letters* 1940, no. 4. p. 309.
5. Letter from Rosamund Fisher to Adrienne Camilloni, April 2, 1966.
6. Adrienne in talk.
7. *The Sketch*, June 23, 1926.
8. Evelyn Jowitt in talk with the author.
9. A. F.'s diary.
10. Volterra in talk with the author at Florence. He has since died.
11. Letter from J. d'A. to Anna Gell, April 14, 1965.
12. As note 2.
13. Letter from Anna Gell to the author February 10, 1966.
14. A. F.'s diary, February 24, 1926.
15. Letter from J. d'A. to Anna Robertson August 20, 1935.
16. Letter from Anna Robertson to J. d'A. October 1, 1937.
17. Letter from Anna Robertson to J. d'A. undated (late).
18. Entry in A. F.'s diary, February 10, 1920.
19. On November 1, 1961 Adila wrote from Bellosguardo to Jelly: 'I admire Bertie Russell and will write to him.'
20. Entries in A. F.'s diaries.
21. Jean Cleland in talk with the author.
22. Letter from J. d'A. to Anna Robertson, July 28, 1935.

The Sisters d'Aranyi

23. Ditto, February 4, 1936.
24. Same as note 8. Further details from A. F.'s diary.
25. The remaining details in this chapter are from a letter of J. d'A. to Anna Robertson, May 11, 1939.

Chapter 19. Last Years
1. Evelyn Jowett in talk.
2. Various letters from J. d'A. to Anna Robertson.
3. Except the Proms, at which Jelly played. Letter to Anna Robertson from Ewelme, September 20, 1939.
4. Letter from J. d'A. to Anna Robertson, June 20, 1940.
5. Sir Donald Somervell was Adila's trustee.
6. Letter from A. F. to Donald Tovey at the time he wrote to *The Times* about the Schumann Concerto. Among the Tovey Papers, Reid School of Music, Edinburgh.
7. From notes in A. F.'s diary. There is a programme of a recital which appears to be in 1948 at the Wigmore Hall, but no reviews were kept, if there were any.
8. November 30th, no year. It contains a reference to the Archbishop of Canterbury's 'Pilgrimage of Goodwill.'
9. *Daily Telegraph*, February 27, 1951.
10. *The Times*, July 11, 1955. The *Daily Telegraph* describes (July 7, 1955) the work as opening in the style of a *Siciliana*; having a rhapsodic development, and a returning to the muted melody.
11. Pierre Citron *op. cit.* p. 175.
12. Programme notes.
13. Remarks by friends in a bundle of letters of this period confirm each other. I think one was Mark Hamburg. A drollery she played at Oxford in 1955 has the title *Variations on the Song 'Ich bin der Schneider Kakadu'* (Cockatoo Tailor, which Jelly said was a humorous song.) My notes ascribe this to Beethoven!
14. Signed M. C. Adila's concert was on October 22, 1956.
15. Letter from J. d'A. to Anna Gell, July 27, 1958.
16. Letter from J. d'A. to Adrienne, undated, written from Walwick just before Jelly's last concert in Bath.
17. Letters from A. F. in London to J. d'A. and Adrienne at various dates in April 1961 and May 1962.
18. Letters to Adrienne from A. F., August 14, 1959 and J. d'A., undated.
19. October 22, 1961.

Additional Notes and References

20. June 16, 1960.
21. September 14, 1925.
22. October 11, 1962. *Radio Times,* undated.
23. Adrienne in talk.

Epilogue at Bellosguardo
1. Entry in J. d'A.'s diary, February 24, 1920.
2. Letter from J. d'A. to Anna Robertson, December 1, 1937.
3. Letter from a friend to J. d'A. 1934.
4. Letter from J. d'A. to Anna Robertson, October 16, 1934.
5. Sir Ralph Hawtrey in talk.
6. *Daily Telegraph,* October 13, 1928.
7. Letter from J. d'A. to Anna Robertson, January 15, 1935.
8. Prof. Sidney Newman in talk.
9. Letters to Anna Robertson.
10. Letter from Kent House, Knightsbridge, December 10, 1934.
11. Letter to Anna Robertson, February 24, 1936.
12. *Hunts & Surrey News,* April 22, 1936.
13. Letter to Anna Robertson, October 22, 1939.
14. Ditto, April 8, 1940.
15. Letters from A. F. to Adrienne, March 24, 28, 1954.
16. Letter to Anna Robertson, April 8, 1940. She says being in this room, which she shared with Mama has done her good.
17. *Bath & Wilts Chronicle & Herald,* March 11, 1954. They played Schumann's *Sonata in A minor,* a Mozart *Concerto in D, Tzigane,* and the *adagio* from the *Concerto Accademico,* with *What You Will* among the lighter pieces.
18. 1949: a Wigmore Hall recital praised in *The Strad.*
    1950: Balliol College. 1951 adjudicates in an International Violin Competition at Brussels. 1952 Aylesbury. Accompanists: Ivor Newton, Ivor Keys.
19. *Bath & Wilts Chronicle & Herald,* February 26, 1953.
20. Letter to Anna Robertson, July 27, 1958. Two were at Hexham, one in Kensington Town Hall on October 9th. The programmes have not survived. She left for Florence on October 30th.
21. In the programme 'Gallipoli' is spelt *Fantasie,* the old-english form. It is possible that this is in fact a separate work from the *Elegy;* British musicians revived the form and the spelling. *The Gramophone,* September 1960, p. 78.

The Sisters d'Aranyi

22. Entry in J. d'A.'s diary, February 1, 1922.
23. She made the offer to Ernest Raymond, but the fund he raised had such a response that her recital was not needed.
24. Entries in J. d'A.'s diaries.
25. *South Wales Daily Post*, 1930, At Pontardawe.
26. *The Observer*, undated. At a Prom.
27. Christopher St John in *Time & Tide*, May 14, 1920.
28. Letter from Arthur Williams and Margaret Read, July 12, 1936.
29. Letter from Anna Gell to the author, June 18, 1966.
30. January 16, 1923.
31. The former at Sidmouth, the latter, I regret to say from Edinburgh.
32. October 8, 1933.
33. But Adrienne assures me both Jelly and her mother expressed great admiration for Heifetz on occasion.
34. Letter from J. d'A. to Anna Robertson, June 14, 1965.
35. Letter from A. F. to J. d'A. and Adrienne, June 12, 1961. She added 'And I will if I ever see him.'
36. Cecil Gray: *A Survey of Contemporary Music* 1924, p. 320.
37. Ralph Vaughan-Williams, *Some Thoughts on Beethoven's Choral Symphony* etc. etc., 1953, p. 69.
38. October 24, 1934. Maisie Kelly married a naval officer of the same surname as herself, but no relation.
39. June 25, 1925(?).
40. Letters from Jan Masaryk at Grosvenor House, July 3, 1931 and July 12, 1932.
41. P.c. from Czechoslovakia, August 4, 1933.
42. April 16, 1912.
43. It is only fair to record that she also had 'an entire and peaceful confidence in Jelly' which also was justified.
44. Letter from George Mallory to J. d'A. on the point of returning from America in SS *Majestic*, April 4, 1923.
45. It is a real Indian Ocean letter. The band is playing sentimentally *Pale Hands I Loved* from the *Indian Love Lyrics*. Stars are in a heat haze. The ocean is dead, unlit. Cinerarias don't like the buzzing fan. The lights have pink shades like a Piccadilly restaurant. Does she read Santayana? About the stars; isn't it positively indecent when the stars are blazing away to be mean of soul and hide one's stuffy head in a humpy skull? He names all his friends now sleeping under them. 'The stars are dim and I blaze.'

Additional Notes and References

46. April 1, 1924. 'Before the Jelapha seated on rocks in bright sunshine beside a stream that gurgles in and out through melting snow.' This letter continues for some days.
47. Sir Arthur Shipley; Tribute in *Country Life*, July 5, 1924.
48. Letter from Mrs Gell to the author, June 18, 1966.
49. Letter from J. d'A. to Anna Robertson, May 15, 1935.
50. Letter from Michael Norris, March 18, 1926. His son John was dying of sarcoma.
51. Letter from John D. Kelly to J. d'A., February 25, 1922.

Selected General Index

Acccompanists 56, 57, 119, 122, 158, 159, 166, 172–3, 208 seq, 227, 229, 239, 271, 273
Allen, Sir Hugh 270
Ansermet, Ernest 124
Arrivals in England 22, 30, 59–60, 84, 89
Asquiths 80, **86–9**, **91–2**, 125, 126, 128, 129, 144, 297
Austria-Hungary **14–5**, 24, 57–8, 63, 69, 75, 83, 109, 129, 237

Bauer, Harold 48, 180, 295
Bax, Sir Arnold 67 & n.
Balfours 59, **63**, **80–1**, 86, 104
Bechstein Hall 63 & n, 115, 121 *and Wigmore Hall passim*
Beecham, Sir Thomas 144
Belgium 89, **164**, 217, 239, 271
Belloc, Hilaire 82
Berenson, Bernard 94
Berlin 27, 32, 35–6, 45, 49, 50, 51–3, 60, 61, 64, **190 seq**, **238–9**, 246
Borwick, Leonard **67**, 84, 89, 105, **109–11**, 120, 121

Boult, Sir Adrian 127, 141, **196**, **201**, 219, 243, 257
Brain, Aubrey & Dennis 166
Bristow, Annie 61
Broadcasting 127, **138**, 167, 173, 182, **195–6**, 198, 201–2, **204**, 233, 234, **240**, 265, 267, 269
Brooke, Rupert 81, 106, 110, 121
Budapest **13–15**, **17–18**, **21–2**, 24, 27, 30, **36–7**, 39, 41–2, 45–9, 64–5, 69, 90, 108, **126**, 131, **136–7**, 204, **236**, 241, 268
Busch, Adolf 95, 200. Busch String Quartet 61, 243
Busch, Fritz 83
Cull, Ole 117

Balvocoressi, M. D. 136–138, 146
Cameron, Sir D. Y. 82
Campbell, Mrs Pat 94
Campoli, Alfredo 91
Cardus, Neville 134, 155, 157

Casadesus, Robert 191
Casals, Pablo **63**, 67, **84**, 155, 160–1, 165, 181, 184, **251**, 263
Cassadó, Gaspar 185, **188**, 250, 271
Chamberlain, Neville 196, 273
Chamber Music **41**, 49, 57, 66, 67, 84, 87, **101 seq, 105**, 173, **185, 226–7**, 238, 256, **258**
Charities 95, **115**, 157, 202, **204–6, 219–20, 264, 283**
Cherepnin, Sasha 220
Churchill, Sir Winston 78, 79, 106, **214**
Classical Concerts Society 66, 84, 105
Coates, Albert 123
Cole, Maurice 229
Colles, H. C. 188, 200
Crowe, Sir Eyre 92

Dakyns, Frances/Bàcsi 61, 93
d' Alvarez, Madame 278
d'Aranyi, Adila *see Fachiri*
d'Aranyi, Adrienne **17–9**, 25, 46–7, **59**, 81, **83**, 93, 130, 140, **141–2**, 186–7, 284, 311
d'Aranyi, Hortense (Titi) *see Hawtrey*
d'Aranyi, Jelly 13, 242, 285
  appearance **47**, 60, 64–5, 85, 102, 116, 123, 134, **135, 148**, 153, 155, 156, 162, 163, 171, **201**, 209, **217**, 231, 271, **276**
  Beethoven violin sonatas, article on 166
  interests 46, 243, 274
  love of places **62**, 96, 126, **149**,
   172, 180, **208 seq**, 211, 274, **275**, 284
  name 22, 75
  nature 20–1, 23, 28, **46**, 72, **74–5**, 95, **129**, 133, 142, 152, **224–5**, 249, 274–7, **279–85**
  playing 39–40, **42**, 46–7, 57, 64, 70, 73, 75, 84, 107, 109–10, 116, 212, 223, 231, **264–5**, 269, 272, 277
  quick study 124, 131, 146, 157
  tours 57–8, 60–5, 69–77, 83, 160–2, 164, 176, 178 seq, 239, 240, 269, 271
d'Aranyi, Toksany **16–9**, 22–3, 26, 30, 47, 59, 83, 90, 130, 236, 237, **240–1**
Dare, Marie 157
Davies, Fanny 67, 101–3, 228
Denekes 205, 224, 263
De Valera 165–6
Douglas, Keith 221, **311**
Draper, *Charles* 145, *Haydn* 125, *Ruth* 283
Dunn, John 67

Edinburgh 74, 82, 123, 127–9, 150, 168, 202, 217, 230, 252, 269, 312
Education 25, 26, 36, 39, 41, 61, 62
Einstein, Albert 205
Elinson, Iso 171, 274
England 17, **30**, 32, 36, **59–65**, 66, **73–7**, 83, 89, **263, 264**
Ewelme 255–6, **262**, 273, 274, 296

Selected General Index

Fachiri, Adila   13, 106, 299
 appearance   85, 156, **217**, **231**
 interests   23, 24, **30**–1, 244, 246, **249**, 255, 262, 265
 nature   **19**, 21, 28, 51–2, 75, 95, 104, **217**, **224**–5, **226**, 236–8, **240**, 243–4
 playing   27, **39**–**40**, 41–5, 55, **218**, **219**, **223**, **226**, **228**, 231, **259**, **260**–1, **264**–5, 306
 pupils   101, 225–6
 social life   222 et passim
 tours   56–8, 60–5, 69–77, 83, 230, 237–9, 240
Fachiri, Adrienne, Signora Camilloni   166, 200, 202, 225, 241, 249, 250–1, **255**–**6**, 257–8, 261–2, **264**, 273, 284, 296
Fachiri, Alexandre   102n, **103**–**5**, 130, 164, 193n, 200, **218**–9, **226**, 235, 236, 238, 241–3, 246, **250**–**2**, 263
Family   **15 seq**, 22–4, 47, 59, **84**, **93**, **106**, 115
Fisher, Admiral William   78
Fisher of Lambeth, Lady   103, 244, 275
Fleury, Louis   145, 243
Folville, Juliette   143, 218, 219
Fried, Oskar   233
France   22, 70–3, 106, 110, 191, 237
Fry, Roger   94, 168

Gaskell, Helen   235
Geoffrey-Dechaume, C-L   163
Gerhardt, Elena   177

Germany   51, 52, 83, 89, **106**, 136–7, **189 seq**, 207, 237, 238–9
Geyer, Stéfi   27, 139
Gicquel, Felix   140–1
Gil-Marchex, Henri   146, 300
Gipsies   24, **37**–**40**, 47, 69
Glasgow   21, 36, 131, **144**
Gloucester   134, **208**, 211, 270
Goossens, Leon   105, 144
Grant, Duncan   94, 224
Graves, Robert   94
Grierson, Mary   68, 233, 296

Haldane, Lord   206, 305
Halstead, Philip   131
Hanson, Edith   102
Harris, Dr W. H.   271
Harrison, Bertram   228, 232, 235, 257
Haslemere   60–2, 73–4, 77, 120, 129, 221, 226
Havana   180
Hawtrey, Hortense (Titi)   13, 16, **17**, 21, 23, 26, 47, 76, 83, 85, **103**, 116, 130, 137, **182**, 225, 240, **254**–**5**
Hawtrey, Sir Ralph   85, **103**, 130, 157, 240, **252**, 273
Heifetz, Jescha   278
Henschel, Sir George   119, 299
Hess, Dame Myra   **92**, 149, **159**, 161, **173**–**84**, 228, **243**, 271, **272**, 303
Hobday, Ethel   119, 166, 172–3, 184n, 229 et passim: *Alfred* 119: *Claude* 171
Holland   56, 129, **164**, 230, 238, 239, 252, 271

317

Hubermann, Bronislav 243, 278
Hungary 14–16, 18, 24, 26, 31, 36, 39–42, 44, 71, 81, 83, 84, 90, 129–30, 137, 138–9, 167, 236, 237, 240
Huxley, Aldous 96–100
Huxley, Sir Julian 96
Hylton-Stewart, Bruce 171, 229–30, 235, 264

Illnesses 21, 23, 52, 89, 116, 124, 130, 210, 233, 241, 247, 251, 267–8, 271
Ireland 60, 158, 164–6, 231, 232, 272
Italy 18, 19, 30, 69–70, 75–7, 91, 111, 155, 224, 229, 236, 239, 257, 258, 260, 262, 274, 277, 311
Iturbi, José 158

James, Ivor 122
James, Henry 94
Jeremy, Raymond 105, 108
Joachim Centenary 167–8, 219
Joachim, Elizabeth/Harold 188, 193, 200: *Gabrielle* 167, 219: *Paul* 238
John, Augustus 162

Kelly, Maisie/Admiral 73, 121, 270, 279, 284, 312
Kimpton, Gwynne 141 & n, 159
Kindler, Hans 145
Klingler, Karl 51, 188
Kogan, Leonid 160, 210, 278–9, 312
Kulenkampf, Georg 194–5, 196
Kubelik, Jan 50–1
Kunwald, Ernst 55

Laszlo, Philip de 47, 163
Leigh-Mallory, G. H. 281–2, 309
Liddells 81, 125, 188, 280, 296, 304
Liechtenstein, Prince von 79, 237
Lloyd-George, David 88
London 32, 33, 49, 63, 68, 74, 78–80, 91, 109, 127, 128, 136, 143, 206, 233, 252, 255, 257, 263, 271
Long, Kathleen 228

The Maharajah of Kutch 245
Maitland, Sir Alexander/Rosalind 82, 107, 128
Masaryk, Jan 168, 280–1
Matheson, Hilda 206, 210
McKenna, Mrs Reginald 193
Menuhin, Sir Yehudi 195, 196
Millard-Craig, D. 304
Morrell, Lady Ottoline 64, 93–4
Morris R. O. 234
Morrison, Angus 228, 229
Mukle, May 145, 227, 243
Murchie, Robert 121
Mussolini, Benito 30, 239
Myers, Rollo 146–7, 201

Newman, Ernest 151, 200, 202, 303
Newman, Robert 153
Newman, Sidney 269, 307
Noble, Sir Andrew/Sir Saxton 62, 81, 105, 219, 273, 303

Oistrakh, David 278
Orlov, Nicholas 172, 220, 243, 244

Selected General Index

Oxford 36, 63, **76, 85,** 93, **96**
 seq, 104, 129, **135, 205,** 224,
 255, 256, 263, 264, 274, 285

Palmstierna, Baron Erik 189
 seq, 253, 269
Paris **71–3,** 126, 129, 137, 138–9,
 140, 145, 147–8, 150–1, 207,
 225, 236, 237
Pernell, Orrea 225, 227, 267,
 307
Piatti, Alfredo 66, 161, 238
Pictures **31,** 47, 59, 60, 64, 72,
 84, **162–3,** 168, 224, **254–5,**
 282
Pierné, Henri 147
Poland 17, 36, **40, 151,** 239
Portugal 161–2, 239
Primrose, William 106
'Punch' 75, 211

Raymond, Ernest 312
Reception at Concerts **42–3,** 73,
 117, 127, 134, **144, 156,** 212,
 221, 270 *et passim*
Recordings **92,** 179, **181,** 185,
 203, **240, 265,** 278, **307,** 312
Reeves, George 116
Reid, Margaret 205
Reiner, Fritz 183
Religion 16, 205, **212,** 222, **224,**
 231–2, **239,** 282–4
Rendall, Dr M. J. **107–8,** 128,
 142, 149, 154, 224, 277, **298**
Richter, Svyatoslav 279
Robertson, Anna (Mrs Gell)
 187, 198, **246–8, 262,** 269,
 272, **274,** 276, 283 *et passim
 after p. 248*

Ronald, Sir Landon 123
Rosing, Vladimir 242
Rothenstein, Sir William 162
Royalty **153–5,** 157, **163–4, 174,**
 219, 244, **245**
Russell, Bertrand 64, 249, 309

St James's Hall 32
Salmond, Felix **92,** 159, **178,
 181**
Sammons, Albert 256
Samuel, Harold **171–2, 228–9,
 243, 302**
Saram, Rohan de 263
Sargent, John Singer 59, 94
Sargent, Sir Malcolm 94, 151
Sassoon, Siegfried 94
Schotz, Emma 205
Schools 107, 115, 158, **179,** 180,
 229, 257, 300: *Charterhouse*
 107, 122: *Eton* 61, 100, 277:
 Northlands 62–3, 168:
 Haileybury 229–30: *Repton*
 100, 159: *Rugby* 121, 230:
 Sherborne 108, 129, 227:
 Winchester 87, 107–8, 128,
 142, 149, 229, 277
Schubert Centenary 181, 219, 227
Schumann, *Alfred & Herbert*
 201: *Clara* 102, 189, 192:
 Eugènie 189, 192 & n, 194
Schweitzer, Albert 205, 224
Scotland 60, 81, 82, 98, 190,
 202, 234, 246, 256, 268, 275
Segovia, André 184
Sheridan, Frank 179
Sherrin, James 256, 260, 273
Siloti, Alexander 128, 208

Smart, Sir George 17
Somervell, Sir Donald 95, 255–6, 310
Sonata Recitals 102, 124, 174 seq *et passim*
Spain 158, 159, 160–1, 163–4, 249
Spring-Rice, Tom 122, **126–7**, 128, **246, 268, 269, 279–80**
Stern, Isaac 184, 202, 278
Strachey, Lytton 94
Strecker, Willy 191 seq
Street-cries 22
Such, Percy 105–6
Suggia, Guglielmina 101–2, 155, 161, 240
Switzerland 83, 124, 150, 202, 225
Szigeti, Josef 40 & n, 166, 170, 178, 301

Tagore, Sir Rabindranath 125, 162–3
Tertis, Lionel 106, **118**, 145, 227
Thibaud, Alfonso 145, 156, 161, 181
Tonks, Professor 95
Trevelyan, Robert/Elizabeth 82, 140

USA 150, **178–84**, 204, 240, 278, 279

Vienna 14, 33, **44**, 49, 59, 130, 236, 238, 239, 265, 268
Vito, Gioconda de 48, 169
Violins 26, 35, 39, 45, 49, **56**, 103, 117, 125, 158, **184** & **n**, 186, 221, 285
Violin-playing, *Joachim on* 48, 50: *Adila on* 48: *Jelly on* 278, 301, 302
Volterra, Gualterio 245, 279

Wales 274, 276, 277, 300
Walter, Brono 238
Weingartner, Felix 133, 155
Weisse, Sophie 62–3
Williams, Arthur **106**, 205, 274, 276, 277, 283
Wilson, Sir Steuart 86, 230
Wood, Sir Henry **67, 115, 127**, 133, 135, 150, 155, **156**, 158, 233
Woolf, Virginia 94
Würher, Friedrich 192, 220, 221, 227, 235, 239, 243

Yeats, W. B. 163, 165
Ysaye 94, 181, 278

Zastrow, Rainer von 260
Zimbalist, Efrem 180

For Product Safety Concerns and Information please contact our EU representative GPSR@taylorandfrancis.com
Taylor & Francis Verlag GmbH, Kaufingerstraße 24, 80331 München, Germany

www.ingramcontent.com/pod-product-compliance
Lightning Source LLC
Chambersburg PA
CBHW052129010526
44113CB00034B/1209